Foreign Travelers in America
1810–1935

Foreign Travelers in America
1810–1935

Advisory Editors:

Arthur M. Schlesinger, Jr.
Eugene P. Moehring

AMERICAN STEW

WILLIAM TEELING

ARNO PRESS
A New York Times Company
New York—1974

134/68

Reprint Edition 1974 by Arno Press Inc.

Copyright © 1933 by Herbert Jenkins Limited
Reprinted by permission of
  Barrie & Jenkins, Publishers

Reprinted from a copy in
  The Newark Public Library

FOREIGN TRAVELERS IN AMERICA, 1810-1935
ISBN for complete set: 0-405-05440-8
See last pages of this volume for titles.

Manufactured in the United States of America

Library of Congress Cataloging in Publication Data

Teeling, Sir William, 1903-
  American stew.

    (Foreign travelers in America, 1810-1935)
    Reprint of the ed. published by H. Jenkins, London.
    1. United States--Description and travel--1920-
1940. 2. United States--Social life and customs--
1918-1945. I. Title. ~~II. Series~~.
E169.T32 1974   917.3'04'916   73-13152
ISBN 0-405-05475-0

AMERICAN STEW

The Author

AMERICAN STEW

by

WILLIAM TEELING

HERBERT JENKINS LIMITED
3 YORK STREET ST. JAMES'S
LONDON S.W.1

First printing, 1933

13 4168

Printed in Great Britain by Butler & Tanner Ltd., Frome and London

CONTENTS

ILLUSTRATIONS

AMERICAN STEW

AMERICAN STEW

CHAPTER I

OUTWARD BOUND

As a small boy in Ireland I remember loving Irish stew. It was no one definite dish. It included fresh meat spiced well, placed sizzling in a pot, and plentifully supported by hot potatoes and other national ingredients.

America—the United States—seems to many of us the same. It is a sizzling pot of many ingredients, the fresh settlers from other nations mixing with the ancient sects, that make the spices in the pot, all made pleasant by the inclusion of the older more national stocks.

It makes to-day no definite nation, only forty-eight different States with hundreds of varying ingredients that one day may boil down into the world's most fascinating nation.

It is a veritable Irish Stew—let us call it the American Stew. I will describe the ingredients I saw, strange and weird, all interesting.

America sends us many strange types, as yet seemingly contradictory, and from them we should learn much, but we do not. The more Americans visit us, the less we know about them. The daily contact does not make us like them more, any more than they are liked by French, or Germans, or Italians. We all misunderstand them, we all try to find the typical American, as we find the typical Frenchman or German, be he poor or rich, in the few that cross our borders.

But if we bother to think, the American that will help our poor for kindness' sake, has little in common with the American that helps because it is one way of

13

getting to know the country's social leaders. The American that tries to crash the gates of the London social world, and succeeds, is totally different from the hunting-box enthusiast, as are the American art lovers of Chelsea, Paris, Rome, or Florence, from the serious students, the Rhodes Scholars of Oxford, the intellectuals of a hundred American institutions visiting our shores—and lastly come the thousands of tourists in groups and parties, shepherded here, shepherded there, and seemingly never anxious to get away and breathe the atmosphere, but only to rejoin the ship or motor in time for luncheon.

These latter always go back to America, some of the others stay—scattered across Europe—and we judge the country then by them. They are usually individualists and apt to be eccentric—they say they cannot breathe in America.

Is it then perhaps a country after all not so individualistic as it is reputed? What is there then in common with all these people and what is there to make a nation, an influence in the world, a contribution to the world?

So far it looks as if only money and lack of any restraint is common. But is not that also typical of what we call democracy?—every type to be free to make a lot of money, everyone to be free of traditions and barriers that impede their desires—be they good or bad. In which case then—if only democracy comes to Europe from America, we must go to America and see what else they hold, what they do not give us—what it is that changes them so constantly, that leaves us always puzzled. Books cannot tell us—they generalise and come to no conclusions, but no book seems to study the different types in America, the types in their own homes.

Since one hundred years ago, when Mrs. Trollope

made her uncomfortable tour, to this day, each book that deals with America makes us laugh a little and pass on. There must be something more in this great continent than that. They send us new wine, that goes none too well in our old bottles. What vintage do they keep for themselves?

I went to see, unhampered by letters and advice from the European Americans, with just some general letters to one or two institutions across the country and relied on the few English I already knew out there.

The mixture I saw was bewildering, amusing, and above all fascinating—real, alive, and worth while.

CHAPTER II

ENTERING AMERICA

IN Vancouver, British Columbia, an oil promoter offered to motor me back to Calgary, Alberta. As yet there is no all-Canadian road across the Rockies, and to get to Calgary we would have to enter the United States and pass through Seattle and Spokane. It sounded fun—I went.

We motored down to Blaine, the border town from Vancouver, and left Canada without the least difficulty, even a murderer can usually get out of the country. Then came the question of entering America. We motored gaily on, and through the town without discovering anything that looked like a border. Eventually by dint of much questioning we found we had gone too far and so motored back to the station.

The Canadian oil man got in without the least difficulty, for him no passport was even necessary, but with me the fun began.

I went into an office where everything possible about me was typed down. The man had a good look at my passport and then asked me: "Where's this place Calais you seem to visit so much?" I explained I often went to France and he was interested, presumably never having heard of Calais before.

All then seemed well, until I found my oil promoter had been talkative as usual. While I had been inside, for some reason or other he told the officials I was a friend of the English Prime Minister—which wasn't true—and was in Canada on a political mission—which was a half-truth. Immediately the man wanted to know why I hadn't another passport—and all that took another twenty minutes.

After that came the only rather silly performance.

I had to pay $8 head tax and I was sent up to the local drug store where I paid the sum to the cashier just like paying for a cup of coffee, got a receipt and was able to enter America. The almighty drug store, it does everything and provides everything in America and it seemed to levy on me the first tribute in the States.

From now on we motored into Seattle mostly in the dark and the next day to Spokane in the same way. My host seemed to have the knack of passing through beautiful scenery at night, bleak flat country in the day, and always to be taking peppermint for colds, or pills for indigestion.

The modernity of the Davenport Hotel at Spokane impressed me, more with the discomfort every country cousin must feel on having to do up-to-date things to which he is not accustomed than with the benefits of labour-saving devices. To brush my shoes I had to put a nickel in a slot and then perilously balance one foot under a revolving brush and try and get that foot covered and then change over to the other foot and get that done, and if there was another second left, jump back to the other foot and get the heel seen to, all before the machine stopped and your five cents' worth was over.

Then I went to wash my hands after this little *pas seul* in the corner and having washed them looked for a towel. A towel! how old fashioned! no, I had to walk over dripping to yet another machine—where I put my foot on a lever and from another hole burst forth a blast of hot air. Over this I held both hands balancing on one foot and eventually managed to get my hands dry—but those little bits of clinging dirt that a towel usually dislodges, they clung on for good—hot air was not for them. I could not help wondering, had I wished to wash my face or neck, what attitudes I would have had to take up to get in line with the blasts of air. For the first time I thanked God I was a country cousin and my worst fears of American up-to-date methods seemed to be realised.

I must however say I never again met these horrible contraptions and only once regretted it—in a Pennsylvanian railway station, where having washed my hands I turned for the paper towel to find I could not get it without the insertion of a coin. By the time I had fumbled in my pocket, my pocket was wet, my hands were dry and I did not need the towel.

One thing, however, made me happy in the Davenport at Spokane, in this city of mining families and great wealth, and that was in each bedroom the washstand provided a special tap through which came iced drinking-water. That really was a boon for hot weather, for whisky parties and just for ordinary thirst at night.

Our next day's ride took us in pouring rain, on muddy slippery side roads and general discomfort, to the border again near Alberta. Here I had a regular row with the immigration officer—of which later on I was well ashamed. But I had not enjoyed my visit to the States and I was just ready for a row.

I had been told I could get my head tax back. But he informed me I could not, I must get it from the bus company with which I had come in. I replied I had not come in by bus. To which he replied I had. I felt I knew better, but it turned out the drug store had put me down as a bus entry. I felt I had been done and suggested America was rich enough to collect her own head tax and not leave it to Druggists and Cigar Stands—and so we continued the argument.

But even now it seems to me futile red tape. America demands a head tax, which is forfeited if you stay longer than two months. But it does not take this tax itself, it makes the travel company with which you enter take it and pay you back if you ever bother to ask for it. If you don't, the Government keeps it. They say it is the only way they have of checking up if people leave the country. It seems to me a very feeble method. If you want to stay you won't mind losing $8 and nobody is any the wiser when you have gone. The railway or bus company cannot be responsible, and if you are lazy you may in any case forget and presumably all America will be excited as to where you are, when actually you are peacefully at home.

In most other countries of the world, the stranger has to register in every town he visits. He doesn't mind if he has honest intentions, and America might have far less trouble with her alien population, a population of over 8 millions I believe, if they had to keep in touch with the local police.

That head tax bother, admittedly only a small thing, annoyed me at the start and again came the same trouble on entering from Montreal the next month, November. Here in my sleeping-berth, in front of everybody I had to tell my family history, how much money I had with me and pay another $8, although I was only going to New York for a week. I must say then, and almost always, the officials, who after all were only doing their duty, were extremely nice to me and made the least difficulty possible.

But I was luckier than the woman in the next berth. She was a Russian with a Soviet passport, and as the Soviet is not recognised in America, no amount of pleading on her part would avail and the train was stopped at the border round about midnight and she was turned adrift into the night. She was well dressed and seemed rich, but no wiles could help her, and it must have been unpleasant, with no trains back and a long night in a lonely station and a forfeited ticket her only lot.

Arrived in New York for one hectic week, I suppose I felt like every other stranger with perhaps this difference: I did not first see the sky-line of New York from beyond the Statue of Liberty. I entered the city through the slums of Harlem and landed underground at the Grand Central Terminal. Of that week my most interesting experience was my visit to Ellis Island. As honorary chairman of one of the English emigration societies, for whose benefit I had been travelling through Canada, I was naturally interested in this much maligned institution and I soon arranged with our New York representative to visit it thoroughly.

We first lunched in the Woolworth Building—which had only recently given way to the Chrysler Building, and which had yet to give way to the Empire State Building, as New York's highest skyscraper—then looked at the heads of Woolworth, the architect, and two other company officials that seem to hold the weight of the building on the inside, and finally hurried down to the pier, where I was given a permit ticket for one day's visit to the island. We went over on a ferry boat—it takes about ten minutes—and looked at the back of the Statue of Liberty looking sadly out to sea, as one who daily feels she is becoming more and more a relic of the past. Landed on the island, we went to the right into a large series of buildings, clean and up to date. Coming over on the boat had been some visitors and also some people who unwillingly had come perhaps to stay.

My guide first took me into a large hall on the left. Here at numberless little tables sat the officials of all the different charities represented on Ellis Island.

When an immigrant first comes to Ellis Island he may be met by these representatives and they may do what they can for him. I understand they are not allowed to see him or her privately until the authorities have fully examined the immigrant. This seems reasonable, as it prevents the immigrant being primed before the interview. After that the representatives of the different charities have access to the immigrant and also of course the deportees and they do a great deal for them. I have seen several people in that room receiving advice, and the societies, charging nothing, use a linking-up system of their own right across the continent which is invaluable.

They have working there no less than thirty-three agencies, such as the American Baptist Home Mission, the Belgian Bureau, the Methodist Episcopalians, the Danish Lutherans, the Hebrew Sheltering, the Irish Emigrant Society—this the oldest of the lot—the National Welfare Conference, the Y.M.C.A., the Daughters of the American Revolution, the Polish National Alliance, the Salvation Army, and the Friendless Aid Society—to name but a few. All these, some of whom have been working there since the Eighteen Forties and earlier, have now amalgamated into one body called the General Committee of Immigrant Aid, and being naturally very strong, they are able to see to it that immigrants and deportees are fairly treated.

They themselves visit the immigrants daily in the detention quarters more than once, give them newspapers, clothes and toys for the children; see to it that there are Christmas parties and Easter festivities and even a party on Thanksgiving Day—though deportees and immigrants may not have quite the same thing for which to be thankful; and they locate relatives in the States—often no easy matter. They often advance railway fares; arrange for marriages and make appeals in special cases. Further, they arrange weekly concerts, have a library with books of almost all nationalities, and I know personally with regard to the National Catholic Welfare Conference, that they have a link-up system in nearly every bishopric in the United States, and their representative, with an office in New York as well as on the island, is on the island once if not twice a day. He himself plays football each afternoon with the detained men—and has a priest to say Mass every Sunday in the large hall, where are also conducted Protestant and Jewish Services.

I was shown the hall, large and airy, with a huge organ presented by an immigrant who made good but started by being detained on the island. In the hall you can take exercise as well as on a balcony outside if it is fine.

The bedrooms, with about half a dozen beds in each, are clean, airy and comfortable. They have central heating and the buildings are as cool as possible in the summer. There are elaborate ticket offices and railway facilities for sending luggage, etc. Beyond are the quarters for criminals to be deported, which again are separated from the rooms where ordinary deportees are detained, until a boat is ready. In the criminal quarters the police looked certainly tough—but no tougher than the inmates—whilst those in charge of the less dangerous element were Irish and amusing. I talked to several and found they varied from English boys from the Midlands to an Egyptian Prince who was being deported for the fifth time. He always managed to slip in again, and was lolling peacefully at the Government's expense, looking regally into space, on a hard bench in the sun.

I went all through the kitchens and the dining-rooms and stole a menu of the day's fare. I do not think, under the circumstances, one could ask for much more.

IMMIGRANT DINING-ROOM

BILL OF FARE

Day—Thursday   Date—December 10th, 1931

BREAKFAST

Boiled Hominy with Milk
Fresh Apples   Bread and Butter
Coffee
Also milk served to all women and children

DINNER

Tomato Soup with Rice
Corned Beef and Cabbage
Boiled Potatoes   Bread and Butter
Cake
Coffee
Also milk served to all women and children

SUPPER

Beef Stew with Potatoes
Apple Sauce   Bread and Butter
Tea
Also milk served to all women and children

For all women and children milk and crackers are served in the detention quarters, between regular meal hours, and are distributed at bedtime.

I went over the hospital on the other side of the island. This hospital is as good as can be found anywhere. First of all it is not a hospital for immigrants or for deportees. It is a seamen's hospital used primarily and almost entirely for sailors, American sailors, and those of other nationalities taken ill in New York. The immigrants who need aid are also admitted free. Operations can be and are performed

23

there, and there is a regular staff of doctors and nurses, and immigrants are brought from one building to the other by a covered passage. There is also a good-sized recreation room.

Here I met one wretched Englishman, a young middle-class clerk I should say, who had come in that day. The matron, a very delightful and sympathetic woman, explained to me the youth had become slightly deranged on the voyage and would have to be detained in the hospital until he was better. This I knew often happens, having come across many cases before, deportees from Canada, people who to all intents were perfectly normal on leaving England—but are so affected by several days at sea that they become temporarily mentally unbalanced. The youth was naturally indignant, but was, I thought, unnecessarily rude to the matron, objecting to be put in prison garments. Of course they were not prison garments, only the ordinary hospital suits of a seaman's hospital. He also talked airily of the trouble he would raise in England. He had only intended visiting America for three months and thought it absurd the authorities should require of him $500 bond, which incidentally he did not look as if he could provide, that he would wire for it at once and that he would write his experiences for the English papers.

It is from slightly hysterical people such as these that we hear of the horrors of Ellis Island. No doubt, once, things were pretty bad, and not so long ago, and no doubt compared with the luxe of immigration quarters about which I have read, in Buenos Aires and Rio de Janeiro, they still leave much to be desired. But compared with the immigration or deportation centres, notably in Canada, and especially Montreal, Ellis Island is a luxurious hotel, run with incomparable efficiency. Nine-tenths of the things said about it are gross exaggerations. I say this not after one visit but after two. Both times I was quite unexpected—on each occasion everything seemed to work smoothly.

The second time, a year after my first visit, the new Commissioner, himself an Italian immigrant by birth and now the head of one of the biggest settlements in the slums of New York, was entertaining the reporters of the different New York newspapers, who "cover" Ellis Island. He asked me also to stop for lunch and to tell the reporters what I thought of the various immigration centres. There were about sixteen present, the Brooklyn Eagle, himself tall, cheerful, round faced, sat on one side and I think the News or the Mirror or one of the tabloid papers sat on the other side.

They discussed the most recent case exposed by one of them, of a Prince acting as a Soviet agent, and the others listened attentively. The Commissioner asked them all for suggestions and nobody had any complaint except the Hearst Press representative, who had not been able to get all the details on a spicy case some weeks before.

My next-door neighbour had just interviewed an English Duke who had arrived that day and found him very democratic and a sport—the Duke of Manchester—and they were all waiting to be on the spot for the arrival next day of Winston Churchill.

These Press reporters who interview you across the continent are the unique product of America, and themselves are usually the most delightful people. They do not often get you really wrong. They know what their papers want, they, themselves, have their own opinions about life, which, as far as I could see across the continent, were rather cynical. Hypocrisy and posing they loathe. They treat such things unmercifully and they get their own back on bores.

25

Treat them frankly, and they in turn may tell you something about the country that does not appear in print.

After this I crossed Canada again and from Vancouver decided to make my final and lengthy visit to the United States. I would travel from west to east and so perhaps gain a new impression of the more real Americans.

My last night after a cocktail at Bell Livingstone's speak-easy, with the lady herself and the plumber mending her drains, I set out for Harlem and some more cocktails at the home of the negress millionairess who, either herself or her mother, I forget which, had invented a means of taking the crink out of negroes' hair.

There I was surrounded by laughter, cocktails, a gramophone and a little gambling, about thirty negroes and negresses, some beautiful and some grossly fat. Amongst them all were three other whites, but they all came from London and were being, at the moment, lionized by the New York foreign society group. We all promised we would not tell where we had been and one left early to dine with Mrs. Vanderbilt. I was the next to go and catch the train for Montreal and the West.

I never saw the negress millionairess again. When I came back next year, she was dead and the very centre and life of Harlem's private entertaining was no more.

CHAPTER III

HOLLYWOOD HOPES

FROM Vancouver, four months after I had left New
York, I set sail for Hollywood.

From Wilmington, Los Angeles, we drove through
endless straggling suburbs to Hollywood nearly 20
miles away but all within the bounds of the same city.
After half a day of looking round under the auspices of
a chain of apartment houses, I finally took a ridiculously cheap apartment with a lovely view and every
kind of modern convenience including a tiled bath
for $12 a week. I had heard of the extravagance of
Hollywood but I was to find it the cheapest town in
which to live of any in America, and it gave me at
any rate more than other cities for my money.

My first afternoon I went up to see a bankrupt
star's house that was for sale. The advertisement said
it was an exact copy of a famous Italian villa. Actually
it was a famous Spanish villa—but that made no
difference. The dining-room and the huge reception-
room were equally elaborately decorated, partly in
Italian antiques, partly in Victorian statuettes and
partly in modern comforts. The bedrooms, three in
number, looked out on a small courtyard with a
playing fountain, and the view was up to those sandy
hills that give such an unreal cardboard effect on the
films.

Next I went for a drive round all the houses of the
famous stars, and then I was taken to a cocktail party.
There were at least sixty people in a small flat off
a courtyard, Spanish style, with fountains playing.
First I was pinioned by two male dress-designers from
Paris who soon found I did not know their favourite
London actors any better than they did themselves,

27

and I saw them no more. Next came an actor who had gone on tour in a famous English war play and warned me while I was in Hollywood to be careful and not go "White Cargo," and in his morbid way detailed to me just what could happen to an innocent youth like myself in such a wicked place. Then two almost-famous actresses spoke to me. And so on, the party becoming more and more a strain, the people talking louder and louder, everybody a little drunk, everybody a little bored. Finally I slipped away unnoticed to have dinner with an English ex-Guards officer, now on and off an actor.

Here was another side. He would not go to such parties but had his own little cottage and there cooked me some eggs and we had bread and butter and jam, and soon one actor and then another came in, all from London, some old and Shakespearian, some quite young, some just an ordinary age and disillusioned and depressed. When an English film was done they would get the jobs of butler or some other small part; Ronald Colman and Clive Brook would insist on that, but otherwise they just sat and hoped for better times. Their little colony just south of Sunset Boulevard, they dubbed "Little Tooting," and there they lived, not happy, not sad, but keeping clear of the international set of "make believe" and preferring to keep out of the papers altogether, rather than get publicity through a murder, a divorce, or the results of a midnight drunken party brawl.

Another night I led the life of a publicity group. Our hostess was rich, the daughter of a millionaire; she had with her a pleasant grass widow, and the wife of a once genuinely famous actor. This actor's wife arranged all her parties and took all the credit in the press for giving them. The men included a well-known English flyer, husband of an actress, another

A Film Star's Beach Home near Hollywood

actor who had made a mess of his contract before coming out to Hollywood and now more or less lived on other people's champagne and sandwiches. Yet another member of the party was one of the films, greatest lovers in the silent days and now was the villain in a series of thrillers.

The invitation was for dinner and to go later to a small and smart dance club. Our dinner became non-existent, as we just drank cocktails and ate *hors d'œuvre* from eight o'clock till nearly eleven o'clock. The woman who took all the publicity for herself cornered me for half an hour in the long baronial hall in the middle of this bijou villa, and explained to me how in the early days anybody that was anybody had lived in the Hollywood Hotel, how Charlie Chaplin would then always read serious books and then talk about nothing else until he had read a new one, how she would never have her babies in Hollywood, but if she had had, she would then have bought real estate and so would now be very rich, that she disliked cinema stars very much and the whole cinema colony almost more. Another lady told me how she longed to have a baby and how she too would have been rich had she purchased land in Hollywood a few years earlier. I tried in vain to hear about the cinema, but nobody knew anything or cared about the subject.

Eventually hungry but well filled with cocktails, and confused about babies and real estate, we all moved off to the centre of Los Angeles—we were then on Beverley Hill, a distance of at least 10 miles—to the Colony Club in the Town House. Here with our bottles blatantly beside us, we continued to drink and to dance and finally had some scrambled eggs about midnight.

One of my partners when the band stopped turned to a new comic star: "How are you, you don't remember me?"—"I'm afraid I don't, you know I'm a star now, I don't remember anybody." A cheerful remark.

Every few minutes somebody well known got up and did a turn, until about one o'clock, by which time anyone who was of importance in the film world had gone to bed. Our little group, however, with renewed strength from the scrambled eggs, motored off on a slightly zig-zag course to Beverley Hills. Suddenly we turned up a dark drive and on reaching the portals of an old English manor house, were met by two dreadful-looking thugs in caps and sweaters—chuckers-out they proved to be—and then the door was opened to show us a blaze of light and behind the doors all sorts of tuxedoed and liveried servants.

Everybody welcoming us and everybody bowing low, we were ushered along an imposing hall to a big drawing-room full of croupiers and tables. We had got to the well-known gambling den run by two Greeks, which appears in almost every book you read about Hollywood life. There wasn't another client there—but that did not detract from the lavish setting. In one room clients could dine or have supper with champagne, all as the guests of the Greeks—then they moved into the different gambling rooms where they paid their dinner bill ten times over. Our hostess played, and lost steadily all by herself for an hour or two—the famous actor's wife lost what she had at another table and then borrowed fifty dollars from the Greek, lost that and then tried to cash a cheque, but the Greek would not do it—she almost begged and then asked him to dinner—but he was polite and firm—he knew all about her financial position.

The lover-turned-villain took me aside to tell me the horrors of the film business, how shocking that it should be in the hands of the Jews and to beg me to write scathingly about it all—"We like that, we want it, we like to be attacked—the more the better."

A little before five o'clock we had some more bacon and eggs—they were welcome; and endless whisky, and finally in broad daylight I was driven home while some of the others, still gay and awake, motored off to Santa Monica for breakfast and a bathe.

All very nice for the papers, all very nice for the outside fringe—but obviously a life that cannot and is not led by anyone that has anything seriously to do with America's fourth biggest industry.

Yet another night I went to a party with buffet supper; hardly anybody in this set ever sits down to anything in Hollywood—and a scenario writer took off her shoes and stockings unbidden, to dance the weirdest solo dances, while in another room far from the madding crowd, Ramon Novarro and half a dozen men held for a time a little court and then went home.

A party in the same house a few weeks before had only been cleared out by the arrival of the police—but this night it was more or less quiet, though the gate-crashing by people who had never laid eyes on the owner far outclassed any London gate-crashing one has ever heard about.

Next day I was amused, when visiting an official at Fox Studio, to find several of the very grandest of the previous night's male guests waiting in a queue for small parts in a new film.

Having thoroughly sampled the publicity parties of Hollywood I went on into a more interesting grade of initiation. I began to be shown the studios. I was taken out to Universal, a little way outside Hollywood, and ran straight away into the working side of the films.

The whole film industry is in this difficulty, that it attempts to please everybody and often ends by making a story unrecognisable and also unreal. All through the Middle West of America, the Secretary told me, they have to remember in their audiences will be strait-laced Nonconformists, and they cannot afford to produce anything that will antagonise them too much—they dub the Middle West the Bible Belt—and many a time has Hollywood bowed before the spectre of the Bible Belt and its reactions.

From the office we went out through a series of small garden walks—like in a model village—and then suddenly we were in an elaborately furnished dining-room, and from there we moved into a bedroom of a different period and then into a large hall and finally into what looked like an aeroplane hangar with number-less arc lamps, strangely dressed people and in one corner a piece of a bedroom. Here Robert Armstrong, all made up, went on time and time again, just doing a few lines with a fat director sitting almost right up to him, with a dialogue writer standing behind and every now and then at his own convenience completely changing the dialogue for the next few sentences. Further back stood a soundman with listening-in discs on his ears.

I took up my position still further back, next the script typist, who grinned at me but did not move, merely remarking, "A script typist is never expected to be polite." My every movement—even of one foot—was jealously watched, and I and all the rest looked on in literally dead silence.

Next, before a new piece was to be shot, a man walked forward with numbers on a sort of blackboard (to place later on each piece of film) and two pieces of wood. When everything seemed all right he dropped the pieces of wood, called out the number of the piece of film to be shot and walked back; then the scene was acted for perhaps two minutes, when the director made an odd kind of groan, and we could all talk again.

The actors would immediately rush into one corner and, with the dialogue writer, discuss what they would say in the next little bit. As the dialogue writer changed the words so often, it would be futile for the actor to learn his part beforehand, so they say, and as a result they see their words for the first time a few minutes before acting them—learn them quickly by heart and then rehearse them before the director, on the scene, and in front of everyone else.

A few nights later a friend of mine, an actress at Paramount, whom I first met in my Oxford undergraduate days, took me to see a scene in her own picture being shot. It was to be a night scene in the Bois de Boulogne. We dined at seven o'clock, the actors all made up since six o'clock, and then we motored to Griffith Park in Hollywood that serves as Central Park, New York, the Bois in Paris, or Hyde Park in London, and took up our positions in the part closed off from the public.

Huge arc lamps and spot lights, like Hyde Park in war time, moved backwards and forwards and then finally concentrated on this girl sitting in a motor with the hero, a Hungarian whose broken English makes him every day more popular.

From eight o'clock until midnight with a monotony that must have driven actors as well as stage hands crazy, a small scene was re-enacted, but never seemed to reach perfection. It all mattered little—though all the extras and the stage hands had had to be paid extra for that evening's work and for two Sundays' work before on the same scene—it was eventually never included in the film.

Such waste you still see at every turn in Hollywood. But the biggest waste is not the stars' salaries. After all it is mostly to see them the public pays its money and their careers are short, their expenses

33   c

immense, and their life by no means the bed of roses it is pictured.

Over and above the perhaps two or three dozen leading stars, Greta Garbo, Ronald Colman, Douglas Fairbanks, Will Rogers, Ruth Chatterton, and the like, there are only in the whole cinema industry about 300 people who are there on a definite contract. For that contract, all these stars and lesser luminaries have to work overtime when required, which will include Sundays and work after dinner sometimes until midnight. The chief reason for this will probably be that in the studio, never so very large, the company wants to get rid of the scenery for one piece in order to put another in production; and if, as happened in that scene at Griffith Park, the picture is going slower than was expected, and yet the scenery must be off the lot by a certain date, then the hectic overtime becomes essential.

For this the supers are paid extra, but never those under contract. Moreover, when under contract you have usually to keep your figure down to the specified weight in the contract and nothing appears more mercilessly on the films than the signs of a hectic night.

By eight o'clock, the star has usually to be on the lot, which means already made up by the dresser, and that takes nearly another hour. And there are few of these leading beauties about whom we read so much who do not get up at six o'clock. They live often a long way from the studio, many of them down at the beach, and have to motor up each morning five or ten miles. From eight o'clock on they will endlessly repeat the same lines, the same acting, until the director is satisfied.

Then they will rush off for an hour's lunch, perhaps to the Brown Derby, perhaps to the Embassy, maybe even to their own homes, but as often as not to a sort of canteen in the studio where they can appear in their make-up and acting dresses and where they will get a not very exciting luncheon on a wooden table and pay as they go out and where they all look ridiculously funny in their different dresses and make-up.

Back they go to act, all the afternoon and, as likely as not in these days of economy, they will be wanted back again after dinner until midnight, and then up again next day at six o'clock.

Is it any wonder people break down, and that a real star who is doing work is not often seen at the hectic parties we hear of except, perhaps, on a Friday or Saturday night, and even then some of them may have to work on Sundays.

For the stars, while stars work is extremely exacting and living is not cheap. They are expected to tip well, have big cars, big houses, entertain not hectically but at any rate with plenty of champagne and whisky for dinner—not cheap commodities in these days of bootleggers—they must keep servants, more than other people, because they are hardly ever home to do things for themselves—they must keep a dresser at the studio, and she will never cost less than $1,300 a year—and servants in America cost a lot of money. And then they must subscribe to charities and help the down-and-out cinema actors and yet try to put something away for the day when they will be stars no more. No doubt that is the reason why the majority of these actors prefer to remain second-class stars—the publicity is not so great, the expenses more normal, the salary steady and liable to last much longer.

Writers seem to come into a different category. I dined one night with a star and his wife, also a star, and at the table was one of Europe's most famous playwrights. He seemed very pleased with his contract which, however, could be broken at a moment's notice, and he intended staying on all through the summer. In fact his wife, he had just heard, had booked her passage on the *Berengaria* to come out to join him. Next day, I lunched with friends at the Brown Derby and the whole room was agog with excitement—that morning the European writer and thirty-nine other writers at his studio had gone to their offices to be told the offices were no longer theirs, they had been dismissed, and were presented with a cheque in lieu of one week's notice. Wall Street bankers had taken over and put in their own friends. Next night again I met the same author—now preparing to leave himself for England, and he told me how he had just finished the first chapters of a skit on modern Holly-wood.

Our host of that particular evening was a humorous novelist. His contract of one year was up and was not being renewed, but during that year his company had accepted almost nothing he had produced, and he felt quite sad about it. Yet each week in came his salary, something like $8,000 a month, and nobody seemed to worry.

That night we had a party typical of the better side of Hollywood—of the real artists that come out to produce, to write, to act, and are serious about their art. One of the world's most famous producers, Cecil De Mille and his wife, were there, some well-known actors, writers and a thought-reader; cocktails first, a good dinner, plenty of champagne and then talk and bridge. The talk was mostly about the next world and the origins of Christianity and the authenticity of the Bible, and it was in no way ignorant talk, and by eleven o'clock everyone had gone home.

That sort of party and the delightful alfresco buffet luncheons so many stars give you on a Sunday, are not often written about because the publicity agent is not invited—but such are the parties frequented by the people who really run the industry, who face the music with regard to the unemployment in Hollywood —who are gradually trying to perfect the machinery and economise as well and who really have an ambition to make Hollywood help educate America, and also help Hollywood interpret what America really wants.

They know only too well what is really beneath all the glamour and the publicity—they know of the 17,000 people connected with the cinema in and around Hollywood. They know that at most 870 are used each day, of which over 300 are the stars under contract, and they know that about 800 out of that 17,000 get an average of three days' work a week—most of them less—and that over 60 per cent. of the juveniles registered in Hollywood get only an average of three days' work a year.

They took me to the different centres where the ordinary actor is taken on. On Tuesdays the men, on Thursdays the women, and on Saturdays the mothers with the juveniles—and woe betide the casting director who says the child is not the most perfectly gifted in the world.

The very greatest care is taken about putting people on the casting list and everything possible done to dissuade the applicant. Yet in spite of that there is this unemployed army of nearly 17,000 on the books alone.

When any company requires extras for special small parts, they ring up the casting office before four o'clock in the afternoon for those required next day— they give the type required, sizes, etc., and there are a group of amazing men who have pictured in their mind's eye almost all the people on the casting list.

Then between four o'clock and six o'clock, these wretched optimistic applicants go to their telephones and ring up the office.

The office has its own Exchange—you give your name—Mary Jones—the operator yells out "Mary Jones" to the group of men—they are immediately supposed to be able to visualise Mary Jones and see if she will fit into any part they have in hand. If yes, they call out "Yes," and she is switched through to the man who wants her and she gets the details for to-morrow; if—as happens nine times out of ten—no man says he wants Mary Jones, the operator calls back "Nothing" and the wretched girl is cut off.

Between these hours so many hundreds ring up, the Hollywood Exchange used to become completely dislocated, so that the industry has had to put in its own private Exchange. For the juveniles, also by law, they have to keep a school for their off hours, and some of the favourite child-actors can be seen there studying the alphabet and what four times four make.

And then tucked away in another part of the town is a small businesslike office for the Motion Picture Relief Fund. Through this office pass many thousands of tragic cases, growing larger every day. No nationality is barred, there is only one rule: you must have been for the last three years in the cinema profession; but that too becomes daily more difficult. So many people now change from vaudeville to the cinema and then back again, that they are seldom three years in cinema work alone. Hard though Mary Pickford works and others too to make the work of this Relief Fund sufficient, it is now quite inadequate.

The misery and the suffering that is under the surface in Hollywood is almost worse than in any other part of America. They are a proud lot, these actors, and it is not an uncommon thing to see a well-dressed seemingly cheerful person collapse on the Boulevards for lack of food and be carried off unconscious.

This industry that throws out a smoke screen of gaiety and butterfly existence, what really is its influence on America?

As yet probably next to nothing—but it interprets, to judge from the box-office receipts, moderately success-fully, the feelings and the interests of a large part of the American population, and this interpretation passes on to the outside world as something essentially American. It offers it to Europe—which is critical—to the British Empire which is trying hard to oust its influence with British films, and to countries like China and India, who get, in many backward districts, no other interpretation of Western life. It thrills them, and they look to this America, as they picture it, many of them for their future happiness.

And yet the people, as far as I could see, who make this interpretation, are mainly foreigners to America or else are American Jews, Americans of only the second generation. This second-generation American, the child of immigrants, I ran up against everywhere as the person most responsible for the misinterpretation of the real American. He is often a Wall Street banker and more often a cinema mogul at Hollywood or a gangster or a bootlegger.

There is a species of a sixth-rate magazine produced in America with an immense circulation. This type deals with hysterical confessions, with ridiculous love stories, and above all with sex. Every prominent publisher will tell you that the market for these magazines is amongst the children of immigrants—the second-generation Americans. The third genera-tion is above them—and it is not really curious that a very large percentage of American films are founded

39

on stories published in these magazines. This second generation seems to spend most money, to be always writing to their favourite star, and always to be at the cinema. They swallow these films and it is for them they are produced. They are a more or less uniform type across the country and a fairly safe market for the industry that is always trying to find something that will sell well across the whole continent and so make bigger profits.

For the rest, the industry is only in its infancy, as indeed in their American citizenship are a large percentage of its patrons. At the beginning of 1931, I found there were only 14,000 cinemas equipped for the talkies in America out of the total of 21,000 cinemas. The industry has still an unknown future, an unknown influence.

The total weekly motion picture audience in the United States is estimated at over 100 millions—and in 1931 it was estimated that over $100,000,000 was annually expended for advertising and exploiting films in the United States alone. If you read the film magazine you will see to whom much of this advertising is directed.

But behind all this are those I met with a serious purpose in the film business. They mean it to be used more and more for educative purposes, even for medical purposes, and they mean gradually and slowly to educate their audiences up to a higher standard of film. Already they are hard at work with many religious institutions across the country and educational institutions and others like the "Daughters of the American Republic," to support by the presence of their members and by public encouragement the more worth-while films. Time too will help them—the more so now that immigration is being greatly curtailed and third-generation Americans neither read the magazines I have mentioned nor care much about the type of story produced to-day.

I found there were many leaders who realised in Hollywood, it is doing more harm than good to the industry as an art, always to try for mass showing of one film and so cutting it as to make it popular to the majority. In the future, like with the stage, they must have separate theatres across the country for separate types of films, even separate films for different districts, and perhaps one day the film world will boast a Theatre Guild of its own. But those days cannot come until films are cheaper to produce.

When that day dawns, Hollywood will still remain the world's Mecca for learning the art of motion picture production, and instead of being to-day the interpreter of what interests democracy with its sex films, gangster stories reacting to college life and Covered Waggons, it will become a leading influence in developing a real American character, a real American spirit. There are many people in Hollywood working to this end, and there are many more who do not care in the least for anything but to-day's box-office receipts.

No matter which wins through, none can say they have seen America, or understand her spirit, until they have seen at close range the types let loose in Hollywood.

CHAPTER IV

CALIFORNIA, CHRISTIANS AND CITIZENS

DURING my six weeks in Hollywood I wandered over many parts of Southern California in search of things typical, and it must be confessed to get away from the artificiality of Hollywood.

The scenery of this part of the world is gorgeous, and unsurpassed in America, but there is little of a Californian type or character to be found amongst the people. The Indians are mostly further East, and the next conquerors, the Spaniards and then the Mexicans, are to be found more in the towns than scattered over the country—large parts of which are desert. Next you have the Americans who came there in the nineteenth century and bitterly resent the modern influx into Los Angeles; then the retired rather better class people from all over America, who have settled in Santa Barbara, or Pasadena, or near San Diego; and lastly you have the great majority of present-day Californians who are retired business people, often with their children, now grown up, and who have swept in from the Middle West.

They have brought with them all the tendencies of the Bible Belt. They have practically no contact with Europe whatever and they have spent the most active years of their life in a hard business struggle or living on the land. Eventually they reach California, and in Long Beach and Venice and other centres they have the amusements which their mentalities require.

But they crave for something spiritual—they have lived on the Bible all their life, and now, especially the women, middle aged and suddenly finding themselves without anything to do, they turn to all sorts of strange religions. You find these sects at every turn in California, and the sects, and the fact that the majority of the inhabitants of the south are retired small capitalists, doing nothing at all, or at most dabbling in real estate, are the two most noticeable things about California—especially Southern California.

Since 1910, Los Angeles has sprung up in twenty years from being the seventeenth largest city in America, to the fifth largest to-day, and the population of the whole State since 1920 has increased over 60 per cent. The boosting of all the cities and the whole country is almost unbelievable and business men are supposed to be flocking to the Pacific.

Yet there is one interesting thing to remember. The acreage of California is just under 100 million acres. In 1920, the Japanese controlled only 458,056 acres—less than half of 1 per cent, and yet in spite of that the latest figures I could obtain—those of 1927—show that these Japanese are responsible, on roughly the same acreage, for the cultivation of 92 per cent of the strawberries, 89 per cent of the celery, 83 per cent of the asparagus, 75 per cent of the onions, 66 per cent of the tomatoes, and 64 per cent of the melons produced in the whole of California, so widely advertised as the fruit garden of the United States. It becomes an interesting set of figures when you have stopped a little time on the Pacific Coast, and realised how little does Eastern America understand the Pacific Coast's interest in China and Japan —how entirely ignorant is Europe of such interest and how equally ignorant is the Pacific Coast, of Eastern American and European problems.

At the same time nearly all the difficult work in the West is being done by Japanese, Chinese, Filippinos, and Mexican pëons—as indeed Negroes do much of the work in the East, and one wonders just what these Japanese think of all the Bible-reading Americans they meet—along the whole coast-line— a coast-line that more than once recently has been scared by thoughts of war with Japan.

Most of these retired Middle Westerners centre round Los Angeles and Long Beach, and, practising every known form of Christianity, they gave me many opportunities of seeing what they like. Undoubtedly the most successful and the most colourful religious personality in Los Angeles is Aimée Semple McPherson, and I had a good opportunity of studying her methods.

A nervous breakdown, nine months round the world, and rumours of the most alarming kind about friction at home, seemed to have made Aimée Semple McPherson even more alive than ever. During my visit Los Angeles, with near a million and a half population, and all its Press, devoted weeks before her return to working up a real enthusiasm. She arrived the day previous to Prince Takamatsui of Japan, and monopolised all the limelight. I was determined to see her arrive, and to be present at her first evening service in the temple the next night.

There were thousands at the station. A special reception truck had been lavishly decorated for the reception, and bands of the Temple valiantly competed with each other as to their welcome.

Descending from the Santa Fé Express was a well-thought-out act. First, outside the station, the coach was detached, then shunted along a siding. All the blinds were pulled well down. Then suddenly Aimée appeared. Beautifully dressed, she waved gaily to the crowds, took one step down and waited for a bouquet of red roses, then another hand wave, another step

44

The Home of Aimée Semple McPherson

down, a second bouquet of roses, and then a quick look round the corner of the train to wave to those who hadn't yet seen her. Reaching the ground, she was surrounded by policemen and escorted through the throng to a waiting well-decorated truck packed with bands, sisters, brothers, councillors from the city, and photographers. Then, but at a sufficient distance, came Sister McPherson's daughter and her bridegroom purser on the ship on which they had travelled. The bands often playing when others tried to speak, added appropriate excitement to the proceeding with such airs as "The Jolly Bunch" and "Here they come!"

After the usual welcome, the evangelist, her daughter and her son-in-law, and also her son, drove off in a gaily draped car to the temple. All this was only a preliminary. Not only preliminary to an official reception that evening—but to her big first temple meeting the next night, a Sunday. Her subject was "Attar of Roses," her audience unique, amazing and rather hysterical.

An hour and a half before the service was scheduled to commence, the temple, holding over 10,000, was already full and some four or five thousand people were waiting hopelessly at the door. The hour and a half passed quickly with such an effective working-up of enthusiasm that the arrival of Sister Aimée seemed almost an anticlimax. Men and women members of the Bible Class had entered at the top of the building and processed to martial music right across balconies, down stairs, and round the stage to the main floor—some 200 in number. They had been followed by about another hundred of men and women —the men in white cassocks with white collars and black bow ties, the women in white dresses with yellow blossoms at their shoulders, and yellow bands in their hair. This formed eventually the choir and lined up to left and right of the stage.

On the stage was a big throne on one side, with a lesser seat beside it, and further to their right three other seats. On these were seated the Acting Mayor of Los Angeles, there to give the evangelist an official welcome, and two of the assistant pastors.

A large mixed band of about fifty people had in the meantime been playing the most martial airs, as also popular ones like "The Blue Danube Waltz," but the average trend of the music was more like the Salvation Army. A type of community singing leader who stood for some time on the stage, in a dinner-jacket, with a trumpeter on each side, asked us all, if we were happy, to say "Amen," and made us sing sometimes standing, sometimes sitting, but always clapping our hands. We sang "Four Square Hallelujah!" "Washed in the Blood of the Lamb!" and then suddenly all shook hands with each other, and I was wished by many determined-looking old ladies and seedy earnest young men a hearty "God bless you, Brother."

At last Mrs. McPherson descended; also, from the balcony right down to the stage, carrying large bouquets of red roses. She leaned on the arm of her son, and was closely followed by the bride and bridegroom who, however, were not allowed on the stage, but were ushered into the main hall, he being still an unbeliever.

The evangelist was all in white, with a silver cross woven on her dress. This was all covered by a blue cloak which, when thrown back, made her look most effective. The first part of the meeting was essentially business. Aimée sat on the throne with her son next her. The Acting Mayor welcomed her. She descended from the throne to thank him and shake hands. She told how she loved Los Angeles, and what she was doing for the needy. Then the curtain went up and we beheld a lit-up electric cross in a huge bed of roses. A large ship of orange-blossoms was then presented to Aimée, and she sat back while a religious concert was given by children and grown-ups for radio audiences throughout America.

It seemed a little incongruous that beside the throne, the evangelist had a telephone which she frequently used. After the concert she came forward and said she couldn't wait any longer. She must tell everyone about how music had just come into her life. On her travels she had composed a lot—in fact, four oratorios of which the first, "The Crimson Road," was already finished. These would take about 3½ hours to perform and would soon be given in the temple. She had also composed a march for the Four Square Gospel and proceeded to sing it.

One could not hear it all, but what one heard came with appropriate gestures. For at the words "Blood-stained Banner" she dramatically turned towards the lighted cross; at the words "Higher, reaching Higher," she did a mild hornpipe, supposedly climbing a rope; at "Preach the Word," she put her hands dramatically to her mouth; at "Unto the East, Unto the West," she looked appropriately to right and left, lifting her hand to right and left eye in turn; and finally at the words "Till the crowning Day" she sprang to attention and saluted dramatically. The applause was long and enthusiastic.

After this came the collection, not only to raise $37,000 for missionary work, but more especially to raise a temple in the Philippines where the Four Square Gospel is prospering, and others in China and Panama. As far as I could see, nobody put in less than 25 cents, and many people put in dollar bills.

47

While this was still continuing, the McPherson son moved to the centre of the stage and made an impassioned if prearranged speech. He told us how, he being eighteen years of age, the Lord had called him and he didn't want to go, but the Lord had persisted, and now he was about to become an evangelist. His special work, however, will be that of assisting his mother in her efforts. At this he resumed his seat and fondly kissed his mother, bending down from her throne. This induced a remarkable number of people to blow their noses in the temple, and there was a good deal of quiet weeping.

Now, however, the real moment had come. The moment when Sister Aimée McPherson was to preach her sermon on "Attar of Roses." The lights gradually went out until the cross and Aimée McPherson were alone lit up. The rather fine stained-glass windows depicting the life of Christ were also quietly lit, but only round the halo over Christ's head. The effect was impressive, and it is a remarkable tribute to her oratorial powers, that though she spoke for at least an hour, there was not one cough and hardly a noise throughout the building from start to finish.

She took us first to Algeria and into the desert. Described the camels, her dress, and her adventures, then how she found an oasis, and compared it to finding, in this world of sin, people leading a Christian life. Later she took us through the Algerian street of perfumes, and described how many roses were trampled and suffered to make that perfume, Attar of Roses. As a sideline she told us how she had bought a bottle and how but one drop lasted for nearly three months. Then she likened this to the life of Christ, His suffering and then the perfume He spread across the world.

She also referred to her own sufferings and the

calumnies that were spread around. But she only referred to them indirectly, with great subtlety,—yet enough to make her audience rustle and long for more. At times she was on her knees, at times, standing with outstretched hands to heaven, she cried, and she whispered. She preached sound common sense, and above all she put in those amazing touches that made you feel you realised why the poor people without too much to cheer them follow her blindly out here.

At the end of an hour's sermon she begged all converted strangers to come down to the stage, and many came. They came accompanied by other Sisters and knelt before the cross while the Sisters whispered in their ears.

The meeting was over and we were informed that the next night the daughter and her husband would hold a wedding reception for their followers and would gladly accept any wedding presents.

I came away realising that this Canadian woman, born and bred in Ontario, though she has taken a lot of money from poor people, is yet giving them in return just what they want. Whether it is a high standard or not, is not the point. It is as high a standard as they can understand. They give their money and get what they want. As for Sister Aimée McPherson, she too gives fully, and one hour spent as that hour must take all the energy out of any woman. She has many trials and much discontent in her temple, but she is a good and clever fighter, and that must always be admired. Nowhere, however, in the world is Christianity preached quite like it is at Los Angeles, and one leaves wondering if one is shocked or impressed.

Walking through the different streets of Los Angeles, you come across many other as yet less successful business—religious ventures—but all seemingly flourishing up to a point. There is Aimée McPherson's former assistant and now rival known as "The Trumpeting Evangelist." She has been able to build or buy quite a substantial church which advertises special Revival Services Every Night and Last Day Messages—which I believe are quite interesting. At any rate she quite shook the Four Square Gospel organisation recently by getting all their Boy Scouts to leave Aimée McPherson and join her.

And then there is the lady bishop who followed Aimée McPherson all the way to London to tackle her at the Albert Hall and each time she rose to speak from her box was drowned by Aimée starting a hymn.

A little further on is the Church of Divine Power —under which is written "Advanced Thought," and then you run into the more practical notice, California College of Embalming—Free Parking for Funeral Business—and if you go nearer to Hollywood you will find the Liberal Catholic Church and half a dozen others.

Beside all this is the more ordinary form of Christianity and you will find the English Church well represented in Los Angeles and throughout California. This is not remarkable when we realise what a large part Canada plays in the population of California and how it more or less holds together, with the aid of the British Consul, the large numbers of British subjects living there at the moment.

Of 386,000 citizens of the United States living abroad in 1930, over 218,000 were living in Canada. On the other hand, in California alone there were living in the same year no less than 450,000 Canadians, over 8 per cent of the total Californian population of 5¾ million.

The majority of them centre around Los Angeles and are in many cases to be found closely in touch with the film industry at Hollywood. A considerable group of retired business men and farmers, seeking a warm climate, are situated around Pasadena and Santa Barbara; but a very large contingent is actually in business in Los Angeles, and yet another contingent is out of work and seeking relief. This group is linked up with the other members of the British colony, a total in Los Angeles County of nearly 150,000 Britishers, and provides with the English some 1,500 souls in Los Angeles that have to be fed and looked after each year. The British Benevolent Society, receiving its annual grant from the Community Chest together with a few small subscriptions, does all in its power to help. Where, however, it is almost powerless is in dealing with cases that are illegally in the United States.

The British Benevolent Society both in San Francisco and Los Angeles does a very valuable work for all subjects of the Empire and is actively supported by the numerous British organisations such as the Sons and Daughters of St. George, The Manx Society, the Canadian Legion and the Daughters of the British Empire.

Canadian societies hold regular dances in Hollywood at which can be seen all the banners of the Provinces and in one corner a replica of Quebec and the Citadel.

But none of these links of out-of-works or more successful people compares with the binding force of the Posts of the Canadian Legion. For Legion purposes, all those who served in the Imperial Forces and are now in the United States, English, Irish or Canadian, are grouped into one Canadian Legion and British War Veterans Association. Out of the twenty-two Posts

134168

they have formed in the U.S.A., no less than nine have been started in California. Their leader is Colonel McDonnell, who started in the War as a private in the original Princess Pat's and ended up on the Headquarters staff. With him I witnessed two impressive sights on Memorial or Decoration Day, May 30. Though this holiday is essentially to commemorate the Civil War, yet the British element joins it, as well as on Armistice Day, to show the friendly spirit felt towards all members of the United States Forces.

We first went down to Pasadena, 30 to 40 miles from Los Angeles, and attended a parade, lasting nearly two hours. All branches of the American forces and the women's services were represented, marching through the town. Near the end came the little group of Britishers with the only foreign flags in the procession—the Union Jack and again the Canadian flag. British uniform, North-West Mounted Police uniform and Canadian Legion uniform all mingled together and the clapping of hands from the spectators was as loud for them as for any group that had passed before. From there we motored back as quickly as possible across Los Angeles and Hollywood to the Inglewood Cemetery. Here in one of the prettiest spots, the British Benevolent Society and their friends have bought a plot of land where about sixteen English and Canadians are buried.

Some two or three hundred men in uniform were gathered under Colonel McDonnell and Colonel McPherson, a former member of the Manitoba Government, and proceeded to march from the cemetery gates to the plot. The procession was headed by a band of Highland Pipers, followed by clergy from the English Church and a choir, officers carrying flags including Union Jacks and Stars and Stripes and uniformed representatives of all the British organisations. At the plot some three or four hundred civilians were waiting. Hymns were sung —the British Consul gave an address, followed by Sir John Adams, who was visiting the Southern California University, and the Pastor. A salute was then fired by a firing squad of veterans followed by the Last Post, sounded by buglers of the British Navy. The National Anthem was sung by everyone and the procession re-formed to depart from the cemetery.

This was only one side of the varied life of this city. Now that I have come through the whole United States, I think it is the most interesting city I found in America, certainly the most cosmopolitan one with, at the same time, a decent climate, a very high average of intelligence, and an atmosphere of its own. I recommend it to anyone, just to potter about in for a few days finding something new each moment.

In 1931, the city celebrated the 150th Anniversary of its founding by Spanish monks. Los Angeles in 1932 was even more the centre of attention. The city acted as host for the Olympic games to representative athletes from all the world over.

In its harbour, you will find the biggest battleships in the American Pacific Fleet, and you will find one of the busiest harbours in America. In the middle of the town, the Public Library and the City Hall stand out in a city where it is a relief to realise that skyscrapers are illegal.

The historic Los Angeles Mission, a few hundred yards from the City Hall, is at the corner of an old Plaza from which stretches a worn paved street, Olvera Street, the Mexican Bond Street of the city. At the head is a wooden crucifix erected in 1781— on September 4—on the right further down is the

53

Avila Adobe, the oldest house in Los Angeles. On the other side you will see the Teatro Torito where the Yale Puppeteers perform daily. Further on is El Navajo—the Indian Trading Post of South-west Indians. There are fascinating shops and fascinating shopkeepers. All round this quarter you are in the heart of Mexican Los Angeles. The cinemas only show Spanish films—though you are only twenty minutes from English-speaking Hollywood—the newspapers are Mexican.

A little further away and you are in a Chinese and Japanese quarter. Move a mile or so in the opposite direction and you will reach the Angelus Temple, the home of Aimée Semple McPherson, and the headquarters of her Four Square Gospel. Another 6 or 7 miles—you are still in the City of Los Angeles—you reach Hollywood studios, Syd Graumanns' Theatre, the well-known Sunset Boulevard and almost parallel with it the Wilshire Boulevard.

Drive on through there and you pass Beverley Hills—the homes of scores of world-famous film stars, and sometimes, if only for a few months, of world-famous authors—past the homes of John McCormack the singer, Will Rogers, and Charles Chaplin, past the University of Southern California, and before you have covered 30 miles you are in Santa Monica and on the coast again.

Come in the other direction from the port, still in this city that stretches 32 miles, and you pass the oil derricks of Signal Hill, the richest hill they say in the world—certainly the biggest oil producer. You are in the centre of the wealth of the Standard Oil, and the Shell Oil Companies—a little further on and you reach the stadium which held over 100,000 spectators in 1932, and in the living-quarters of the city, away from the homes of the cinema celebrities

54

Mexican Crucifix, Los Angeles

on the other side, are the homes of the Los Angeles millionaires.

Outside the city you have Pasadena, Santa Barbara, San Diego; to the north the famous ranch of Randolph Hearst, to the south the ranch of Al Capone, and also the Huntingdon Library housing "Pinkie," "The Blue Boy" and other famous pictures and rare manuscripts.

Hidden away in different parts of the city are places like the Cocoanut Grove at the Ambassadors Hotel, and the "Brown Derby for lunch or dinner." Add to these innumerable small eating-places built in the shape of a huge coffee-pot or a bottle of milk, a large painted owl or a yellow hen, and then drink from a bar cut into the middle of a vast wooden orange innumerable drinks of orange-juice, almost free, oranges being so common, and you will realise that you are only a few miles from orange groves, walnut and grapefruit ranches, and that every day you can explore something new in this city.

No district can offer half so much to see or do in the United States, or offer it so cheaply. The best of everything comes at some time to Los Angeles, not only because Los Angeles includes Hollywood —but because it has grown and is growing faster than any city in America.

I do not think it is any exaggeration to say all this or to add that I think the city in one respect deals with the unemployed more efficiently than any other city of similar size in America. There is of course a Community Chest and there are large numbers of charities working with it—but no charity is empowered to help a needy case until they have first sent him to a Municipal Clearing Bureau.

I spent a morning here in their basement office. The men sent by the charity or coming on their own are closely questioned by an expert, who decides first if they are legally citizens of the United States, next whether they are legally eligible for relief in Los Angeles or should be helped by Los Angeles societies, and finally what work they can do, and what society could help them most. They are eventually sent to that society—though it need not be the one from whom they came. Before this, while the Municipality so to speak has them under their thumb, they give them a short medical examination and decide whether they must just suffer the pangs of a bath and a little cleansing up—or whether they need more careful treatment.

Naturally thousands of unemployed the country over flock to Los Angeles and California for the winter, and it is up to the city and authorities to protect their taxable citizens from having to support these people from another district.

Some of them told me the trains are now raided by the police as much as fifty miles outside Los Angeles, and all the unrequired visitors are given a night in the police station in the city and then given twelve hours to start back again! The city is not unkind about it, nor are the judges—as after all, the advertisements the city puts out about flourishing industries, wonderful climate, oranges and lemons to be picked off the trees, are as largely responsible for the influx of unemployed, who can live on less food in such a climate, as they are for the refined Middle Westerners and their religious idiosyncrasies.

Most of the city's European foreigners I met when mixing with the Catholics, and a fête I was taken to, brought them together in full force.

The fête, as often everywhere, was postponed a week because of unsettled weather, and then it was held on a Saturday in brilliant sunshine. The object

56

—a home for Catholic working girls whether in the films, the factories, or the office.

Motoring down to Los Angeles from Beverley Hills, we passed the Spanish-style Church in Hollywood, built where the famous Franciscan Missionary, Fra Juniper Serra, once said mass and which now is under the care of the Jesuits. Here on Sundays with masses every hour, you will see the church crowded with Italians, Hungarians, Irish, Americans, Germans, French, Negro and every nationality, and perhaps more than anywhere you will notice the number of young people. We passed one of the oldest of the famous Mission Churches and on along the Boulevards till we came to the Catholic Cathedral, as fine a building as any in America.

The fête was in a unique place. Not quite a private residence yet not a public park, but something between the two and typical of the novel ideas of American millionaires.

In the older part of the town, this group of private houses formed a small cul-de-sac park, perhaps ten houses and about thirty or forty acres of ground. All this has gradually been purchased by E. L. Doheny. He is said to be the richest man on the Pacific Coast. From a poor boy working in gold mines, he very literally struck oil and is to-day as big an oil magnate as any and a prominent Catholic.

Having bought all the houses around his own in this park, he pulled down a few that seemed in the way and the remainder he lets at almost nominal sums to his own personal friends, prominent Catholics and such public leaders as the head of the University. They are all friends, and all use the park with their own bit of private ground as well. All this was thrown open for the fête for the Catholic Cathedral, largely supported by Mr. Doheny, which is built at the next corner conveniently near.

Like a large garden party with many people not Catholics but often Episcopalians or nothing, the place was filled with admirers of Catholic work. Bands played at almost every corner, and often their music clashed with each other. But Hungarian national costumes and Tzigane orchestras were perhaps most noticeable. There is a very large Hungarian Catholic colony in Hollywood and they had mustered in force. The tennis court, covered over, was another dancing centre with tea served around it and priests and nuns and the Sisters of Social Service mixed with the throngs on all sides. Jackie Coogan ran the children's entertainment, and many famous film stars were to be seen helping as mannequins or by purchasing freely. It is worth remembering that Hollywood, day in, day out, in the full limelight, no matter what happens, is also a strong centre of practising catholicism.

The many nationalities represented in the colony are for the most part Catholic, and include the majority of the actors, actresses and the even greater number of people one never hears about who actually produce the pictures.

But when you get more out into the country, you must be impressed with the Catholic background of this part of America. Old Missions everywhere, Spanish names, crosses here and there, and slabs inserted in buildings, monuments erected on the roads to commemorate the lengthy tramping of the old-time monks bent on the conversion of the Indian.

I often got out to the country for the week-end, but never to a pleasanter spot than Santa Barbara and its Mission. You are not far from Hollywood and Los Angeles and yet the people are in a different world. At the different villas, the owners are still "at home," as you see on their cards, first and third Thursdays, or second Mondays, and it is almost impossible to be admitted without letters of introduction.

While I was there, there was a yacht anchored in the harbour and on board a very rich English widow; but she had no letters, though a well-known name in business, and nobody would call. This greatly upset the shop people and the local hairdresser was terrified such a good customer might leave. However, she did not, and committed the even more shocking crime of entertaining lavishly the cinema colony from Hollywood. Santa Barbara looked disapproving and gave its usual Sunday suppers at the Montecito Club.

I dined one Sunday at the Club with an English lady, yet the Deputy-Sheriff of Santa Barbara, and her husband, one of the original Directors of the Canadian Pacific Railway. The other guests were all, I gather, pretty well known, very quiet people from Boston, Montreal, Denver and Washington. They played polo, some, and others the piano; they were all great friends of Lindbergh, and they all had gorgeous villas. We walked round the buffet table in a queue, filling our plates to the brim after hot soup, and then, after tons of food, moved into the hall and watched a Will Rogers film, and then home to bed.

Their Club is magnificent—far too big for such a small colony—and now more or less in difficulties for lack of members, and their whole life is unique on the Pacific Coast. This is the centre of rich people who are really Americans and have been so long enough—both rich and American—to be almost unrecognisable in many ways from the same type of European—and yet they have a difference. They are brighter yet more sincere and somehow cleaner. There is a freshness about them that is a tonic, and a liberal spirit that yet is terribly conservative about their friends—but money means nothing to them—they like you or they don't—and kindness to the foreigners in spite of a hundred bad experiences is to them almost a religion. This is not just Santa Barbara—I hardly met a soul there for more than twenty minutes—but later I met the same type across the country—and I only mention them here because it is one of their best known haunts in America.

Diplomats say the three social centres of America are Washington, Long Island and Santa Barbara—and from the point of view of the Pacific Coast it is their only haunt. The better class Californian from the south is more apt to concentrate on Pasadena. Santa Barbara embraces all America.

Easily its most interesting landmark is the Santa Barbara Mission, the largest that is still held by the Catholic Church. The monks show the visitors round regularly and show with great pride their garden where you will find 4,000 Indians buried at seven feet apart in graves nine feet deep. Each is buried in his blanket. Near by in tombs lie 500 Spaniards.

In one villa I found one of the three original Stewart pictures of Washington from which is taken the likeness for the One-dollar bills. It shows very clearly what trouble Washington had with his set of false teeth—the mouth sagging pathetically. A second picture belongs to the Boston Athenæum and is now in Washington, and the third is in the possession of Lord Rosebery—having been originally purchased by his Rothschild grandfather.

From Los Angeles I went by stage bus as far as San Francisco and eventually on to Seattle, and all the way through Southern California I was on the road of the Spanish monks—El Camino Real—one of the prettiest drives in America. First the country is hilly and sandy and not very interesting. But then come the most attractive gorges, canyons bringing you down from San Fernando to Ventura, through orange and lemon groves. Here you find oil derricks stretching right out into the sea, and you continue along the coast from Santa Barbara until you turn into the Gaviota Pass, which is surrounded by hills covered in bush, like huge, soft, dark, moss-covered rocks. All around St. Ynez is attractive and you begin to pass many fine-looking horse ranches as you approach St. Luis Obespan, where I spent the night.

I was starting my journey through a country first Indian, then Spanish and intensely Catholic, but now overrun by Middle Westerners with a thousand strange religions. The Spaniards at least fought and prayed—the monks cultivated and irrigated the land —but the present crowd is too artificially prosperous to think of fighting, they just pray and play—the prayers do not work on the land and the players can do little for themselves—and beneath them are the workers who cultivate the land, the people from the Far East—the Japanese, the Chinese, the Filippino.

The Christians of California may be largely in the majority and they may be a peace-loving Bible-bred set of earnest human beings—but they seem only to be adepts at taking in each other's washing. The main work of the south of the country is done by people who distrust and certainly despise the white Christian of the Pacific Coast. Theirs is another religion, theirs is another philosophy of life, and how California will fare in the problems of the Pacific that are only vaguely understood or imagined to-day will be as interesting a development as any in America in the next hundred years.

CHAPTER V

TIBETAN BUDDHISM, AND EGYPTOLOGY
AMERICANISED

"WELL, you see," she told me, "Max Heindel got all his information from the Twelve Elder Brethren in Germany."

"Ah," said I, "and are they still alive?" She looked at me a little sadly and a little vacantly.

"Alive! Yes, you would say some are. The others are with the living dead. You could not see them. But they are all alive."

"Quite," I quickly replied.

"And where is their centre?" I tactlessly persisted.

"Their temple too is in Germany—if you have the eyes to see—you have not. Even I cannot see the temple. The naked eye cannot. It is only visible to the full-believer."

The conversation was getting beyond me. Only the night before I had attended a gay party at Hollywood. And here I now was, at Mount Ecclesia, Oceanside, not far from San Diego—seeing—or rather not seeing things—with a lady that seemed otherwise sane, on the edge of a cliff overlooking the Pacific. She was English, this lady, and her brother had been Captain of Winchester and her nephew was now at Oxford, but she had come deliberately to California to practise the teachings of Max Heindel and the American Fellowship, and altogether as she looked you through and through, I thought her an alarming person with whom to be alone on a cliff. In no way would I contradict her.

And then the materialistic touch appeared. I asked why had they purchased fifty acres just here when Germany was their spiritual home. "Ah," said she, "that is due to astrology. We know there will soon be changes in the earth and California will become the centre of the World. So we have invested in land here."

Shade of the real estate promoter! Even astrology would back up California. But there was no doubt about the beauty of the position.

Here on a hill less than two miles from the main highway that to-day runs 2,000 miles from Vancouver in Canada to the borders of Mexico and that one day will stretch from Alaska to the Panama Canal, they have built a white temple into which but a few of their members can enter. It is only for the fully initiated, and is a Temple of Healing. From beside it you look down to the Pacific Ocean on the west, and to the east along a beautiful valley with a trail that leads to the old mission buildings of St. Luis Rey—the old Camino Real. As I stood with my guide beside this fine domed building looking at the sun setting across the Pacific, she explained to me their religion.

Max Heindel, their founder, had a few years previously gone to Germany where these Twelve Elder Brethren, some living, some living dead, had told him now that democracy was coming to the fore it was no longer wise to keep secrets guarded and he must tell the world all about the Rosicrucian beliefs. With the aid of the living, and the living dead, and no doubt with his own knowledge of American mentality, they so arranged and brought up to date this religion, that, as they now advertise it, it is suitable and sufficiently modernised for Western consumption.

It would seem to be mainly a study of astrology, and the application of the latter to healing the sick. The Fellowship—which has a senior rival further up the coast—is now concentrating on healing, and this is done mainly in the temple—into which only a few

63

of the colony can enter. They are trying to make a healing-chain around the world, and for this purpose all their supporters, wherever they may be, are supposed to think of each other at 6.30 each evening—regardless of whether it is Pacific time, Eastern time, or Greenwich time.

When you are ill too, in another part of the world, you must write once a week to the temple and say how you are getting on, and you must write in ink because the ink fluid will form a contact. This struck me as an ingenious way and indeed a modern method of getting more people to join the Oceanside order, and to prevent mere distance stopping the work.

So successful has been their organisation that they now have a large staff of secretaries, most of them working voluntarily, and speaking many languages, who work regularly at Mount Ecclesia and keep in touch with the sick the world over. Across America they have many branch offices and are preparing to build at Oceanside a large hospital in which, however, all the doctors and nurses practising must believe in astrology and have a very clear knowledge of the effects of the stars on people's lives. For the rest, their religion holds little that is new.

Perhaps their most up-to-date idea is that the spirit escapes from the body at death—that it is a form of ether—and they would prove its escape by the fact that a doctor in Boston recently weighed a body at the moment of death and then immediately after, and found the body lighter.

They consider this ether spirit, or soul, is imprinted with all the doings of the being during life, and that during the three and a half days after death, all your past life, imprinted in this ether, develops before your eyes and you gradually disappear into different degrees of after-life, and atonement, until eventually you are

The Rosicrucian Temple of Healing in California

A Rosicrucian Cottage

reincarnated after roughly one-third as many years again as you spent in the world.

During the three or four days in which you are seeing your life—if you die as a child, it must be a very slow and long-drawn-out film—your body must not be disturbed and there must be silence in your house. Thus if you are killed in an accident, things in the next world are very difficult for you—and in any case the modern method of embalming is strongly rejected at Oceanside, and it is recommended that the body be left on an ice slab in temporary cold storage.

At first the dead person does not realise he is dead, and also during the first few days or weeks it is easy for him to get in touch with the world, and if while alive he has daily examined his conscience, then when he dies he can have a sort of holiday during the period other people are going through purgatory. Needing no food or sleep, he can do twenty-four hours a day of good and later will be many steps ahead of others in his reincarnated form, and of course much nearer —though the Rosicrucians do not say so—to the Eventual Buddhist Nirvana.

From astrology they take most; but many of the smaller details come from Buddhism, especially the esoteric kind practised by the Lamas in Tibet; a little comes from the *Egyptian Book of the Dead*, and no doubt a certain amount from Plato's *Republic*.

But all this we do not hear, we are only told that the light came to Max Heindel in Germany, and now the money is coming to California. This much must be said about Mount Ecclesia, they make very little of money. They charge remarkably little for stopping there—fees for lectures are merely voluntary gifts, and it is probably only on the sale of their books that they are really making money. They have a colony of over fifty people, who live in small cottages on the property and are mostly women, and nearly every-one does voluntary work in keeping in touch with their really huge volume of mail. They run a vegetarian cafeteria and have a small chapel in addition to the temple, and now are busy saving money to build the hospital which may have some very interesting results. No doubt they make money, but they are not mysteri-ous, and in this they differ from their rivals whom I visited a few days later.

The rivals form the Rosaecrucian Order, or to give it its full title, the Ancient and Mystical Order of Rosae Crucis—A.M.O.R.C.—and are to be found on the road from St. Luis Obespan to San Francisco, at a town called San José.

They are not so easy to find, as they live on a side street off the main road, having nothing like as impos-ing an estate as their Oceanside rivals. I first heard of them in Los Angeles, in their small office where they hold lecture classes every week, and everything was extremely mysterious.

"Was the order alive in England?"—"No, it only existed in secret—but if I joined I would later be told of some of its members," and so on.

Finally I was told about the temple at San José, and I broke my journey there to visit it. It consists of two long low buildings, of a pink colour, reminiscent of a Hollywood film studio—but behind it is a perfect replica of an Egyptian arch—which would give the clue to the whole or almost the whole of the teachings of this organisation. Inside, one whole building is given up to a large private post office—from which they send out endless supplies of literature and adver-tisements and from which they send out the various lessons which presumably, if he continues to pay his fees, will one day, by correspondence course, make the interested person into a being with the knowledge of the Pharaohs, the Lamas of Tibet, Euclide, Count Cagliostro and even Baron Chaos of Prague.

There is no doubt, however, that Americans are intensely interested in what these people profess to teach—and many times across America, I had only to mention them to people to find that they knew a lot about them and wanted to know more.

Their museum is the most interesting thing in the building. Here they have the Benediction Stone reputed to be from under the temple under which Moses appealed on behalf of the Tribes of Israel, and here also are priceless scarabs and work from the tomb of Tutankhamen, as well as interesting gifts from the Emperor Francis Joseph of Austria to his brother Maximilian of Mexico, showing his knowledge of the mystic signs of the order. You can also see the Silk Collar of Masonry that was worn by Napoleon the First, and several other interesting links between Egyptology, Freemasonry, and, they claim, Rosaecrucianism.

From the museum, you enter the actual temple, a large, square, dark and very cool room with a low ceiling. The lighting is very subdued, and though all sorts of religions and mystic practices can be carried on by Rosaecrucian branches, throughout the country, I gather here alone are held the chief rites—as in a sort of holy of holies. At the far end from the door, lit up from behind, was a large cardboard Eye—The All-Seeing-Eye—and behind it very dimly lit up was a painted wall. It looked like the Egyptian Desert, with azure-blue sky, silver stars, and pyramids. All around the room, placed in what seemed to me Masonic form, were Egyptian thrones, and large numbers of mystic signs.

In one corner I was shown the Initiation Room, which was very dark. On one wall, however, was a

67

picture of Christ lit also from behind, and with the reflection I was able to see in another corner a gramophone.

Outside attached to the post office is their own printing press from which they send out their endless supply of literature. They seem to me infinitely more mercenary than the Oceanside ladies—though they too no doubt do not starve. But at San José—unless in recent months prices have come down—they charge "in accordance with the ancient custom" as it is put on your application form, $5 as a contribution to the Rosaecrucian Foundation, and you promise to pay $2 a month as long as you remain a member—that is $24 a year. The application form which is supposed to be sent you as an invitation—presumably somebody having said what a sympathetic soul you are—but which is lying outside the museum door for anyone to take, is very uplifting in its promises—but at the end are the ominous words, "Be sure to send your remittance with this blank."

Then over and above that you have to pay for your books—which they produce fairly frequently and which I must confess have the most appetising titles and are well advertised—*Rosicrucian Principles for the Home and Business*—costs $2·25—*Unto Thee I Grant*, price $1·50, tells you the Secret Teachings of the Masters of the Far East, and I gather is translated by special permission of the Grand Lama and Disciples of the Sacred College in the Grand Temple of Tibet. And then there is *A Thousand Years of Yesterdays*, which boldly professes to be "The Story of the Soul," and explains in detail how the soul enters the body and how it leaves, where it goes and when it comes back to the earth again and why . . . a revelation of the mystic laws and principles known to the Masters of the Far East and the Orient for many centuries and never put into book form as a story before this book was printed. . . . Fascinating—Alluring—Instructive—"You will learn more about the mystic principles of the Orient in reading this book . . ." and so on.

They say Catholics, Jews, anyone can belong—even Popes and St. Thomas Aquinas were members—and they gaily explain away the Immaculate Conception and the Resurrection for $2·90 in the *Mystic Life of Jesus*. There are a lot of other books, and people across America lap them up with relish. As their Order is secret and until you pay your dollars you cannot know what they really teach, I am unable to be positive—but in their pamphlets they claim Freemasonry is only a branch of their more Ancient Order, and they speak of the laws of Karma. They deal a little with Astrology and there is enough spoken about health and right living both at work and morally to seem that they are also dabbling in that much abused science of Tibetan Buddhism called Tantricism.

If one were to hazard a guess, one would say the more intelligent people are interested in Oceanside, whereas the less literate, not alienated by the money side of the teaching, are interested in the promise of business success cleverly offered at San José, as also by the mystic element—dear to so many American business men, and the historical background—which at Oceanside they say makes them out of date but which, whether it be a true claim or not, attracts many people across America longing for ancestors or a link with the past, and especially from Pennsylvania, where the Rosaecrucians claim an original American background.

They claim their Order can only exist in any one country for 108 years. Then it dies or goes into retirement—as to-day in England—for another 108 years. Then it starts afresh. In ancient times in

Egypt, the more learned people decided to hold private classes to pursue their learning, and they commenced these classes under the auspices of Ahmore the First, who ruled Egypt from 1580 B.C. to 1557 B.C. Gradually the Order developed until it took its present physical form in the reign of Thutmore III, 1500 B.C.–1447 B.C. Later on, according to the San José offices, Egypt's most enlightened monarch of this era, Amenhotep IV, 1367 B.C., gave the Order the teachings and writings they use to-day.

Many people it seems came from outside countries to study with the Order—and then when thoroughly versed in its teachings, went home to start Chapters of their own. The list of members claimed by the present Order at San José as their more distant and more immediate "fathers" is distinctly impressive—especially as one stands and looks at the present buildings in a side street in the living quarter of San José.

Glancing through the list we find Solomon, Pythagoras, Democritus of Thrace 460 B.C., Socrates of Athens 470 B.C., Euclides 399 B.C., Plato of Athens 428 B.C., Aristotle of Thrace 385 B.C., Episurius of Athens 341 B.C., Cicero 79 B.C., Seneca 70 B.C., lodges in Toulouse and Montpelier in the twelfth century—others in Tibet and China, in Cologne in 1115, under Charlemagne in France, on the Gold Coast of Africa in 1799, in Mauritius in 1794; fairly modern "fathers" such as Francis Bacon, Earl of Verulam, Joseph Balsano (Count Cagliostro)—whom, however, they eventually turned out of the Order—and then Benjamin Franklin and Thomas Jefferson.

But where the history becomes of particular interest in studying America is in its first advent to that country. Perhaps I am wrong in saying first, because these Rosaecrucians claim from old manuscripts in their possession, that one member at least landed with an early expedition from Spain in California in 1602 and deposited a Rosaecrucian stone—which may be a reason why they are at San José to-day—but at any rate the first really historic landing of Rosaecrucians was in 1694.

They are reported to have come together in England and in Holland and to have selected pioneers from their number according to their professions and trades. All had to be able to contribute to the knowledge and experience required, and in the winter of 1693 they set sail in their own boat the *Sara Maria.*

It is interesting to note that they travelled under the auspices of Francis Bacon's old Lodge in London known by the Greek word Philadelphia—and you can still see in Philadelphia part of their first home on Mystic Lane in Fairmount Park.

In America they claim to have established the first complete printing plant and they made their own paper in the first American paper mill. They published the first American Bible and they started a Sunday school, sixteen years before one was established in England. In addition they started mills for grinding corn and factories for making organs, and they established the first botanical gardens for the purpose of preparing herbs and medicines for advanced medical practices.

In their college rooms the Declaration of Independence was translated into many foreign languages so that the different colonists could read it. They started the propaganda for negro slave emancipation —and one of their members, after whom a square is named in Philadelphia—Rittenhouse—established a world-famous observatory.

Such was the work done by these early mystics, and according to their rules, after 108 years—in 1801— they went into secret retirement—only to emerge again in 1909. This is the claim of the organisation at San José. They claim to have received initiation from their brethren in France, and to be the representatives of all the old orders and people to whom I have referred. Whether that is so or not has nothing to do with this book. There are many other organisations that claim they are the real mystic inheritors.

Be that as it may, none can deny the existence all through the eighteenth century, especially in Pennsylvania, of the Rosaecrucians and other mystic bodies, and undoubtedly they did practise many arts and sciences then considered extremely advanced. Most famous of their temples was at Wissahickon—known as "The Woman in the Wilderness," and here forty of them lived a mystic life about which it is really fascinating to read. At first they called themselves Pietists and settled mostly at Germantown outside Philadelphia—but they were essentially Rosaecrucian, though later on the terms began to be loosely applied, and we find much of what the modern Rosaecrucians claim to have been their work actually the work of a sect at Ephreta in Lancaster County, Pennsylvania, that were in many ways more Mennonites than Rosaecrucians.

The present-day teaching, as far as one can gather, at San José and at Oceanside, besides much that comes from Egypt and something that comes from Philadelphia of the eighteenth century, has also a large amount of teaching copied from what is believed to be the teaching of the esoteric lamas in Buddhist Tibet.

First of course comes the teaching of Rebirth; then you can notice the ideas about what happens immediately after death—the different other-world lives lead —the accumulation through numerous lives of a sort of fate for your future, called Karma; the suggestion that much can be done by the right pronunciation of certain words—which in Tibet is known as Mantra —Word of Power—and is also the Greek idea of chords in music and the more scientific modern theory of sound waves—but it was magic in many lands one hundred years ago. And then you have healing which may be classed with Tantricism in Tibet and the herb doctors from the East.

Moreover you have much that was practised by the early Christians before certain Councils stamped out such esoteric teaching—which is perhaps why the freedom-seeking Christians of the seventeenth and eighteenth centuries dabbled so much in these doctrines in Pennsylvania—and lastly you have the modern Democratic method of making it all understandable to the American public.

Wherever you look in history or even in the East to-day, you find that these teachings, now so much advertised from California, were previously only taught to people who through constant watching and much preparation had been proved to be capable of understanding such teachings and not going insane, as they well might at too much psychic knowledge, and the teachings were taught to nobody who had not a proved mentality and power of understanding.

What, on the other hand, is happening to-day? The Western method—the American method as some would say,—to be more accurate, probably the method of Democracy, is to let anyone know a garbled version of partially true doctrines, and learn it by post without anybody who gives that knowledge being certain of anything concerning the correspondent beyond that he is sending two dollars a month.

Through the knowledge given him he may practise vices, herb cures, communications with the other world—enough if he is slightly unbalanced to send

73

him completely off his head; and in short what all the world has always admitted to be knowledge dangerous to all except the extremely intelligent is now to be administered wholesale—and at that in a potted version across the continent to gullible men and women.

Behind it all is something that strikes me as essentially American. From those days of the seventeenth century down we find a strong mystic strain in the real American, a keen interest in things esoteric, and it has gone on right up to this day.

Here we see the combination of the two, the mystic string being played on by the democratic touch, and it probably does more harm than good. But when such mystic orders can go on quietly throughout the land—as they do more in America then any other land in the world, then are we likely to see more and more in America the production of new so-called inventions and numerous scientific discoveries.

For those who study what was known of old in the East, have a great advantage over those too practical people who have no time for such things. The real American is intensely mystic and interested in religions; and though swindlers and adventurers may profit immensely by the gullibility of so many millions of her citizens, yet it cannot be a bad thing that a nation wants to know about the other worlds. It is far better than to be like so many Europeans, just drifting towards a lazy cynicism. As the years go on I feel America will become more and more interested in things mystic and, if you like, in their application to science, with probably amazingly profitable results to herself; but let her try and guard against overstressing the democratic side of such teachings—which are essentially not for the people of ordinary intelligence—as she seems to be doing to-day in California and also in New York and in the South.

I cannot do better in ending this chapter than by quoting from *A History of the Jews*, describing the years just after the death of Jesus Christ.

"It is difficult for us to understand just what was going on in the civilised world at that time. A great hunger seems to have taken possession of all the races, a hunger for faith, for religion. It was a tired—a dying world—a world that had lost its best blood in wasteful wars of conquests. And in its last hours it gulped thirstily from every cup of faith held to its lips, hoping wildly that some one of them might contain the elixir of life. In the lands around the Mediterranean there was almost an orgy of belief-making in those years. All sorts of Gods belonging to all sorts of religions were fused together —even their names were combined—and sacrifices were offered to them all at one time. Not having complete faith in any one God, the people tried to make use of them all."

And to anyone who looks, such must be the impression of much of the Middle West and the Pacific Coast of America in the depression of to-day.

CHAPTER VI

SELLING REAL ESTATE IN SAN FRANCISCO

From San José to San Francisco was only a short run in the stage bus. And as I came into the city and discovered that the wealthy district is called Menlo and was founded by Burkes and by Blakes, I was suddenly homesick. Menlo Castle in Galway in Ireland, now burnt to the ground, I have known all my life, for it was the home of my great-grandmother, a Blake, and of my cousins, and was only a few miles from my own Burke home, Ower. As I looked at the Menlo district advertised as the home of millionaires I thought of the old eleventh Blake baronet in Galway, my great-uncle, who had been so poor and owed so much money that he had to be a Member of Parliament.

In those days a member could not be arrested for debt. But when Parliament was dissolved and you had to be re-elected again then things were worrying at Menlo. The Baronet could not be arrested in his house, so he would not go outside the estate—except of course on Sundays, because again on Sundays you could not be arrested for debt. And lastly, in order to represent Galway again in the next Parliament, he must address the electors.

But that was simple. Menlo Castle was on Lough Corrib, which goes up to the bridge from which you can see the salmon leap, in Galway. And so he would row up to the bridge and harangue the electors from a boat. But he never dared to land. And all the electors, who often were in the same position and could sympathise, always elected him again, for they respected old families and sportsmen. And we too, the Burkes, nearby, were no better off, and when a

76

few years ago the Sinn Feiners burnt my home down, my father always said it took such a long time to burn because it was so damp.

Here in San Francisco were the descendants of the Blake and Burke peasants that had been our tenants and had called the district after their old home, and now they were rich millionaires, and I found many interested in the history of their clans at home.

I passed on in my bus to a small hotel, and later went out to see the many parks, and also the fine tower erected by the Burkes. Everywhere in America I ran across Irish people tremendously keen on their links with Ireland and also those of Anglo-Saxon descent. As one man, a FitzGerald, put it to me: "We really love the old country and we pretend we do not mind your criticism, but we do, we are sensitive about it, and we really do want your praise just sometimes." And certainly if you look at San Francisco you will willingly give it. I think I know no cleaner or more beautiful modern city.

This bus visit was really my second—as on the way down to Los Angeles my boat had stopped here two days, coming through the lovely Golden Gates, and I had been ashore to see friends then in San Francisco and we had been to theatres, hotels, beautiful antique shops and really superb museums.

Now however I was more serious about the city, and I only paid one visit to Archbishop Hanna, the Catholic Archbishop, and one of the most influential characters on the Pacific. A delightful man, tall, very breezy and kind hearted, he had studied for some years at Cambridge, been many years in Rome, and was one of the best educated of the bishops I met in America. With a powerful Irish flock that greatly influenced the city and another large Italian contingent, he is their ideal leader and I believe everybody loves him. He sent me round the more obscure parts of the city with two native sons of California and I was shown the old Mission Church, the Italian fishing quarter, the site of the great Exhibition and finally the Russian Church.

Here I had a long talk with the Archpriest, who told me of the number of Russian refugees who came out through Siberia and are to-day in San Francisco; and we talked of that part of the country a few hours north of San Francisco called Sebastapool and Russian River, and such names, where still stands a church built on the spot nearly a hundred years ago where the Russians landed and made a half-hearted attempt to colonise California themselves and make all that and Oregon into a Russian province as Alaska was to be. Had that been Russian before the gold rush came—what different history the world might show to-day.

I also visited the very large Chinese quarter where many a writer has got his material for the most blood-curdling tales of San Francisco, and then the docks and the Irish quarter.

But I was to get my greatest joy in San Francisco in the sale of real estate.

At my hotel sat a charming old lady at a desk and all around her were notices that a real estate firm would have much pleasure in showing you San Francisco for nothing. Grand, thought I. I've already seen it, but why not another trip, and I can compare notes.

Next morning in bed I received an elaborate invitation and was asked to be ready at ten o'clock when a closed car would await me at the door. It was up to time and the old lady took me out, introduced me to the gentleman-chauffeur and to a nice-looking young man behind and to a lady quietly dressed, I should say about thirty years old. At first I thought the man behind was like myself interested, but soon I found out that he too was a salesman and the lady was his particular charge, as I was to be of the driver.

We were told of the wonders of the city, and as we drove out I realised we were destined for a new plot of land that was to be sold out in lots.

On the way my intelligent lady friend behind, who knew what she was talking about, being a school teacher from, I think, Massachusetts, asked some tactless question about rates and the high taxation of land. This the driver thought might frighten me, so he switched on the radio in the front of the car, and the lady's remarks behind were effectually drowned. We stopped at Stanford University and were shown a few sights and then proceeded to a small bungalow park which the driver had recently helped to develop. The man behind asked him the right questions, and in a perfect state of mind to buy at a moment's notice we landed up at the estate nearly 30 miles from San Francisco, but which somehow would one day be the centre of the city.

At the moment, however, it was just one flat piece of waste with a clump of trees under which was pitched a tent. In state we drove up to a sort of temporary landing-stage when our number was taken and we got out—our driver and his friend disappearing. Roughly there were about sixty people like ourselves, all out in cars at the expense of the owner and nearly all as amazed as myself. The lady and I promised to keep together and if anyone almost made one of us bid for land, then we would pinch each other to stop. Soon we were all ushered into the tent—at one end of which stood a large auction platform and behind it a lit-up map of the bottle-neck, that is San Francisco.

We were all put at little tables and given food that was called lunch. It was not a large meal—but it was sufficient to support us through the coming ordeal. After we had finished we were each given an identity number with our names on it and then a small man— a great salesman I was told and a former Revivalist preacher—got up on the platform.

He took off his coat and waistcoat and was ready to get down to business. For one whole hour without a moment's pause that man talked on—sometimes he yelled, often he whispered—he would produce a plan, catch the eye of some nervous female, rush down from the platform and show her the plan—then rush through the tables, still talking, always talking. Hotter and hotter he got, more and more fabulous seemed the prospects of the wonderful district, more and more extravagant became his superlatives.

Snatches I caught that were perfect—"Yes, ladies and gentlemen, this is the Golden Land—but here also are fifty-nine other minerals—and then there is agriculture. . . . But above all water is king,—yes, ladies and gentlemen, water is king. . . . There is white pine, enough building material for generations—oil too, that is the black gold—and the greatest landlocked harbour. Here is the navy, here are pleasure ships, here commercial ships. The harbour could hold all the commercial ships of the world. . . . Life here is sweeter—age is longer—money is more—and birth-rate is higher. Indeed, ladies, this is the 'City That Knows How.' As in human beings there is a heart, in cherries a stone, so for California is San Francisco. Never forget God stopped making land— and we must propagate not fish, ladies and gentlemen, but race, indeed we must push up the value of land. . . . Each year there come through here eleven million cars, and twenty-four million souls. Railways

are coming, dirigibles will make this their base. . . .
Remember in everyone there must be two qualities—
Faith and Vision."

As he screamed and gesticulated and as he developed
before our wondering eyes the plan of the estate, the
business section, the residential quarter and the
amenities, many became excited, more began to
weaken, and then in one last frenzied appeal to "buy
now before you leave to-day" he stopped and we were
all whisked out into the open.

One by one our mentors swooped down on us to
ask us what plot we wanted and where. Wretched
people, protesting, were carried off in cars to different
parts of the estate to choose their holding, and by a
radio machine the central booth was kept informed of
the sales. Every few minutes a bell would ring and
through a loud megaphone we, the doubting ones,
would be told that fresh plots had been sold.

People from Australia, from London, from New
York, from New Orleans and from Buenos Ayres
started to buy—plot after plot began to go—of course
on easy terms—and more and more I felt I was a poor
sport or a fool not to take up some piece of this amazing
bargain.

Now a sort of general-in-chief decided it was time
the lady from Massachusetts and I should part—we
were being a damping influence on each other, and he
descended on us with a bland smile, and as I was
English, for me he provided a small Canadian from
Toronto to do some real selling. To the wretched
girl he presented a formidable female, not unlike a
policewoman, who just marched her off to a tent to
question her as to what she could really afford to buy.
I was driven off and shown around the land. The
plots marked off with pegs were shown me here and
there, but I still made excuses, and at last they realised

I would not fall and I was taken back to the clump of trees and left there.

It was three-thirty and vaguely I had been promised to be returned by four o'clock. Now however things were different—people were no longer polite—they were just gruff and they kept me there in the hope I might relent until nearly seven o'clock. And then the school teacher and I were returned to our hotel, but with an ill grace—and yet they should have been content—out of sixty people present, over twenty lots had been bought, and they told me every day they took out people to that property and went through the same programme. On the way back my driver confessed to me if he was buying real estate, he would never buy in San Francisco or Los Angeles. It was far too high in price. His suggestion would be Vancouver in Canada, or Honolulu in Hawaii. And so we said good-bye—each admiring each a little bit for neither having fooled the other.

And all this crazy advertising. Has it not brought about the present depression as much as anything else? Has it not created a demand for things required by nobody? Has it not pushed beyond the bounds the essentially American idea of liberty to every man to do what he likes? Interpreted by the advertisers this means to develop slip-shod when and where you like without any thought for the benefit of the whole. This real estate selling, this boosting of a city, I found across America, and every city, every State, had in it elements let loose on the world, who boosted to a ridiculous degree their own area, and to gainsay them was to be backward, to have no local civic pride—and the result inflation till the bubble bursts and all that was good beneath looks like another bubble to many to-day.

Even the more subtle advertising has gone too far.

It may pay, but only for a short time. There is no need to stand still, but equally no need to go crazy—and the cruder advertising, especially in the West, makes life often hideous. Your concerts on the radio are spoilt by requests to buy tooth paste—Amos and Andy in the same way lose their attraction, the best and most soulful tangos may come to you through the courtesy of the latest ginger ale.

And as you travel through romantic Californian scenery, besides frequently being reminded that you need a shave you will see on most farm-houses that Dr. Pierce's Pleasant Pellets are good for liver complaints. While away in the forests of Montana you will be hit by the remark, "This is God's Country, don't turn it into Hell," when it would have been just as useful and less vulgar in such really majestic surroundings to be asked to be careful about forest fires. And lastly as you stop at a gasoline station, there is no need for such brilliant wit as the following:

No CREDIT—
    CREDIT means BUST—
        BUST means HELL—No CREDIT
                No BUST
                No HELL
                    THANKS.

And yet such a notice is sound common sense—and if it were practised a little more in America, that biggest free trade area in the world might still be prosperous. There is no doubt that in America the lower middle-class element is most strongly entrenched in the Middle West—and it goes in for such advertising and falls for it. They say they like pep and they consider the East of America "just sleepy." But their pep brings on such a nervous state, such a determination to get rich quickly and allows so much unhappiness that it is not surprising such things exist as I saw on the west coast— Eccentric religions, real estate lunches, gambling dens and debauch clubs. They all lead to the centres that come in the two chapters to follow.

CHAPTER VII

"THE BIGGEST LITTLE CITY IN THE WORLD"

EVERYBODY insisted that before continuing up the coast from San Francisco I must go inland and see Sacramento, and, above all, Reno in Nevada.

I started out by stage bus again and had a variety of characters as companions. First a sailor who told me of life in the navy, then a drunken old Irishman who tried to instil into me his hatred of England. Whenever he opened his mouth, he said, in England it lost him his job; and I could well believe it, though he meant that his Irish brogue went against him, and he explained to me how many thousands of Indians Lord Kitchener had shot down in cold blood—of course that had never been published, but he knew—secret information.

Later I was joined by a cheery soul going home to Indiana after three years in Hawaii. He hadn't told his family he was coming, but if he didn't lose too much money in Reno he'd wire them so as not to give the old woman too much of a shock. In the meantime he offered me neat whisky out of a bottle in his left-hand pocket. I refused and so he offered me some out of the right-hand pocket, saying it was better. But as I again refused he shook my hand warmly. "Sir," said he, "I see you are a gentleman of education, you do not accept drinks from strangers, you are wise." By the time we had reached Reno he was fast asleep on my shoulder.

It was one o'clock in the morning of Friday, June 5, as I stepped into Reno. In a minute I was in one of the two main streets, and an amazing sight struck me. Here were cars packed all along the street on both sides, like market day in England. Every window was brilliantly lit and signs outside the different doors told you that this was one famous club and that another. As you looked inside you still saw hundreds of people wandering about drinking openly and playing every kind of chance game—crap, fan, roulette, black-jack, and the wheel of chance.

If there were hundreds inside there were almost as many outside, gathered in groups, talking, talking all the time. I moved on to the Golden Hotel and was lucky to get a room. The town is always packed full, either for divorces or for gambling, and many a person gambles all night for lack of a bed in which to sleep. All over the west excursions are advertised to the freest and gayest city of America, and part of the fare provides for sleeping in the train while in Reno, as hotel accommodation would be impossible. The Golden Hotel was thoroughly Victorian in furniture, and the taps of the water-basin in my room were in the shape of devils' heads. To turn on the water you squeezed the devils' ears.

The valet who brought me to my room was quite communicative and was very interested to know if I had come to get a divorce. If so I must be sure and see the manager, as eventually he would have to swear that I had been six weeks in his hotel and he must know me personally.

Next morning I was on the streets by eight o'clock. All the gambling dens were still open and some of the inhabitants looked a little bedraggled. But they never close day or night, and when a new gambling den is opened there is an elaborate ceremony in which the key is solemnly carried to the river and thrown in, as a sign that it will never close its doors.

As I eat my breakfast I read about the murder the previous Wednesday in the club across the street. The man who ran it had an argument with another friend and told him he must leave the club. This the man did but returned an hour later. The moment the manager saw him return he took out his revolver and shot him dead. Of course the manager was arrested; but next day, Thursday, after a trial lasting eleven minutes, he was acquitted of murder. His defence was self-protection. The man, he maintained, was most unlikely to return except with a gun to settle the argument, and in case that might be, the manager thought he had better get it over first and fired. Several of the people in the street seemed to be carrying arms as well, and I felt at last in the Wild West and suitably thrilled, and wandered down the street to the small, ordinary looking county court where Reno settles her divorces.

Inside there seemed remarkably little evidence of bustle or fashionably dressed crowds or even of litigants at all. I went into the office and asked the clerk if there were to be any divorces that day and if so when and in what court room. He seemed annoyed at the question and said there were none. I suppose the disappointment on my face was very obvious, for no sooner had he said this than a woman clerk leant over to me and said she thought there might be just one about 10.30, and when I told her I was a student from Lincoln's Inn in London and very interested to see the procedure, she insisted I go up to the judge's room, knock on the door and go and have a chat with Judge Moran, who deals with the divorce cases.

This I did and he welcomed me warmly. A rather small, stockily-built man with white hair, he was extremely affable. His room was very much like that of any lawyer, the walls covered with bookcases, filled with yellow-bound legal reference books and case histories. He put me in an arm-chair and for half an hour talked about the law in England and

87

America. He strongly recommended me before practising at the English Bar to spend at least a year at Boston or some other centre and study American legal methods about which English people know so little and were always so critical.

I made a tactical error when discussing with him the divorce of a peeress, which was shortly to come before him, by suggesting that such a divorce might not be considered legal in England. He naturally replied that he could not see why a divorce granted by him should not be good in law anywhere. He took great care about divorces. We then discussed a previous Scottish case that had come before him, and finally went into the library together to look the case up, and he asked me to take the volume and read the case in detail during the day.

He was interested that I was Irish, as he said his father had come over from Ireland and his mother came from Liverpool, while he himself was born at sea when they were emigrating to the United States. His father's family used to keep an hotel in Dublin, which I knew quite well, and I smiled to think what his good Irish Catholic relatives would think if they knew their kinsman was one of the two most famous divorce judges in America.

As there was to be one divorce case that day which he was trying he invited me to come in with him. As we walked in, everyone in court stood up, and before they were allowed to sit down again I was brought forward and introduced to the counsel for both sides. The Judge then put me to sit in one of the three seats reserved for distinguished strangers within the bar.

Outside the bar there was room for about sixty listeners, whilst inside was the judge's seat on a raised platform but without any coat of arms or emblem of any sort at his back. To his right a few

THE DIVORCE COURT, RENO

A GHOST-CITY IN NEVADA

steps down sat the clerk of the court—who was a woman—and to his left, not quite so many steps down, was the witness seat, you could not call it a box. Facing the Judge were two more seats for the counsel for the defence and the counsel for the plaintiff. To the right of the clerk on the other side of the judges' entrance were the three seats for strangers, where I was to sit but where I did not find it easy to hear the witness. The rest of the room, which was well lit with large windows, was behind the bar and for the general public. Nobody wore any kind of uniform, and the whole room was dark and panelled, and the procedure from start to finish, though dignified, was extremely informal.

The case was one of a man seeking divorce from his wife and the suit was defended. First of all the plaintiff and the witness were sworn. Then the witness called to the seat was asked to give evidence of how long the plaintiff had been in Nevada. The witness was a well-dressed attractive-looking middle-aged woman, and I gathered she kept a dude ranch near Reno, as so many do, for the more well-to-do litigants. They come there and while away the necessary six weeks, riding, gambling and generally enjoying themselves, and the owners of the ranches make quite a reasonable profit. The lady therefore, when business is good, appears fairly regularly in that court to testify that her clients have been with her the full six weeks. As she took the oath and proved her own residence she looked up smiling at the Judge as much as to say "Isn't this a joke: you know I'm always here." But Judge Moran took it all very seriously and satisfied himself, no doubt for the hundredth time, that she was herself a *bona fide* citizen. Next came the plaintiff, who pleaded gross cruelty on the part of his wife— mostly mental—but never produced one witness to prove it nor seemed in any way to be going through anything more than a mere formula. His counsel— who incidentally was a woman—just asked him the requisite number of questions about date of marriage, etc., and when the wife had been most cruel, and then sat down.

Up got the counsel for the wife, who incidentally was a man, and begged leave to read a sworn statement in defence for the wife, taken in Washington, but again without any question of witnesses. The wife just pitched into her husband in the statement and stated more in detail where and when he had been rather difficult, and after about seven minutes of this the counsel sat down with a final request that the husband be divorced, not the wife, and that suitable alimony be allowed. The husband denied nothing and agreed he would pay. Whereupon the Judge said that was all right, refused to divorce the man from the woman but instead divorced the woman from the man.

He then turned to the counsel for defence and asked him what he was doing for the rest of the day. The counsel tactfully said nothing very serious, whereupon the Judge pointed out that he was in a hurry to get off to a funeral and perhaps counsel would take charge of me and show me a bit of the country, the ghost cities of old mining days, and a bit of Reno. All this while the Court was standing for the Judge to leave. It was all settled and we shook hands and I departed with counsel. The divorce had taken ten or twelve minutes. We went downstairs and the counsel paid the requisite fees, so that the divorced man could get married again that afternoon if he wished. Earlier in the day he had been fined in another part of the building for being drunk and disorderly in the town the night before—altogether for him a busy day.

That we must remember was a defended suit—one of the more difficult ones—which are always set aside for Fridays—the undefended ones which take about two or three minutes are usually dealt with earlier in the week—starting on Mondays—and at the rate of about forty a day. They calculate that a good year in Reno brings in about 2,000 or more divorces, and the cost is not excessive—the only real expense being the six weeks in the town, which is not exactly cheap for lodgings or food or amusements.

As I walked down to his office with my new-found friend, he explained to me a little of the development of Reno and Nevada along its present lines, prefacing his remarks with the statement that he and the other bigger lawyers of the town concentrated on divorce as easily the most profitable business, and that though Reno received all the publicity, it was only one of many county towns in Nevada, in all of which you could, and many people did, get divorces just as easily.

Vaguely I had realised that the United States were only held together loosely by the Federal Government at Washington—but here I was to realise for the first time how very separate is each State. I had just come in from wealthy California, and now I was in a State of 100,000 square miles, nearly twice the size of England, but only with a population of 90,000. This population had to keep up its roads, its State Parliament and Civil Servants, and carry on in many ways as an independent country and could get nothing of the wealth of California or the Eastern States. Its capital, Carson City, had only 18,000 inhabitants, and in Reno itself there are only about 19,000 residents. All this might have been very well, but unfortunately almost all the State is one huge desert covered in sweet smelling sage-brush.

Its only great asset, mining, brought it in the old

days of gold and copper and silver and lead a great prosperity. But to-day those mines are all closed down, and the State is at its wits end to know where to turn for money. Not perhaps just for to-day, but in looking into the future, for unless something brilliantly clever is done, it is likely to remain, through lack of water, one of the poorest of the States. In the beginning, when the California gold-rush was on, the Nevada Government, in order to keep some of the people in Nevada who were passing through to richer California, passed a law that you could become a citizen of Nevada after one year's residence—which was at that time a great innovation. Later they brought this period down to six months' residence. The result was a number of prospectors stopped in Nevada and found the present mines. Those that made wealth like the Mackays, and the O'Briens, later moved out, leaving the poorer ones behind, and now that many of the mines are worked out and others are closed down for lack of producing profit, we find a population of miners and descendants of miners that are almost as tough as their ancestors of seventy years ago.

It is a population that hates laws, and in that, for the moment, the State has found its fortune. Having no water for the land they will at least have alcohol for the body, and the State has passed laws making itself wet. This means no State prosecution can take place for making or selling or drinking liquor—it is only a Federal offence and for such offence you can only be arrested by Federal law officers. As there are only two Federal officers in the whole 100,000 square miles that is Nevada, and as nobody is in sympathy with them, it can well be understood that most people know where they are and know when they are coming.

Drinking, then, in Nevada is fairly easy. Next

comes gambling. Against that there is no Federal law, and as Nevada has now passed an Act making it legal in that State, she bids fair to become the playground of America—which of course is her aim to-day. But just for the moment, with gambling and drinking in full swing, though she is the most wide-open State in America, yet the element that is playing is a very rough one and murder and crime are rampant. The gold-rush element is still too strong to make Nevada a fashionable playground, though just one spot—Reno—is trying hard to gain that position, and here her weapons are publicity and divorce.

As a whole the State is making much more money out of gambling and general lack of laws than out of divorces—though that too is naturally bringing in for periods of six weeks people rich enough to spend their money at the gambling tables and they have chosen Reno as their centre. It was an enterprising divorce lawyer who first saw the possibilities of the six months residence law for people in other States who wanted to be divorced, and he advertised it plentifully in the East.

Further publicity came to it when Mary Pickford and her husband Owen Moore got divorced, and finally the Government saw the possibilities and cut down the period of residence to three months. Soon other States saw the gold mine that might be theirs and equally cut their residence period to three months. Nevada retaliated by cutting this still further to six weeks, which is the present position. One or two other States are talking of following suit, and my counsel friend told me Nevada would then have no hesitation in cutting the period still further.

She quite openly states she needs the revenue—but even so the divorce business seemed to me precarious. Even at that time people were talking of easier methods

93

and pleasanter climate in Mexico, and yet others, disliking the limelight of Reno, were beginning to combine a pleasure trip to Europe with divorce in Latvia at Rega.

And that, my friend told me, was how gambling and divorce and temporary prosperity has come to Nevada. As against it he put England's attitude towards silver, which has ruined Nevada's mines, the further fact that Irish leaders had taken large sums of money from the many Irish miners in Nevada to help the cause in Ireland and, that usually, when you got rich in Nevada, you went away. He told me practically the only form of sport or hectic life now forbidden in Nevada was cock-fighting. Yet every Sunday, cock-fighting clubs met in different private farms and carried on gaily. The Governor of Nevada himself possessed some of the most valuable fighting cocks and loved the sport.

We motored out to the lawyer's farm near Reno, first for lunch, and there I was given neat whisky to drink—they call it straight whisky in America, and while drinking it at only a quarter the rate of everybody else, I looked over the causes for divorce to find they were desertion, cruelty, mental or physical—lack of proper maintenance, adultery, non-consummation and also lunacy—after two years. After that I forgot about divorces and prepared to see the other side of Nevada.

From the lawyer's farm we set out to climb the many mountains of Nevada and to see some very wonderful views, but before starting my host asked his son to get him his six-shooter revolver—necessary, he explained to me, nowadays against hold-ups and also against bears. To an ordinary peaceful Londoner this was getting more and more thrilling: hold-ups, bears, neat whisky, gambling dens open day and night, murders, open-air boxing and wrestling promoted by Jack Dempsey, turtle races and cock-fights, a plethora of divorces, week-end excursions from all over the west with no hotel accommodation, just sleepers on the trains—could one feel further away or could one ask for more?

We motored past some geyser hot springs, where in the old days the miners used to take baths, cramped with rheumatism from mining, and they told me that mixed with salt the water tasted like chicken soup. Further on we came to Carson City, the State Capital, with only 18,000 inhabitants and yet boasting a large Chinese quarter and a Mint where gold coins were formerly made from nuggets from the neighbouring mines.

And then on through the hills to those ghost cities that give such a dead atmosphere to the whole place. Past town after town that once had been big and flourishing but now was totally or almost totally deserted—the neighbouring mines closed down or worked out. It made you realise how terribly wasteful in the first flush of wealth has been the American as he passed through the country—but again you realise he was not necessarily an American—he was probably a European, usually Irish, just out from his own country and with no feelings for this new country, or an Easterner who felt nothing very much for this West, and in any case thought its riches unlimited.

Here it did not seem difficult any longer to understand one type of American—the spendthrift and the incurable optimist. They may for the moment have overspent and overproduced, but almost as certain as anything can be, their assets are still largely in the soil, and if, as it seems they will, the inhabitants of Western America learn to go more slowly and to put by a bit and save, then with such a healthy clear-minded population they must develop into one of the world's greatest nations in history.

So at least you must feel when you stay some time in this vast country, and so I felt as I travelled through one specially deserted city—Virginia City. On one side of the main street were small modern shops in which the reduced population of 150 souls made their purchases, and then on the other side of the main street, and stretching away, were huge great houses, some almost palatial, but many without a roof. These were the houses of people like the Mackays, who have now moved on, and head vast telephone and other concerns across the continent.

But here, fifty, sixty years ago, they lived in state, they bought their horses from the Czar of Russia— they paid Jenny Lind huge sums to come and stay and sing for them. But had the present inhabitants any post cards of these ruins? Good gracious, no. They only sold photographs of the side of the main street that is still standing. Dressed in clothes reminiscent almost of Victorian days and prosperity, the men would talk willingly of the past and also of the undoubted future for these 150 who had stuck it out—but the present—of that not a word.

Eventually we got back to Reno—in time for me to catch Judge Moran before he left his office, and after a last talk we exchanged cards and I was free for the evening. It was now getting dark and as I moved up one of the biggest streets, fast filling up with cars from the country and with single ladies out for the evening and with numerous men with broad-brimmed hats and with coats sometimes reminiscent of old gold-rush prints, I saw the arch over the centre of the street lit up and it blazed out the city's boast, "The Biggest Little City in the World"—a really cheerful welcome.

All the night until at least three o'clock in the morning I went from night club to night club. They were nothing but gambling dens, wide open to everybody, and the stakes played were usually anything from ten cents to a dollar. I could not tear myself away. Never have I seen a more fascinating study of human nature. There were farmers and their wives in for the evening, there were Canadians, foreigners and people from all the States of the Union. Once a woman next me nearly burst into tears as she was losing so many dollars, she said, she could not afford to stay the whole six weeks to see her divorce through, and this was only her first night. Another man put on his last dollars and then had nothing for a bed, and people were chucked out bodily by powerful armed ruffians. By the time I went to bed my pockets were weighted down, for at the Wheel of Chance and Roulette I had won my whole fare from Los Angeles to Seattle, and paper dollars in this part of the West are almost unknown.

Here you get the huge heavy dollars produced in the mines of the district, and it is a great grievance here as in Utah that the silver dollar is not used in the East so to increase the use of the mine's products. As now and then I went out to get air and walk around, I found the streets crowded as ever, and down the dark alleys were small ominous-looking little groups that would put you on the floor for nothing and take your winnings gladly; and in the cafés, many run by Chinese, you found people rushing in for a bite of food and then rushing back to gamble, whilst in and out amongst the crowd zigzagged many a drunken man, for drink seemed plentiful and easy to get.

A few miles further away the smarter people in river-side clubs were doing exactly the same on a larger scale under the auspices of such well-known club queens as Bell Livingstone, but they could not have offered me half the fun or excitement that I obtained from this real Western crowd—a crowd that often comes to Europe on a conducted tour and then looks out of place and terrible—but here is fascinating and very real and in no way incongruous—with plush furniture, cheap Victorian prints and two-storied houses but little removed from the shack of fifty years ago.

And when next morning early, I left at six o'clock to go back to Sacramento, I could not help but feel the fascination, as we slowly climbed the gorgeous Sierra Nevada mountains and looked down on Donner Lake, and I thought of those many people that in the old days were snowed up and died of starvation and cold as they came across this pass to seek the gold that was on the other side.

And then I read of the neighbouring small town of Placerville. It seemed so dignified and rich. It is, it seems, a small and flourishing town that has an annual sort of fiesta. But less than one hundred years ago this dignified Placerville was called Dry Diggings, and to it many people flocked to make their fortunes. It indeed became so prosperous in that way that the name was soon changed from Dry Diggings to Hangtown, and as Hangtown it continued to prosper if a little violently, as its name implies, and now that it has settled down to a dignified old age we treat it with respect as Placerville.

And from there I passed on into California, across the only State boundary where my luggage was examined. It was for infected fruit—none of which California permits to pass her borders.

CHAPTER VIII

PRISONS AND THE SING-SING OF THE WEST

As we motored through Carson City, Nevada's capital, my lawyer guide took me to see the State prison. Considering the 90,000 State population, the prison was naturally not large—but even so it was filled to capacity and boasts an interesting death chamber and in its grounds some fine specimens of prehistoric animals. The prisoners do a good deal of handicraft work and this is for sale in the outer office where we had to give up our revolvers.

After going through the cells and the grounds, I was shown the spot where in the old days condemned men were shot. There had been a firing squad of three men and always with a dummy bullet for one of the three, and with the sights so set and everything else arranged that they must hit just over the heart, be the men frightened or not. I gathered this method of execution is still practised optionally in Utah, as it is part of the Mormon creed that if you slay a man you must atone by the spilling of your own blood, and shooting is the only effective method for practising Mormons. I believe the Mormons in the old days practised blood-spilling for quite minor offences—at least that is one of the accusations against the leadership of Brigham Young that his enemies brought forward.

Now the method of execution in Nevada is by use of a lethal chamber. And I believe this is the only State in the Union that practises it. Some still go in for hanging, but the majority use the electric chair. I had a good look at the lethal chamber. A small room with a large window. At the window sit the twelve witnesses required by law and they look on

99

at what is happening.   Inside are two chairs, should
there be more than one prisoner to die.   The man
is brought in and strapped to the chair.   Everybody
else then leaves the room, which is hermetically closed
up.   Two holes are kept closed by a string which is
then cut and the lethal gas drops from a tank into
some concoction which is already in the room and
with three breaths the man is dead.   It is seemingly
quite painless.   The gas is then removed through
another hole opened for the purpose, and later the
body is taken out.

Besides this there was nothing of great interest in
the prison—but it was a very different matter when
next day I visited Folsom Prison, 100 miles away
near Sacramento in California.

I had got a letter to the Warden from a politician
in Los Angeles, and it worked wonders.   I went out
by bus—the only other passenger, a woman, going to
visit her husband—and passed through first a delightful country covered with fruit farms and vineyards
and then out into a more barren undulating country
on which the sun poured down unmercifully its scorch-
ing rays.   In the middle of this loomed up the long
high turreted walls of Folsom, I believe, the largest
prison for second-timers and desperate criminals in
America.   After the usual formalities at the outer
gate, the Warden telephoned through he was ready
to see me.

At the gate they told me that Sing-Sing has 2,000
inmates, Folsom nearly 3,000, and that there were
over 130 murderers serving life sentences, and six
others in the condemned cell awaiting execution.   To
reach the Warden's office I had had to pass through
high walls and had been watched from every corner.

The Warden explained to me he could not take
me around at once as the convicts were having lunch

and should I be brought in, they would certainly start a howl with clanking of plates, which no number of guards could stop. Nearly all of them were desperate characters, each one of whom had served at least one sentence before, and they didn't care very much what they did and strongly resented any visitors seeing them at irregular hours. The Warden, a big, burly, hearty individual, talked for nearly an hour about prisons and reform in America and then eventually sent me round to see the cells.

One block holds over 1,000 convicts, two in a cell, with washstand and any photographs or magazines they require. From there I could just see the corner of the solitary confinement cells. Here go those receiving extra punishment and also all those who have just come in. For the first week they get bread and water, the second week one meal and the third week two. Next I saw the outside of the condemned cell. Here are confined the men condemned to die and even with appeals pending which may take a year or more to go through. They are never allowed out of that cell and nobody sees them but twice a day when their food is brought in. They are hung in the same room, but moved out the day before the execution, so that the portable gallows may be erected. When the hanging is over—witnessed as prescribed by law by twelve people—the other condemned are moved back again.

The dining-rooms are huge with a fine kitchen. No knives are used at meals except on Sundays— all meat being previously cut up. The concert hall is nearly as large as the dining-room, and some few years ago was the scene of a famous riot. Here they were preparing to stage a show on July 4, when visitors and relatives visit the prison. In the yard from twelve to two o'clock, a band was practising and numerous

convicts—black men as well as white—were playing
or taking exercise.   Near by is the chapel, used by
all denominations, and the library.

The guard, whenever he entered the yard or anywhere where there were groups of prisoners, took a
club, and in no case would allow me to walk through
them.   "You never know what they might not try
to do."   I gathered again strangers are not welcome.

Through more barred gates and we were on the
edge of the quarry—here worked the most desperate
characters, while more peaceable ones were allowed
on to the ranch surrounding the prison.   The boiling heat beat down on the prisoners all the time,
but their regulation garb guards a little against this,
even to that of those who have tried to escape or
are otherwise out of favour and who wear for a year
a special striped suit.

The lash is forbidden in California—confinement,
and at worst, solitary confinement with bread and
water, is all that can happen to a prisoner.

The hospital is most elaborate, with very small
wards, and no freeman could have more comfortable
quarters.   The nurses, themselves convicts, also sleep
in barred cells and somehow there always seem to
be enough efficient trained nurses, as there are also
enough cooks, who have committed crimes to make
these grim communities self-supporting.

From the hospital I thought I could find my way
easily back to the Warden's, but the guard said "No."
He'd better "highball" me across, else I might get
a pellet from the watchman.   But when I saw what
he meant and realised across every strip of open space
I covered, I was being watched from a sniper's tower
and that a gun was trained on me, I felt a little nervous in case of accidents and no more cheerful when
the Warden showed me his little book of horrors,

including stories of all the murders, photographs of those who had been hung, with details of their weight and how long it took for them to die.

I left the prison feeling that if that is all the punishment meted out to the toughest criminals in the land, including 136 murderers, at worst a week on bread and water in solitary confinement—it is perhaps no wonder crime is prevalent all over the country, especially when it is not so easy outside a prison to find regular bed and food.

I could not help contrasting it with some of the sentences I heard given in a Canadian Court—nothing like so long terms of incarceration at the expense of the State—but plenty of healthy stripes of the lash which the prisoners dreaded much more, and not just one set of stripes but a series to be administered at given intervals so that having once tasted it, they knew what to expect again in a few weeks or months.

In contrast I gathered various American societies were even then busy trying to get the lot of these good-for-nothings made easier and I could not help smiling as I rode back to Sacramento at some of the regulations for the officers and guards dealing with 3,000 criminals. Rule 9 reads:

"Within the prison grounds the guards shall refrain from whistling, scuffling, immoderate laughter, exciting discussions on politics, religion or other subjects, provoking witticisms or sarcasms, and all other acts calculated to disturb the harmony and good order of the prison."

Rule 10:

"In their intercourse amongst themselves, the officers and guards of the prison are at all times to treat one another with mutual respect and kindness that becomes gentlemen and friends, and are required to avoid collusions, jealousies, separate and party-views and interests amongst themselves, and are strictly forbidden to treat one another with disrespect, or to use any epithets."

It all sounded to me as if the guards required were to be men suitable for a diplomatic salon or a seminary, rather than to guard and put the fear of God into a few hundred murderers and a few thousand degenerates.

From there I went back to San Francisco to visit a still larger prison, St. Quentin—one of the world's largest—with accommodation for nearly 5,000 prisoners—and it is nearly full.

It is however meant for first offenders, fraudulent millionaires, faulty District-Attorneys, foreigners, even a few more murderers and the general lot of any prison. Across the bay from San Francisco, the prison is beautifully laid out and in a very lovely position. At the end of the dining-hall is a platform on which the prison band plays during meals. Smaller States with less variety amongst their criminals have to forego music at meal times, as indeed have most of us less fortunate beings, but at St. Quentin there is such a variety of professional talent, that the prisoners have little opportunity for being bored. Constantly too they have classes for free improvement in any art or craft, and even those who stutter have a doctor who comes every week to improve their speech.

This is all perfect and very right for the young man in prison for his first offence, unless indeed it makes him want to come back again—but why should elderly fraudulent District-Attorneys and other sharks have all the same pleasant advantages. Surely humanitarianism is going too far, and if reforms are essential, here seems to me scope for at least one.

I was interested in an English boy who, not finding work in Canada, aged 19, had had the enterprise

to decide to hitch-hike down to South America—
hoping to find work in the Argentine. In three
weeks he had got as far as San Bernadino near Los
Angeles in California, when he fell in with two other
hitch-hikers. They had got a gun and persuaded
him without thinking much to help them hold up
a man in a motor. This done they obtained five
dollars from the man for their pains, and later this
youth went back to untie the man and let him go
—but he found he had already gone. As they walked
through the next town they were arrested and this
boy, who had so bad a stutter he could hardly speak,
was sentenced to "five years to life" at St. Quentin,
and the Judge added he was convinced he was a
dangerous criminal. A few strokes of the lash and
the boy deported would cost California far less than
five years in prison and would save one boy from
five years in the company of other criminals and from
the waste of his own youth.

Almost all the officials saw this and agreed when
I mentioned it—but red tape intervened and it was
impossible to do anything. As I understood it, the
State has appointed a group of well-paid men to
examine cases of prisoners and remission of sentences
—but no case can be touched until eighteen months
of the sentence has been completed, the cases must
be taken in rotation, and for some reason difficult
to understand, the Committee had got so behind-
hand in dealing with the cases that it would be nearer
three years before this youth's case could be touched.

In the meantime I left him working his first year
in the jute mill, depressed to a degree, a youth with
all the very best references from English employers,
who had never been in any trouble before, and who
now was beyond help through the action of a local
court in the heart of California where the prevalence

105

of crime had petrified the countryside into an unreasoning hysteria.

While I talked over this case with our Consul-General I came across one of the most interesting characters in San Francisco, the British legal adviser —a fascinating old gentleman over eighty years of age. He is, I believe, the only British subject allowed to practise law in America—because he was already practising before the Act was passed forbidding any more aliens to be called to the American Bar. When quite young he had entered the Austrian army from Ireland and later had gone to America to help the Emperor Maximilian in Mexico—but when he landed in New York he found it was too late, the Emperor had already been shot and so he continued through to San Francisco, and still a British subject even to this day—started to practise law.

It was a few months later before I again visited a prison. This time it was in Montgomery, the capital of Alabama in the South. Nothing could be more different. Here in the heart of the cotton plantations in a thinly populated State I found no less than 150 men serving life sentences for murder —but they and all the rest of the prisoners were garbed in smart white suits, which they make themselves. Everything was cool, comfortable and spotlessly clean.

In the large dining-hall one whole side was set aside for the negroes, one for the whites. In prisons in the South they are all separated. But up above in the condemned cells were eight negroes awaiting the result of their appeal against the death sentence.

There were 150 murderers serving life sentences, but these eight negroes were to be executed because they had raped two white women, themselves female hoboettes, on a freight train. Such is the law in the

South and it naturally differs completely from the North and from the West, and as naturally such a sentence was causing intense racial feeling not only in Montgomery but throughout many parts of the North where many of the 15 million negroes are living completely free—and to-day it is known all over Europe.

In the West, however, where the negro is almost unknown except on railway trains, these cases would cause no stir of interest and more and more one realised how vastly different are the four ends of this continent we try to think of as a nation. They have so little in common as yet, and for such a country a great faith in its future is essential.

To-day, without great reason, it seems to be lacking and already the results are disastrous. Crime, resultant insecurity and then uncertainty about graft, and the efficiency of certain hitherto unquestioned institutions and the increased practice brought on by prohibition, of evading laws wholesale, which eventually leads to evading taxes and the like, such things strike a foreigner forcibly and such things you hear frequently discussed across the country. Yet nobody seems to consider a possible reason for all this crime —the amazing comfort a prison life offers. People seem to think once the prisoner is clapped behind the bars, everything is over. And yet in no country have I seen such pleasant prison life in certain States; though a few States are disgraceful—as witness the almost true film "The Chain Gang."

No wonder a man down and out with his back against the wall, entitled to no dole, uncertain what will happen next, just takes something preferably with a gun and he is almost certain of five years steady, not excessive work, with, if he is in California, perhaps music at his meals, which too will be good regular meals, and a bed and a regular life. Others of course hate the lack of freedom, but that is all there is to hate. We may hear of the third degree and no doubt the start is unpleasant—but once the prisoner gets settled in, he seems to have a pleasant life.

This does not apply to all States, and in Harlem they told me of States in the South where negroes are sent to prison for next to nothing and then hired out to local farmers almost as slaves.

But if that is so the State is not Alabama. As we passed through the prison kitchen, my friend, a former head of the Chamber of Commerce, stopped for a chat with one of the men and gave him a tangerine. The man he told me was in for thirty years. He had been a real estate salesman, wealthy and well known in Montgomery, but he had defrauded a lot of poor widows. The guard and my friend both talked of him as otherwise "quite a decent fellow." And I found that feeling in all the prisons. People are afraid of crime in America, but they rather admire the criminal. He has just been found out, so many others have not.

Later we motored out to the farms and the dairy and we talked to the negroes working there—"trustees" they are called. Just one or two in each place, left alone there to work all day long. They would never escape. One, now fifteen years in the jail, said he would just like one or two days of freedom, and my friend strongly advised him to stay where he was in these days of unemployment. He was certain he was very lucky to be in prison and the negro agreed, "Yeah boss, dat wat d'other chaps dey tell me."

And later on the wife of our Consul-General in a big seaport told me in her husband's presence, and he did not contradict her for exaggeration: "When we first came here I was given the name of the most reliable bootlegger and his telephone number. He was doing time in prison—but the telephone was in the prison and he had his own private line and was still carrying on business from there, and we also got our drinks delivered within a couple of hours after telephoning to him in prison."

When such things go on after people have already been sentenced, when no corporal punishment is even administered and when within a few miles in another prison eight men are to die for having violated two women of the road, because of a difference in colour, and when it is nothing out of the ordinary to have in each State from one hundred to two hundred murderers leading a quiet life at the State's expense, one I think begins to understand why it is that crime becomes daily more popular in America and daily more difficult to suppress.

After all, Al Capone is at bottom a greater hero to the youth of America in many ways than Washington and certainly more up-to-date. And when Legs Diamond was killed and I brought the news up to the office of my lecture agent in New York, all work was stopped for a few minutes and later my taxi-driver insisted on carrying on a long conversation to see what I had heard about it.

Still later at a lunch where were two of New York's best known hostesses, one a daughter-in-law of a former President and a well-known Editor—the Editor had the latest news about the murder telephoned through to him, so that the ladies could know and he himself decide how much of the latest news from Germany could be squeezed away.

And then again in Universities—it is the speakeasy visit that always seems most fun. And so on it will continue, until not the catching becomes easier

—but rather the punishment becomes quicker, and as Gilbert says in the "Mikado," "they make the punishment fit the crime" and not the pocket of the criminal or the criminal's desire for a temporary home free of cost and worry.

CHAPTER IX

THE PACIFIC HIGHWAY

FROM Sacramento I started the last part of my motor ride to Seattle and then Vancouver. The night before I left I walked through the few small streets—boulevards would really be the proper name —and as I looked through the green leaves of the trees lining the streets to the clear sky and moon above, and then as I turned towards the electrically lit dome of the Parliament building, I felt suddenly back in the capital of one of the smaller States in Europe, some State that only recently had left the age of brigandage to vote on equal terms with France and Britain at Geneva—perhaps some State that still for all its outward appearance of culture and civilisation had its brigands but a few miles away hiding or not even hiding in the hills.

And somehow it does not seem so very different now. Here, less than one hundred years before, lived a Swiss, one Captain Sutter, and on his farm Marshall found gold. From then began a rush to California to find the gold they say the monks knew all about long years before, but wishing to civilise the Indians and to keep away the inevitable riff-raff, had kept as knowledge to themselves. But with this riff-raff had come to Sacramento a group of what we would call younger sons—educated but poor young men from Eastern America. Between them they saw the necessity of a railway and they scraped together the nucleus of a fund to start it. They were Crocker, Stanford, Mark Hopkins, and Huntingdon. They made their fortunes and they left their impression. It was here in Sacramento they first lived and in contrast to Dry Diggings, Reno, and other centres, they made Sacramento a dignified and a beautiful little capital.

The sort of life they led and their artistic outlook can be seen and imagined in the one substantial house left of their period which now they call the Crocker Museum. The steps of the stairs are covered in studded brass, the walls show copies of every historical subject, and nearly every famous picture in Europe. Later these solid business men moved on to San Francisco, and made of it the seaport and money centre of the Pacific Coast. The Crocker Bank is to-day world famous, the Huntingdon Museum in Southern California, housing the Blue Boy and Pinkie, holds also some of the world's literary treasures, the Mark Hopkins Hotel looks out over the Golden Gates and the bay to the endless future and possibilities of the Pacific, and the Stanford University, the most famous of the West, gives Presidents to the United States and an interest in politics lacking in most of the State Universities in other parts of America.

But these are not the only families this little town has produced; there are the Hearsts who, not content with the wealth of one generation, have made with the press a power for themselves or for their head that is world famous, and then the Ogden Mills family, who have with the Whitelaw Reids become famous in Diplomacy and are now taking an even greater part in the country's political life, so that it would probably be no exaggeration to say that this small, clean but quite unexciting town, capital of the potentially greatest State of America, has given in recent years more Empire builders to America, if one will admit that the United States are but a loosely federated Empire, than any other city of its size.

And nearby you have lawless Nevada, with its deserts, Folsom Prison with its thousands of criminals, the sweeping downs, fertile lands, vineyards and forests, and in its middle this little town with a Parliament building of great dignity; one fine hotel, a Chinese quarter that stretches right up to the capital; old Fort Sutter, to remind you of the Red Indians and Mexicans and ordinary highwaymen and bandits; and near the Capitol a State Museum full of relics of gold-rush days and of manuscripts that give the full history of California.

They remind you that it once was Spanish, then Mexican, and only a part of the United States long after the Colonial Days of England and the Declaration of Independence.

In Sacramento you can understand, I think, better than anywhere else in California, the type of person—uninfluenced by the more recent influx from the Middle West—that has made such a mark on American public life, that eventually found its best outlet in San Francisco; and that is to-day continuing there and in Los Angeles, making of both great world-famous seaports, and of one at least a great banking centre. These people too are making of themselves millionaires, that show in many ways a more picturesque appreciation of European culture than their Eastern prototypes and a greater knowledge of how to enjoy life temperately.

From here I went on to Eureka, and Grants Pass, through the Redwood Forest area high up above the Pacific Coast. To look at these giant trees, centuries old, is to look on one of the most magnificent sights in America, and it is the beginning of the lumber country which is as different in its climate, its scenery, and its people, from California as can well be imagined. Through Oregon and Washington, we drove along some of the wildest and most beautiful bits of coast road I have ever seen, and if it was a striking change from what I had seen before, it was no more striking than the variety of the inhabitants of the bus.

There were two quiet students going back to Seattle from a Californian holiday. There was a farmer as noisy and as vulgar as could be, who was completely captivated by two thoroughly coarse women, I gather a vaudeville turn, on their way, travelling night and day to Portland to act during the Rose Festival. There was a quiet old Englishman who lived in California and was troubled by the menace of the Jews, and there was a woman with two children who had travelled from Salt Lake City and was going to join her husband in the lumber business in Oregon, and there was a commercial traveller and a school teacher on holiday.

We broke down once and spent endless hours waiting for a relief bus in the forest and it seemed as we passed through almost every town that they were *en fête* for a visit of Elks, or Rotarians, or some other holiday-making fraternity.

In one town I spent the night in a small inn and was amused to hear two tough-looking individuals with some mine samples in their hand, discussing how much they were going to get out of the "sucker" who was sitting in the lobby and seemed interested in their mine and in buying a part share. But most of the towns were given over to lumber interests, and I heard later that so bad are the times and so many the unemployed seeking work in the camps that the owners are not always bothering to take the proper precautions against accidents to their men—knowing that if the man's leg is chopped off, there will always be others at hand and that life is becoming terrible in many of these camps and the trade unions are almost powerless to help.

At length we reached Portland in time for me to see

the last two days of the Annual Rose Festival. Even the real estate venture of San Francisco had not made me immune to the amazing boastfulness of some American cities and the superlative praise they always give themselves, and to this day I always leave an American city duly impressed with its wonderful future, its unique position, and if it's a seaport its obtaining all the advantages of protection from inside and yet somehow of trade with the outside world; and so I foresaw a wonderful Portland, but above all in the immediate future a great city suitably bedecked for its annual unsurpassed Rose Festival. In my humility I felt carnival in France and poor Italian small towns would not be comparable—but I was to be disillusioned.

As we drove into the town about six o'clock in the evening, we found ourselves in streets simply covered in streamers, papers, cardboard boxes and a thousand and one other signs of a procession that had left the maximum amount of litter. I went straight to the Portland Hotel where I found men looking intensely self-conscious in the most amazing concoctions of coloured garments imaginable and a few minutes after my arrival appeared the Rose Queen—the Queen of the Carnival who was calling on the hotel. With her came a number of maids of honour. They were prettily dressed, but the whole sight was spoilt by the man accompanying them—a fat man in a tight-fitting white suit belted, and with a straw hat, looking for all the world like a prosperous salesman at the seaside.

Later on, as it got darker, I went into the streets— now crowded again with sightseers in from the country and deposited by various excursion buses from neighbouring towns. I watched with interest the town's leading band, beautifully garbed. Their uniform was of orange with blue knee-breeches and leggings, with an orange stripe. They wore peaked caps with ospreys. The leader, an impressive individual, twisting a baton, varied this dress by wearing a black bearskin with orange osprey.

Now in the town of Portland there are the usual traffic signals. Red to stop, yellow to get ready, green to go on, and down the main streets you meet these signs every two or three blocks. The band and the bandmaster with true civic spirit decided they must obey the signals and so would start off a grand march with a perfect swing down an empty street until unluckily they met a red sign. Stop, the band marked time and then the green, and on again. It looked too ridiculous as this happened block by block and the poor band could not get up a proper swing at all, nor could the small urchins following it as they too reverently stopped before the regulating signs.

At one sign we found a radio already playing and advertising the advantages of a local tooth paste. As our band had stopped with the signal, the band leader, now keyed up to a fever pitch of excitement, danced a cheerful step himself to the radio tune, bearskin and all. The tune stopped, he twirled his baton. Yellow sign, then green, and we were off again. More than once alas the band was out of tune, but under the circumstances I suppose that was inevitable.

Then came the famous much advertised Mardi Gras Procession—it was a Friday—but that made no difference to the name. Everyone of the floats I think was an advertisement for some kind of goods and the whole thing left on me a terrible feeling of depression —one float advertising a brand of cigars had a gramophone on the front gaily playing "Il Bacchio." Paper was thrown about lustily in every direction and the noise of squibs and crackers grew hourly more deafening. I went into the local gardens where

Lincoln's statue looked down broodingly on a crowd that could hardly move and in the distance played a band giving a concert of semi-classical favourites. Inside one of the halls was an excellent flower show, the best part of the proceedings.

And then I walked down a few streets, it being nine o'clock, to see the Chinese Baby Prize show. Here in the Chinese quarter, prizes were to be given for the best baby. It being night by now, it must have been difficult to deal with the babies. But there was a large cart in the centre on to which the lucky babies could be hoisted for the crowds to see. It was raining slightly and a band played cheerfully so as to keep the babies awake. And then so as to drown the squeals of the irate prize-winners, everybody started community singing and I went home to bed.

Wherever I turned these bands, these radio loud speakers were at work and all, it seemed, "by the courtesy" of some shop. You never were allowed to forget business. Exhausted I stopped at a shop to get an ice—but finally succumbed to tasting what was evidently the popular dish of the festival. It was called a "Hostess Banana Split."

Next day a new and really magnificent bridge was to be opened at St. John nearby by the Rose Queen, which would link up two parts of Oregon, and I went out there in the morning to see it.

The little town of St. John is hoping for great things from this bridge and already is preparing for growing prosperity. It struck me as if every town sees in itself a future city of skyscrapers and one wonders just where this all will end. The rain was pouring down and obviously the ceremony was going to be shorn of much of its beauty, so I left early and continued on my way to Seattle, but in a much less comfortable bus.

Out on the highway, we continued along the most

wonderful roads and through absolutely gorgeous
scenery, but I was relieved to get away from that
tawdry festival. You could not help but be angry,
first at the ridiculously exaggerated claims of its beauty
and originality, and secondly at the overdoing of the
publicity and at the greedy unnecessarily rushed
development within the last few years of a country
flower show that no doubt in its early years was
completely charming; and had not advertisements and
democracy stepped in like a bull in a china shop, it
might have developed into something distinctive and
with a tradition like carnival at New Orleans, instead
of into what we would consider a flower show tactlessly
given at Margate or Southend on August Bank Holiday and completely swamped in chewing gum, squibs,
tooth paste advertisements, men's fancy-dress parades
and "Hostess Banana Splits."

I had only a few days in Seattle and I never regretted
anything more. To begin with, the town is wonderfully situated and has made the very best of its opportunities. Not unlike San Francisco or Genoa in its
position, it consists of a series of hills on which are
placed skyscrapers, and when a hill or large rock is
in the way, they just blast it out. In fact most of
Seattle is the result of blasting hills.

Here most people of the North and many other
parts of America too, look for the New York of the
Pacific, though naturally San Francisco and Los
Angeles deny it. Especially the latter which claims
she is nearer the Panama Canal, has as good advantages
for China and Japan and has a wonderful hinterland
and climate. San Francisco has to admit her geographic position does not help her much towards
expanding—but she relies on her skyscrapers, her
position as a banking centre, her harbour and her
reputation. Seattle points to Alaska, and to herself

as the most northern port of the United States and as the nearest in mileage to China, Japan and Siberia. She also claims a wonderful hinterland and a good harbour. I was amused my first day in Seattle to see a large poster telling of all the wonderful advantages of Portland from the hinterland along, I think, the Columbia River. This struck me as odd—not being accustomed to seeing one American city or State doing anything to boost another. But at the end was the remark that all these advantages, if real, could be taken away from Portland by the country just boring a tunnel through a mountain and Seattle would become the more convenient outlet. It is true and will probably happen—Seattle being to-day more influential than Portland.

All California had seemed so almost tropical and so Spanish—here in Oregon and Washington it seemed another nation with other ideas, other traditions and almost rival ambitions—you have behind you the traditions of the North-west, the fur traders, the lumber, the fisheries, and early nineteenth-century French immigrant influence—the Hudson Bay Company and the scene of the early fame and fortune of the Astor family.

They made their money here and then invested it in real estate in New York, which turned out immensely profitable. To-day they might well realize and put back the money in Seattle and perhaps within one hundred years make as much again—but nowadays people in America will not look ahead one hundred years—only foreigners in their midst do that. Ten years is far enough ahead for the average man, not over keen on family stabilization, living just for to-day and to-morrow.

I talked a lot to Seattle Church leaders, to business men and to journalists. The latter told me a good deal about the Chinese problems of the town and asserted that there is more underworld life in Chinese Seattle, more opium smoking and more secret societies than in any of the more famous cities, such as Chicago or New York. Certain it is that when Al Capone came to Seattle a couple of years ago to investigate the possibilities of making that city the centre of his activities on the Pacific Coast, it was the powerful Chinese Tong that refused to let him poach on their preserves.

The Tong was originally a Korean organisation to combat Christianity and support Confucianism; now in the United States it is a huge and powerful secret society under the control of wealthy Chinese business men, operating chiefly in Seattle and New York and carrying on an underworld existence that shuns the limelight given to Sicilian Capone, works infinitely more systematically, is wealthier, more powerful, and capable of deeds that make racketeering pale into insignificance. Nothing did I want to do more than follow up the various lines of enquiry that were put at my disposal, but it would have taken far longer time than I could afford and I had to leave it alone for the time being.

Another less exciting but equally alarming problem for Seattle is that of the Filipino immigration, and it worries the Catholic hierarchy on the Pacific particularly.

The Philippines being American territory there is difficulty over restricting the entry of Filipinos. The better class ones do not come so much, as the type which is more or less that of single men. To-day on the Pacific Coast there are about 7,000 Filipinos. They are all small, extremely vain and lazy, but willing to work for so little that like the Mexican peon they are replacing the ordinary American in unskilled positions. They seem keenly anxious to go up to Alaska—but they are not strong enough and usually return to Seattle with signs of consumption.

Seattle is perhaps not as seriously affected as California, where these youths take jobs as house-boys and also for working on the land. Here it seems there have recently been many race riots initiated by whites against them. But it does become a serious problem for the West when one realizes that 30,000 Filipino couples to-day on the Pacific Coast, breeding families of an average of nine children as they do, would have no less than twenty-one million great-grandchildren. It may not quite reach that figure, but the tendency is towards large families, and the Filipino is apt to marry white girls of not very strong mentality. The result is not a good breed. After all, the fifteen odd million negroes to-day in Eastern America are said to be descended from no more than 750,000 slaves, and the mortality then was ever so much greater than now.

This, is the negro problem of the West—the Filipino. It is not really appreciated in the East, any more than is their colour problem in the West. No one again is looking much ahead and the business man wanting his dividends increased is out, as he has been for generations in America, to get the cheapest labour and if necessary import it. America is only united about the Philippines on the one point that they are her first big colonial problem, and it was fascinating for me, brought up on colonial talk, to see the reactions throughout America to this problem.

While passing through these different towns, I had begun to notice in the telephone book my namesakes and I had a longing to get in touch with them. Still I could not but remember Edward Marjoribanks when he did a lecture tour of America a few years ago. He saw a Marjoribanks in the telephone book, rang him up and suggested this man might like to meet his English namesake and perhaps relation. The other replied he would and it was arranged that after that evening's lecture, the man should come up to the platform and make himself known. He did, but he was a negro. Fearing some skeleton in the family cupboard might appear, I kept away from the telephone and finally with a friend, who had come down to meet me, I drove on across the border (everyone laughed at me when I called it frontier) to Vancouver in Canada for Polo week. From there I was to go into the Canadian Rockies to visit the naked Doukhobor Sect and then to work my way down into Montana to attend a Writers' Conference and Summer School at the State University—that I had read about in Los Angeles.

And as I left the Pacific I heard no more of the problems of migration from Asia and little of the development of the Pacific; and I was still too far from the eastern side to hear of European problems or to meet anyone more than mildly interested in them— I was moving into the Middle West—the backbone of America—the part that Washington can never wholly ignore and that, buried between the two great coast belts, bothers little about the outside world and looks only down to the development of its own soil and up to heaven for the development of its own soul in some future existence—in short, I was moving towards the Bible Belt, towards Main Street and perhaps to-day the real America, the one Europeans scarcely ever see.

CHAPTER X

FROM NUDE DOUKHOBORS TO SUMMER SCHOOL
IN MONTANA

Tucked away in a valley of the Columbia River near to the Canadian Rockies, in a district appropriately called Brilliant, I discovered a religious communistic colony of several thousand Russians. They call themselves Doukhobors, the Russian for Spirit Wrestlers, and they have an extremist branch of less than one thousand a little further away on the American border, called sometimes the Sons of Freedom, and at others the Black Hundreds.

On my way from Vancouver to Montana, I spent a few days with the thousands at Brilliant. Only a very few spoke English and they all welcomed me as some curious phenomenon, staring, and then shyly gathering around me. And then a braver boy, who had been sent to school, would speak to me in English, and if I went alone near to their bridge over the river or to their school-house, or to their railway station, up from apparently nowhere would jump two or three youths, watching me carefully, for they feared their Black Hundreds brethren, who might, they said, blow up their much-prized bridge.

These thousands came from Russia many years ago under the auspices of Tolstoy, and they thought that perhaps they would find more freedom in Canada than in the United States. Therefore they went to Saskatchewan, but some of them went naked to meet the Lord in the snow and were sent to prison, and finding many other things that did not suit a government apt to be slightly Scotch and Presbyterian in its outlook, they moved to British Columbia, and made a veritable garden out of a wilderness in the most beautiful surroundings possible.

But their tendencies here too were unpopular, and to-day they do not know which way to turn.

They have looked to Colorado for a home—but are now more interested in Mexico. Some that are only half practising are already in Southern California and others are scattered through the East, but I found the main body at Brilliant near the Kootenay and on the Columbia River.

I stopped at the nearest inn two miles away and I visited them in their villages which consisted of two houses each village, and in each house lived over forty people with one room for two people, and they have their communal kitchen and a wash-house behind where on Saturdays they bathed themselves and their clothes. Their leader they believed to be imbued with the Spirit of the Lord and he could, and did, do with them what he liked. With him worked a Committee of Elders, but he had enemies, and no one knows who is responsible for the blowing up of his father, of the schools in the neighbourhood—for the Doukhobors will not send their children to learn of capitalism,—or who is most responsible for all the accusations made against them from outside.

As they receive no money payment for their work, and as they all work hard on their fertile land which originally did not cost them much money, and as they are almost self-sufficing in their organisation, they are not popular in the neighbouring towns, neither with the shopkeepers nor with the farmers. They have naturally in their frugality grown extremely wealthy, and it has perhaps made them a little careless of their religious life which should be Spartan in the extreme. Thus they are criticised as hypocrites by their opponents, and by those more rigid who have broken away

124

DOUKHOBORS IN PROCESSION

A DOUKHOBOR COTTAGE

and are living near Grand Forks, ten minutes from the American border on the railway line to Spokane.

After some days with the Community at Brilliant where I ate only fruit and drank no alcohol, I went on to Grand Forks and they met me in their camp, a disused mine where they are living on the bare necessities, those Sons of Freedom, and they told me of the religious beliefs they practise to-day and which they practised in the Caucasus.

God is in every one and you must take no oaths and be subject to no country and to no potentate. You must not pay wages for land because all the earth should be free, and what is mine is thine be it in the produce of the land or anything else that is essential, and so their neighbours sometimes say they steal. And they do not believe in marriage, for you should live only with one woman at a time and with her no longer than while you are in love. And you should keep no money for yourself, neither should you eat nor drink too much. Above all you should daily humiliate your flesh by stripping naked when you feel most the call from Heaven, and you may work naked in the fields and you should also occasionally go naked before those that have evil minds—for that tempts them and it is good they should be occasionally tempted and get used to it.

Considering that one lady, known as Old Bottlenose, and weighing over 300 pounds, was there at the moment with many friends not unlike her in figure, I could well understand it might upset one's temptations. And then they told me if they are arrested for non-payment of taxes or because they will not register births and deaths, then, as it is written in the Scriptures, "If a man ask for your over garment, give him also your under garment," so they again strip naked, and though they should not resist, Old Bottlenose and others occasionally kick violently the police—but that is often only after the police have douched them with itch powder.

And then and there some twenty of them old and young stripped completely naked before me. And after having taken all their photographs at their request I finally left them to catch the train for Spokane.

Arrived there, it was the 4th of July, and there were squibs and other things let off around me, and I could not help, as I entered a drug store, but wonder if the impractical life of the Sons of Freedom were not infinitely more to be admired in its simplicity than the unbeautiful existence of a holiday in a city. Or as a compromise, whether the Doukhobors at Brilliant on their great holiday the 29th of June, had not shown in their prayers and their dresses and their singing and their picnics, the signs of a new era towards which we are all moving. It was some months before I saw a good answer to this and it was in another religious communist colony in Iowa. Next morning I arrived by train at Missoula in Montana for six weeks in the State University.

I had only heard of the University Courses through an advertisement in a writer's magazine which I had seen at Los Angeles; this had advertised a Writers' Conference for a fortnight and a Summer School for yet another four weeks. It seemed to me a good way of knowing first an American University and secondly some of the country's writers. Yet when I got there that Sunday morning in July, my heart sank and I felt a little like my first term at school. And this time I knew nobody and nobody knew me. I had heard by wire that I was to have the room next and share a bathroom with the Dramatic Critic of the *New York Evening Post*, one John Mason Brown. Luckily he was delightful, but I did not know that yet.

I was welcomed on the whole very well, rather as a mysterious oddity, and for the first few days I was able to watch everyone without being very much noticed. The Writers' Conference had as its nucleus a Writers' Colony, most of whom came from the twin cities—Minneapolis and St. Paul—and consisted entirely of women. Many were wives who had the idea, rather strange to a European, that to enjoy your holiday you must get away from your husband. All were intensely keen authors, but so far more or less devoid of success. There were perhaps some fifty of us.

A very charming old lady led the group, and, as she herself put it, bumbled along. Next in importance came a really well-known playwright and authoress who was no doubt correctly convinced that if I did write a book on America it would be a bad one—and then came a lady who wrote cookery books, and another who put cookery recipes to Mother Goose rhymes. Otherwise the fifty-odd ladies were still hoping.

To make us all more hopeful, we had with us the Editor of a Regional Magazine—which is the type that requires good stories with a distinct local atmosphere, but never pays, as you just write for it for the general kudos gained. We also had the poetry partner in the publishing firm of Longman Hill, and the author of a best seller at that moment, later to become the book of the month in England—Mr. Struthers Burt. With him came his wife, herself an equally popular authoress, and all these people with a great sense of humour, or else intensely bored, lectured to us regularly from 8 a.m. through the morning, the afternoon and into the night.

They told us how to write, how not to write, and in between went out to lunch with the local Rotarians. Sometimes they and we were entertained for coffee, cakes and gramophone by some local Don, or more daring, we went to drink whisky with "the County," from under the table at a local café, and then to sing sonnets or quote Shakespeare to the full moon or to some small spur of the ever-present Rockies.

At other moments these wretched authors sat in tiny sitting-rooms and read the plotless outpourings of pretty maidens, elderly spinsters, and mature mothers, and later, in a twenty minutes' private interview, would tell the unbelieving ladies that their stories just lacked that little something, and everyone felt exhausted at the effort not to hurt.

And then again, which was worse, we would sit around perhaps under a tree, or else in the women's drawing-room, and listen to one another read their painful efforts. I remember a lumberjack thriller by a lady in the seventies who strongly disapproved of drinking and swearing, the poetic outbursts of another in blank verse for over an hour on "de man dat did her wrong"—the usual story of black and white, and my own appalling efforts that made people laugh and cry at unintended moments.

And lastly to cheer us all came a Jewish Rabbi to lecture on the Talmud, and after him the Chancellor of the University, to help whose oratorical efforts we had to have both a piano solo and a violin piece before and after the inspiring speech, and so half fill the hall.

At last it was all over and we were all very happy. No one had sold anything, but many had hopes and we all cheerfully adjourned for an outing in the country. Eight motors full, we headed for the mountains, but soon stopped to see a shack now fifty years old. Here the vigilantes had hung just half a dozen outlaws, and at least two ladies wept at the ancientness, the romance of the relic. Later we stopped again to look at the geographic features, and then again for lunch

BRILLIANT, A DOUKHOBOR VILLAGE

PETER VEREGIN'S DOUKHOBOR TOMB

near mountain goats, and later still to cook our supper and tell camp stories near a buffalo range, and then motor home, just a few singing, but the majority in dignified silence.

Next day I escaped to an Indian pow-wow 40 miles away, and there, in their tee-pees which they had brought on their carts and many in more modern motors, I talked to these Indians and their squaws. Poor souls, the older ones with the most wonderful heads and faces, seemed like children and seemed sad and now almost out of place, and the younger ones in ordinary day clothes, seemed only a rather dark type of American—perhaps just Mexicans.

As night came on, you heard the sound of bells in the tents as these warriors of old put on their full regalia and one by one they came out summoned by the Chief, and entered the big central tent. There were a few, but only a very few, of the type of American trippers that come to Europe, and on the whole the gathering was as Indian as one could find.

Perhaps forty men were dancing—wild, frantic, excited war jumps, with weird chanting noises, and the monotonous drone of the drums went on, never ceasing. The dust covered them in a sort of mist, but through it all you could distinguish the old chief in a large sombrero hat, and a sub-chief from Coeur D'Allein. There were representatives from Idaho, and Utah, from other parts of Montana and from Dakota, Flathead Indians, Chippewaks, and Mexicans and even whites married to squaws who had turned Indians and wore their feathered dress. Plumed heads danced with real porcupine heads covering members of the snake tribe; and most beautiful in garb and movement was a mute hermaphrodite who never missed a dance. The leaders urged on the lazy ones with whips, and towards midnight the whole scene, with the squaws dancing in the middle, assumed a savage aspect.

I began to look towards home, but it was impossible to find any kind of car, and a booth-holder from Seattle, giving me for luck two pieces of copper from a local mine, bade me come on with him into the nearby village where there was to be a dance, after which I might get a lift. It was after midnight and the dance was in a barn, every soul was Indian or half-caste—it was the new generation, and they danced to three instruments at five cents a dance, and mostly round dances, so that more people would put in their nickels. Drink was procurable and the more Native Indians began to look less pleasant and so, devoid of tooth-brush and pyjamas, I woke up the hotel keeper, who was sleeping through it all, and, paying my dollar in advance, settled down to safety if not sleep.

When I returned to the University next day—where none had missed me—I went to hear immediately a lecture by a well-known author on Indian subjects, on the local Indians that I had met. It seems they move about during the summer from one of these pow-wows to another, and after all, you cannot expect a hunter by nature to turn in two generations into a farmer. It took a thousand years in Europe. To-day the Indian finds himself at his worst. Even the average full-blood Indian of 50 years of age knows nothing of his old customs, and gradually these are being lost to an America that in another fifty years will curse this generation for letting die out unrecorded the most fascinating customs and ideas of the original settlers. Here, just east of the Rockies, the Indians neither catch fish nor do they care to eat it, and until quite recently they were divided into "King George men" or "Boston men"—over a hundred years too late.

Their religious beliefs make a rather pleasant and simple philosophy. They believe in one God, who however did not make drink; on the contrary He is to them rather a good sportsman, that at times, however, is apt to play practical jokes, but He is always very polite—and so are they. God's greatest manifestation is the sun, and on earth, His most interesting product, the grizzly bear, a piece of whose heart they always try to eat, for they admire him very much.

Amongst them are still many secret societies—the most exclusive of which are the "Fighting Bulls." They have an unwritten law that amongst them mothers-in-law are never mentioned.

One of these days when we know more about psychology and things of the other world, we may marvel, if we have enough recorded of them, how much closer to the realities of nature were these simple people than we who have strayed off into so-called civilisation. Back to this civilisation I came when I started to move into the world of Missoula that was typical of Montana, a little of the Middle West, and more so of the sons and grandsons of pioneer farmers the world over.

The town was almost run by Higginsons, Dalys, McCormacks and FitzGeralds—but as a whole the State has almost as many Poles and Danes, the former in the mines, the latter on the farms. The Governor's wife, with a Danish name, showing the democracy of the whole system, coming to the University for some lectures and finding no bedroom free, camped out in the bedroom of two girls until later in the week a room was found for her. She had visited England on a round Europe tour, and the day in London had just given her time to see the changing of the Guard. Her official home at Helena, the capital, she told me was "turreted Tudor," and she was the type of American that any Britisher would always like to meet—tall and naturally dignified. She was ready for any kind of amusement the University was ready to provide.

But the University did not mix much with the owners of the railways, the mines, the real estate, the ranches, and the banks. The latter worked at business all day and on Thursday with wives and all departed to the County Club for dinner. First of all you drank in your own house so as to get to the jumping-off level and then you appeared at the Club— armed with your own favourite flasks.

On arrival I was greeted by several ladies with "Ah, we know all about you. You're here as a British spy." This, presumably, because they still keep an old fort in Missoula, once used against the Red Indians, and have now also got barracks and some troops. Another lady, much amused at my funny name, disagreed with me that I could be Chinese because she and her husband had been quartered in China for several years. Neither could I be English, she said, because I did not say "cheerio." All her English friends said "cheerio" and I suppose "chin chin."

Later, after innumerable drinks, we sat down to a dinner at a long table, forty of us, and in between each course got up to dance violently round to a victrola. Afterwards dancing and drinking and garden walking were continued. The drink was kept in the lockers and changing room and most of the party were to be found there. Upstairs we danced now to a piano, and the main piece of furniture was a modern tapestry scene of an English hunt. There was a good deal of kissing and hitting on the back by the women, and we eventually moved off to a house in the town where more drinking was continued until about 2 a.m. The

women had now quietened down—but some of the
men, though not rowdy, were sleepy, and these were
removed more or less bodily.   One gentleman told me
in a kind-hearted way that "It's a great relief to find
you are not one of the usual impostors we get from
England."

On the whole I think the Indian pow-wow was more
dignified.   About the same time I was taken to a
political meeting—actually a taxpayers' meeting, and
the two main speakers were the Democratic Congressman and the Republican Ex-Congressman.   You
might quite easily have been at a farmers' meeting in
England.   The speeches were partly sentimental,
partly practical and wholly political.   On the platform
was a working man as Chairman and some farmers
of French Canadian origin who with their parents had
come lumbering in the past, from Quebec.   The
audience was distinctly one of ratepayers, and I noticed
two University professors who were reputed to be
interested in real estate near the University Campus.
The most noticeable thing in the speeches was, that
however Socialistic the Democratic Representative
might become in his speech, and however much he
might dread the advent of Communism due to the
reactionary methods of Federal Republicanism, yet
both he and the Republican speaker united in defence
of the small capitalist.   In fact I could see but little
or no difference in the fundamental ideas of either.

The Democrat may pretend to the working man
that he is a Socialist, but unlike real Socialists he is
at heart an active defender of the small capitalist,
though not of the Big Banker and Big Business Man;
and at heart his working supporters, hoping that if
not they, at least their sons will be capitalists, agree
with him.

In the meantime the Writers' Conference was over

and we were continuing with the last four weeks of the Summer School. For this I had to be registered in some subject in which I should nominally try to get a credit, which would help me, it seemed, towards an eventual University degree. There were a variety of subjects and I chose English History, in which I had already got my Degree at Oxford, and swimming. I must confess I did not often get the opportunity to attend the former class, especially as I was apt to feel angry at the lecturers' interpretation of the Irish position, the Dominions, and the House of Lords. On the whole he was very fair, but it was essentially a surgeon's dissection of an evidently unhealthy body.

The idea of the Summer School seemed to be, roughly, that the ordinary student could get in a few more credits and so get his degree earlier, and that State School teachers throughout America could also take courses that would enable them to get more salary and better jobs. In fact unless these teachers attend a Summer School each year they eventually get dismissed. To get your degree you take credits which make up four years' work, and you can take them at the rate of one year's credits at any separate University —so that you find undergraduates with a bent for travelling doing a year in Montana, a year in Boston and another somewhere else.

The result is no doubt a potted and pointless education and the whole system seems to mean learning as little as possible of as many subjects as possible and then going forth to teach other people just a little less again of all the subjects learnt before.

For the teacher, he or she goes to any University, Montana or Hawaii, it matters not, as long as there is a Summer School in Session—and at this particular course I met teachers from Iowa, New York, Boston, Duluth, Minneapolis, Kentucky, Idaho, Seattle, Spokane, California, in fact from all over the country. They seemed to study everything, and one day I went in to listen to a class for Public Speaking.

There were twenty students, ranging in age from 22 to 40. One huge burly male gave us ten minutes on the problem of "Married Women Teachers." Next came a fragile, youthful female whose voice, pitched all the time in one key, gave us nearly a quarter of an hour on the advantages of capital punishment—she was bloodthirsty to a degree. Next came rolling along a middle-aged buxom dame who, in a deep not-to-be-contradicted voice, boomed forth anathema on prohibition and the Eighteenth Amendment, and she was finally followed for another ten minutes by a very prim middle-aged female, as thin as the first was fat, who spoke on that all-engrossing subject for teachers, "A defence of snobbery."

Such was the educational side of our Summer School; everybody dabbled in a dilettante manner in whatever subject pleased them most and everyone was deadly serious. In the morning we could breakfast up till eight o'clock, we lunched at twelve and dined at six. All our meals were cooked and served by fellow students, and almost all the work in the University office and in manual labour in the grounds was done by students trying to work their way through college.

As I bathed each evening at five o'clock it was quite natural to see rushing into the swimming pool, huge muscular youths, originally Danes or Germans, who had just finished making a new path or cleaning out refuse in boiling summer heat, their day's labour over, and hoping in a few minutes to learn enough of swimming—they had never even seen the sea—to get a University credit from this cooling process. They spoke to me with a certain fascinated interest in one who had come so far, and if there was in many of them an almost childlike simplicity there was at the same time such a clean unsophisticated outlook on life that it put one to shame; though when I asked one man from Kansas City what there was of interest in his city, he could only answer with pride, "There's a fine Kiwanis Club," but that same man had never drunk liquor or been to a speak-easy in his life.

The smarter set was different. They knowing their London, their Paris and the Riviera, took me gaily round to what speak-easies or road-houses the country offered and bemoaned the boredom of Missoula. But on the whole this very middle-class crowd was intensely earnest in its outlook on life and had a spirit for fighting poverty that made you sometimes nearly speechless with admiration. The most menial task was not too low as long as it brought in money so that you could be educated.

In term time in this thinly populated State with its University buildings and schools scattered all over the bigger towns for political purposes, so that no one place should get full benefit from the influx of students, there would be some fifteen hundred pupils, of which six hundred would be girls; the first year they would live in College, and many of them could so ill afford the expense that they went out and worked as servant girls in private houses, as nursery maids, as stenographers, as anything, and then when possible attended a lecture and did a little study, presumably with a brain already dead tired with physical exertion.

The food they got was brought down to a minimum of cost and somehow never quite filled one—yet the names made up for the insubstantiality, and to this day I never shall get over the thrill of eating "Dyna Mite" and "Veal Birds" and above all "Shrimp Wiggle." And the result of all this? They told me of those who had taken their degree in Law and many of these were begging on the streets in other Montana cities to-day. Though many went back to their farms, others were discontented with their lot, by learning just so little and yet just so little too much, and were unwilling to help at home or went to glut the market for white-collar jobs, in the position of clerk or salesman.

The Dean of Women and the leading professors hotly defended the system that urged on these people to greater intelligence and effort, and perhaps they are right—but you must set against that the potted unsatisfactory education, the disturbing atmosphere, the constant stress on games and petting parties between the youths and girls at night, the making of teachers out of people so little qualified, and the fact that to get such an education, large numbers have to work so hard to keep themselves in college, they cannot give their brains to any leisured thinking. But no doubt this has been debated a thousand times; I can only tell of what I saw.

Amongst the teachers the men seemed infinitely pleasanter and more natural than the women. The latter's affectation and veneer of gentility became at times extremely boring, and meal-time was such a polite adventure, you always felt like resting later on. Never could you stretch yourself one inch for the food, and the words you used were always dignified and almost Old-English. Though one was supposed to come in to meals and leave when you had finished, you always had to catch everybody's eye at table before getting up and ask leave to be excused.

You could not be introduced until the other man had definitely caught your name and caught it so distinctly that he could say "Pleased to meet you, Mr. Teeling," and in the meantime your hand was dangling aimlessly in mid-air, for he would not clasp it until

137

he had your name in its every syllable, and to arrange all this we had a regular hostess for the whole Summer Session. I gather she came from one of the best Walla-Walla families—the smart town in the State of Washington, and she helped a few other enterprising teachers produce "Hay Fever," by Noel Coward, which everybody agreed was "refreshing" and so English.

Only on one occasion did we all join together—town and gown—and that was for a luncheon party jointly given by Rotarians, Lions, and Kiwanies to Tom Mix, travelling through with a circus. These three Clubs, inevitable in almost any big town in America, represent the vitality of the place, its every phase of business and public existence, and here they were all gathered together at their best.

They expected from Tom Mix a racy discourse on cinema or circus, but this dapper medium-height rider in his 10-gallon hat and his full cowboy rig, told us first of his boredom in visiting Europe, his feeble attempts to learn French and his difficulties with the knife and fork as used in England. All this delighted such a Monroe Doctrine audience, and then he got them into an ecstasy of civic pride and joy when he held forth at length on President Hoover, Mr. Stimpson and all these other less intelligent politicians who were worrying themselves about Europe.

He used the argument, so popular in these parts of America, and not easy now for politicians to combat—that the bankers instead of lending wholesale to Europe and South America should have saved some money and some thought for the more than 40 millions of their fellow countrymen living out there, west of Chicago and even Kansas, and should have tried to save their banks and their farms and their enterprise and that without the risk of war. But then he went more extravagantly ahead and advised a still higher tariff, not a tariff just round the United States, but one around Montana alone, and all would again be joy and prosperity. The audience loved every minute of it, and Will Rogers talking of the Presidency or Charlie Chaplin turned economist, could not have done better.

A few days later I went not to his circus, but to a local travelling fair show and found myself back, at least in mind, in England and Ireland. The yokels stared open mouthed at the fattest lady in the world, at half men and half fishes, and a Polish American challenged everyone to a wrestling match. My Seattle friend who had helped me out at the Indian pow-wow, brought up the local strong man, and the Pole had no desire to fight him. But the crowd insisted and in we went for 25 cents. But each time anyone was hurt we were all shot out again, and the ire of the Pole was terrible to see; he hurled buckets about, broke chairs and swore, and then we went in again for another 25 cents' worth.

Soon I ran out of cents, but my friend was taking the gate and he let me in for nothing. I had a grand evening of sham fighting and everyone else felt the same.

Next day some students motored me up to a lake in the hills where friends had a dude ranch, and there I spent the week-end. On the way we stopped to put up poles advertising along the road a new café at the lake, and my friend got a few dollars for himself for his effort. The ranch was delightful, owned by a retired Colonel, with only two dudes from Boston, who knew far more of England than I did, and had done the Avon, the Severn, and the Thames in a canoe.

We rode in the mornings and bathed, and in the evening we went to a dance in a barn and drank

Mountain Dew. The notices on the walls included "Gum spoils the floor," a practical suggestion, and as we drove through the forest we were warned against forest fires with the bright inscription, "This is God's country—don't make it Hell." After each dance, arm in arm we paraded round the room in circles, never resting—perhaps in order not to catch cold.

Next day I lunched with a lady whose mother was the first white woman born in Montana. My last experience was to broadcast through Montana and Idaho from the Missoula Radio Station. I gave them what they said they wanted for thirty minutes, an English voice and a talk on London, its palaces and public-houses. Before, came a youth and girl from the University, earning a few dollars with a rendering of the Indian Love Lyrics and the Moon Rocket; and after me the following typical advertisement:

"A rare opportunity is now offered every R.Q.V.O. listener. A large finance company who make loans to dealers and manufacturers has just had to take over a hundred thousand figures of the 26-piece silverware of ——, guaranteed genuine Nickel Silver Sets made by ——, world famous manufacturers of high grade silverware. The Set includes 6 each of table spoons, tea spoons and forks, one sugar shell, one butter knife, 6 crown hand forged silver plated knives, all packed in a handsome container with the ——'s printed guarantee. You can buy one of these beautiful sets for only $3.50. Don't send any money but get your order to the Radio Station right away. Phone 5744 or send us a letter and we will forward your order to Chicago and your silver-ware will be sent parcel post pre-paid. Phone us right now."

And then we had a gramophone record and it was all over.

Later they took me in to see a Fraternity house. Each year, it seems, old members of the Fraternities scattered through the State look out for likely youths about to go up to the University. They warn the present members, and these youths are quickly entertained on arrival and, if thought suitable, are asked to join. Your qualifications may be good athletics or wealth or whatever the Fraternity stands for. You then go and live your University life in one of these houses. At Missoula they had their own dining-room, their own servant and common sitting-room, and there were about eight beds in each bedroom—doubledeckers, four on top of the other four. . . .

And so the average undergraduate lives. The Fraternities and the Sororaties all have Greek names and are linked up across the Continent, making a series of almost secret societies to which you belong for the rest of your life. It does not, in these State Universities, help you to meet others outside your set, and also you are apt to become too snobbish and too clannish, and to work in peace presumably you must go to the College Library—almost the only central meeting place of the University—and there when it closes at 9 p.m. the men meet the girls and they go off motoring in the hills or down to the banks of the river or to the cinema or to dance, and there may be a petting party.

Such is the type of life in all its variety that I led and saw during six weeks of midsummer at the University of Montana. The President and his wife and most of the professors were delightfully kind to me, asking me constantly to their houses and explaining all I wanted to know. The life was in every way different from the University life I had known—but the people that led it too were different. Different in a thousand ways and yet probably at bottom, if only they knew each other, these enthusiastic middle-class and often almost peasant students and teachers—whose struggles to carry on would in themselves make many a novel—

these people would probably have more in common with the English farmers and with the suburban University students of the English Midlands than with the peoples of any other country.

They have all the pluck, the doggedness we admire, and we in turn are not only not as effete as they think, but just a little longer educated and just a little more experienced and just as fond of our liberty. But their interest in Europe was only academic, that it affected them they would not believe, and their remedy for all troubles was to get further away from Europe and have a higher tariff, for their belief in themselves is phenomenal—these people of the still unharnessed West.

What I saw was the ordinary life they led. But then there was that new side they did not understand. There was unemployment. The rumbling of the misery of those others passing through each day, on freight trains, was at their door; and I gradually determined my next step was to spend a little time with the hobo, the down-and-out, those unemployed without a dole.

CHAPTER XI

BY FREIGHT TRAIN TO WYOMING

Soon after I arrived in Missoula I climbed to the top of the hill that is behind the University, and lay there thinking how I could get to know these people who seemed so shy of me, and where I should go afterwards. And as I lay there, looking over Missoula, into the distant forests, and down to the gap through which the river wound and where the Indians used to war, there came a dishevelled, fair-haired and pleasant-looking youth. But his dress was alarming to meet alone on a mountain.

He wore a large sombrero, a black jumper or pull-over, with many holes, and a pair of corduroy trousers of a light brown colour, and in his hand he carried a branch of a tree that he had turned into a stick. He was a hobo, in the almost regulation kit. He was 18 years old and sat down beside me to talk. When he heard I was English he asked me if we celebrated the Fourth of July in England.

"Why, no," I answered, "hardly that; after all, it's your feast-day for having got away from England—why should we celebrate it?"

"Gee!" said he, "I never thought of that. I thought every country celebrated the Fourth of July. I thought it was some battle."

After a few minutes thinking all that over he asked me—"And do you celebrate Mothers' Day?" Again I had to reply, "No."

"Say, I'd hate not to have Mothers' Day," he went on. "Last Mothers' Day I begged a lot in the town I was in because I wanted to get enough to buy something to send home to Mother—but I couldn't get enough."

And he went on to tell me much of his life. How at sixteen he had left home because there was no work there, and how he had wandered up and down the country, and he was making for the Pacific Coast. It was cold in the winter in the East, and not easy even to beg bread. Sometimes he got a job but less often now, and in no town did anyone want a wanderer like him. He often tried to beg money to write home, but he hardly ever got more than enough for his food and he could not afford a stamp. He thought Al Capone was a sort of god because he financed a whole bread queue in Chicago; yes, most hoboes liked Al, he was good to them. I suggested a sort of Robin Hood. He thought perhaps—but he'd never heard of Robin Hood—and his ignorance was striking.

He asked me if there were railways in England, and when I said yes and they were much faster than those in America, he was amazed, and then grew more excited when I told him the unemployed were looked after systematically in England and given a dole if no work was to be found, to which he answered—"Say, the United States can't be so perfect after all."

Then he thought again a long time. "I was born in America," said he, "but my parents they come from Poland. I'd like to see Poland and England too," and he told me of life as a hobo.

You travelled on freight trains, mostly by night, sometimes more than a hundred people on each train, and many were old men sixty and seventy years old who had done this since they were twenty, and they were covered with animals and never washed; but now the majority were young fellows that did not like it and had to do it, and it was dangerous. Sometimes he had seen men fall off, and more often, walking from one freight car to another, they had slipped and been cut in two, uttering horrible cries.

All this he had seen and he strongly advised me never to become a hobo—but if I wanted to go back to England he would come with me, and we would meet in San Francisco. He was to be in Missoula for a few days, for he would sleep in the jungle down by the river and I promised I would go there and see him. A day or so later I went.

They were living down by the river bed, these hoboes, under a bridge and along the banks. They had the shelter of the trees, and one of them from floating logs was building himself a small hut. Many of them would stay here for days and nights, preferring the open air to the Salvation Army hut. Others, sometimes fifty or sixty of them, would come here off the trains in the daytime, would beg food from the shops and the houses and cook it here, would strip naked and wash in the river, would shave, and would rest. Yet others I found drinking canned heat—and my friend would not let me near them for they were drunk and in a fighting mood. But most of them were pleasant enough young fellows, keen for work they could not find and gradually getting desperate at the monotony and the degradation of begging and privation.

One week over fifteen hundred of them were in and around Missoula, and the Community Chest—the only organisation to help them—was at its wits' end to know which way to turn. Missoula was near the forests and this year there were more forest fires than ever—they said these hoboes started them to get work. However, all along the lines in these jungles and hobo camps—for they were everywhere in America, passed the word, that this was the season for fires in Montana and Wyoming and Idaho, and daily it was no uncommon sight to see more than a hundred men on a freight car as it slowly steamed through the station, and near the forest ranger's office there would be perhaps two hundred fellows sitting, waiting, waiting, hopelessly waiting for work.

One day, determined now to join them, I walked along the line, some two miles towards the mountains to see where people waited to jump on and off, and on the way I met a sixty-year-old hobo. His shoulder came out of his torn shirt, he had a two days' growth of beard, a black old hat, a stick, and a bundle. We talked. I was in an old grey flannel suit and I asked him which way the train came for Butte. "Say, young fellow," said he, "I wouldn't travel like that if I were you—too fine clothes, you'll get hit on the head certain," and thinking me already a fellow hobo, he went on to tell me his story.

He had been selling insurance—and his own policy had not been a bad one. He had sold insurance in Seattle and in Vancouver and he knew Canada well and he thought me a Canadian. And then his wife had died, and he himself fell ill and had an operation. He lost his job and to pay his bills he sold his policy and to-day he could find no work. Gradually he had sunk lower. And he told me he had an only daughter and she was grown up now and a school teacher—yes, and at the moment, he said, she was doing a Summer School course there at the University at Missoula, and she allowed her father all she could, ten dollars a month, and at night sometimes she slipped away from the University and walked up the line and sat and talked with him, under the old tree, with some old clothes hung from a branch, where he and another old man had made a dwelling, and when she went back to her school, he would tramp that way too and perhaps she could find him a hut for the winter.

Then he looked at my clothes. "I envy you them. When your clothes go you lose your morale, I've lost mine altogether. Ten dollars a month—it just keeps me in tobacco—I beg the rest." And as I went along I thought of the many pretty girls I sat next at dinner, different each evening, and I thought that one, any one, might be the one that slipped away, perhaps, with part of her dinner in a hand-kerchief, down the line, to her father living in the river bed, down under a tree.

At the University they tried to persuade me not to go, so many people they said now got killed for their money, and once I hesitated when a Canadian was beaten to death on the line half a mile from Mis-soula, because the men walking with him thought he had a Legion pension in his pocket—but this was ten days before I should leave and the Community Chest encouraged me and introduced to me two regular hoboes who however could not wait until I was ready but advised me to carry a revolver—which I did not do—for caught with one you inevitably went to prison.

And at the Salvation Army hut I bought for 60 cents, all included, a filthy old black hat, a black moth-eaten pull-over, a blue "payday" working man's shirt, an old pair of corduroy trousers, a belt and a washing bag in which to carry my belongings. All for 60 cents, which did not seem bad. That week-end with some members of the Phi Sigma Kappa Fraternity, I went out to the country and we hung out my new-bought clothes to kill the insects in the sun, and on Monday in Missoula the President of the University's wife presented me with a blanket and a tarpaulin for the journey.

I changed at the Phi Sigma Kappa house, got some drinks for our evening meal at the local speakeasy and with five friends and the Republican ex-Congressman motored down to the station in time to catch the freight train at 10 p.m. from Spokane to Butte and the East.

In my washing bag I carried my grey flannel suit and a few other things and on me only one dollar. My trunks had been sent on to Wyoming and five dollars by letter post to the post office at Butte—Montana.

A short distance from the station I said good-bye to my friends, put my pack on my back and made for the bridge. There was a policeman near, but he did not seem to notice me. Down the steps to the station where the freight train was already waiting. It was a clear moonlight night and hoboes were moving along the track from both ends to the train. It was in the station, but no officials happened to want to be about or to see anything and I followed a youth up the side of a lumber car. It seemed the easiest, the only open car, and though I had been warned lumber was dangerous, that with the jolting of the train it often moved and crushed the pygmy bodies lying on top, yet it seemed more or less safe as it was held in place by a wooden frame.

As I reached the top I saw the whole car was covered with bodies of sleeping men who had probably come through from the coast. Gingerly I stepped across them and reached the end of the car where the youth had lain down and I lay down beside him. Almost immediately the train moved out. I had only just been in time. My neighbour felt cold and so I gave him my blanket and covered myself with the tarpaulin. This immediately made a friend, and so we remained through the night. Soon it got bitterly cold and the jerking of the train and the moving of the hard wooden boards underneath me made sleep impossible.

But the moon shining high above the hills made up for much and my new friend told me how he had come through on the train from Spokane—how suffocating had been the tunnels and how the night before three tugs had boarded the freight train armed with revolvers, and high-jacked the hoboes. They had proceeded from car to car and made, as they boarded each car, all the men turn on their stomachs and stretch out their arms. They had then systematically searched each one, taking any money they possessed over one dollar—perhaps the first for months —fighting forest fires—these creatures knew they would make a haul and they got away with $100. My friend they did not rob because he had only 13 cents. He had been working on a fruit farm near Walla-Walla. This surely was the lowest form of villainy to rob these almost down-and-out men of all they had.

Indeed it was a train load of depressed hoboes that travelled with me that night—but as we stopped a little further on, at an evidently recognised spot, more and more men got on and our lumber car began to be uncomfortably full. The conversations were amazing to listen to and one man told another that "Nowadays we must be thankful for anything and mustn't complain too much about the Salvation Army —one has to put up with it," and the others reluctantly agreed.

As the sun got up it became pleasanter and soon as we crawled through the hills basking in a warm sun, it became extremely pleasant. I got used to the double time of the logs as the train rushed down hills, but was surprised when my friend admitted that thanks to the blanket he had "had the best night in years." I did not like to confess I had had the worst.

Soon others came along to join us. One fellow lived in Soult, and was heading for Omaha—but he found these freight trains too slow—he was impatient and soon would jump a passenger train. The others seemed to think this risky—it was so simple on a freight on the main line and nobody bothered.

After all it was a cheap way, while saying nothing of moving labour from one end of the country to the other. It would be too cold to stay in Montana all winter and yet they wanted extra workers there in the summer. The Companies said nothing. They did not want their trains to find obstacles on the lines and have accidents. But my friend warned me about other lines, less pleasant, of prison terms and no questions asked and of rough treatment on the Santa Fé.

And yet others came along and wondered what day it was and by calculating back to the day they left Spokane, came to the conclusion it was Tuesday morning. In this way we crawled through the station yards of Butte, and there hiding in other trucks were men and also women hoboettes, waiting to board our freight. It was now eleven o'clock and in a boiling sun I said good-bye to them all—they were all going East, and I slipped off the lumber car. My friend shouted to me that 10 cents had fallen out of my pocket where I had lain and he threw it after me, and I started off towards the town, stopping for a few moments in the jungle to know from other hoboes about the trains to Livingstone, a side line that was not so easy to ride—but the only way to get to Yellowstone Park, which was next on my list after Butte.

For Butte I had letters to the manager of the Anaconda Company and I was determined to go down a mine. But before going to the offices I would have to change my clothes and shave and in this suit I could not enter a decent hotel, so I moved into a workman's hotel where I paid 50 cents for a three-bedded room in which to change.

As times were bad I was left alone. Changed and more respectable I went up to the offices, and it was soon arranged that I should go down the Mountain Cone Mine next morning at 8.30.

The Anaconda Company is like many another company in America—run by wealthy men—wealthy beyond the dreams of the average European. These companies are superbly organised right across the continent and control their subordinates in so many different ways that it becomes extremely difficult ever to get anything done of which they do not approve. There may be democracy, there may be individual liberty—but these large companies with their fabulously wealthy founders really rule the country. One of the local Copper Kings, by name Clarke, is reputed to have left a fortune of over 100 million dollars.

The company controls everything in the town of Butte and in a sense controls the State of Montana. They own the copper companies, they own the lumber companies, they have a brick company in Poland and large interests in South Africa, South America, and the neighbouring State of Utah, and in and around the State of Montana they control no less than seventeen different newspapers—in which the events in Russia are invariably relegated to the bottom column of the second page. There is of course no press censorship in Montana—officially.

The Manager told me to cope with the depression the workers are employed two weeks at a time and then one week off—thus employing the maximum possible of workers. The extras are employed by the Montana Power for installing their new pipe line. Nobody is employed who was taken on after January 1, 1929.

I tried to find out what the Company did for their employees, as they comprised practically the whole of the town of Butte—but was told they do nothing at all. Here I must say I found them different from most other big companies in America. After work hours, the company does not in any way interest itself in what the workmen do.

The net result is that Butte has the reputation of being about the wickedest city in America. To begin with it is extremely ugly and dirty, as no doubt any mining town planned in the nineteenth century would be—but Butte never gives the impression of having been planned at all. With a not very large population it manages to have over 500 speak-easies, a few of which I visited, and there is one whole street to which the representative press of a agency took me to see all the sights, where behind every window on each side was sitting a half-naked woman, beseeching you to come into her "home." As we passed, they all pulled up the curtains, and batoned on the windows with little sticks. This tapping noise soon got quite loud all the way down the street and made one think of Chinese quarters. These too, my press friend told me, exist in quantity, and the Chinese live with white women and make Butte one of the chief centres of the American dope traffic.

Incidentally he told me the unemployment problem existed in an acute form in Butte, but was being hushed up, which made me all the more surprised when I went in search of the local Community Chest. I found it in the County Jail just next the prison bars, and hardly a cheerful place for a man to come for help knowing that the police might immediately lock him up for vagrancy. But in any case it did not matter, as in spite of unemployment and in spite of wretched people passing through the town, the Community Chest, the only charity organisation of Butte, was closed for three months, and the secretary, the only official, had gone to California for a month's holiday.

Admittedly a town like Butte cannot be expected to look after people from other towns, but then other towns should not send people off to be looked after *en route* to their destinations. I remember an example from Missoula and wondered what would have happened then in Butte. These people originally from Minnesota had been packed off from Tacoma, Washington, in a car purchased for them for $50, and given enough petrol to get out of the State and a few dollars to buy some more. The whole family had arrived plus their household goods in Missoula and had to be helped on their way.

Had they arrived in Butte, they must have gone to prison and the sergeant in charge would hardly have been sympathetic judging from my reception. I showed him my letters and credentials and got no answer—he did not even bother to stand up or look up—I repeated my question—finally he looked up and snarled:

"Young man, we are a Republic—we don't believe in charity—everyone can do as they like. If there are unemployed, it's their own look out—Good morning," and he continued to read his paper. Feeling like a snubbed Soviet emissary I departed and next morning in greater state was taken down the mine.

The workmen, I gathered, work in twos, and some are on contract labour. They may earn as much as $10 a day, but the average ordinary pay is about $4.75

a day. Most of the 750 employees are either Cornishmen or Irish and there are a few Italians and Swedes.
The Cornishmen go by the name of "Cousin Jacks."

Later in the day I returned to my flop house, re-
dressed as a hobo and started off for the station. As
I tramped down the hill I overheard a man say, "Lot
of Bums in town to-day," and I felt happy that my
dress was recognisable.

As I crossed the railway line I fell in with a youth
about 18 who was going the other way. He came
from Milwaukee and was jumping freights all the way
to Seattle, then down to Portland, San Francisco and
back to Milwaukee—just to see the country. He paid
no fare and begged for his food. He had a job waiting for him when he returned to Milwaukee next week.

And then I went on to the line that went to Livingstone and Gardner. There were several others sitting there, the sun was setting, there was quiet and
a coolness after great heat and we watched as the
engine shunted backwards and forwards piecing the
freight together.

I joined the two best-looking of the bunch and
they said I could travel with them. I told them my
tale—that I was a Canadian on the way to Mexico
to find work and that I hoped to get money from a
sister in Salt Lake City, and they believed me. They
told me the Company did not like us to board a
train until it was ready to move and when it was
we got into the only possible car—a disused coal
waggon—because there was no empty box car.

They helped me in and they complained because
it was dirty for they had both had a wash that day
in Butte. One whom the other called Jack and was
about 25 had blisters on his feet and broken boots
and no socks—and I gave him a spare pair of mine
that came from Hawes and Curtis in London, and

he looked suspicious and I said quickly that I had
begged them off a lady back in Montana somewhere,
and he was still reluctant because he said he didn't
want to "take them from a fellow," but if anyone
needed them he did, and then his pal, who had bigger
boots, offered to swap those with him as they might
pinch his sore feet less, but he would not. He was
new to being a hobo, having been an oil man in
Arkansas and only two months on the road.

And nearby was another youth in rough clothes
but with silk socks and he did not like our looks, and
while the train was moving he climbed over to another
cart and sat on the rim near the wheels of an oil tank.

Slowly we crept up over the hills over the Great
Divide that cuts off Pacific America from Atlantic
America, and it began to rain and to get colder.
My friends and I got in under the tarpaulin, and
it gradually got darker until we reached Whitehall.

Here they attached some more freights and it included an empty box car. Jack went forward to explore and Tom, his pal, stopped behind with me.
He was dressed like a Dutchman with brown cor-
duroys, a blue payday shirt, a light scarf and a peaked
hat, and he said very little but was tall, dark and good-
looking, about 30 years old, and when we moved on
to the box car he saw I was not used to climbing out
of freight cars and took my sack, helped me down,
and they all pulled me into the box car.

Here it was cold and dark and the others collected
the papers that were lying about, for the last travellers
had used them—papers wrapped round you being a
great aid to warmth—and they shook the papers to
make sure there were not too many insects and lay
down to sleep. But Jack and I rolled together in
my blanket and to Tom I lent my tarpaulin. At
first I did not sleep at all, lying flat on a wooden

155

floor that shook violently as we climbed up and then down ridges of the Great Divide. But then the tiredness of adventure eventually forced me to sleep, and about one o'clock I was rudely awakened by the shouting of railway police—"Bulls" they call them, telling us to look sharp and get out.

We all thought we were being arrested—on the contrary the box car was going no further—we had reached the junction at Logan and nobody wanted us to stay in the town—so we were told to wait till the next freight started for Livingstone in about an hour.

It was pitch-dark and we kept together by the tracks. Nearby was a house and one of our friends, a Pole by origin, went to the house and got himself some food. Later he came back and told us how he made silver rings and peddled them and so made a living—how he had offered one to a woman in Butte and she had been willing to repay in kind— but he had refused, not wishing to miss his train, and he boasted how he always fooled priests and got money and food out of them—but that now he felt lonely as he used to travel round for five years with an English Cockney with a great sense of humour, who slipped between two freights and was killed last week, and my friends told me that type disgusted them. "He ain't got no shame always being a Bum." At last our train came, and not much liking the looks of some of the others, one of whom showed his revolver, we three settled down in a gondola. But I could not sleep.

First Tom told me how a friend of his had once lain in a gondola—not long ago—and the gondolas open downwards to let out the coal, and it had not been properly closed and when they went fast it fell open and his friend fell under the wheels and was quickly

killed. We walked round the gondola testing each
piece—but as the train went faster and as I lay on
the floor I felt it might open and for the first time
felt really frightened.

Then again as dawn approached and we seemed
to mount higher into the mountains—it got colder
and less pleasant and the sun appeared, and as we
stretched ourselves and felt hungry, Jack said: "Oh
God, I'm just about ready to throw my hands up,"
but Tom answered quietly: "I'm just about ready
to make the other fellow put his hands up." And
I felt I could certainly not blame him.

It was 6.30 a.m. We were nearly in Livingstone
and we jumped off because one of us had been caught
like that at Pocatello for stopping on too long and
searched to pay his fare, and as I went into the town
I heard there was no train that day to Gardner—they
only went once every other day and my money was
in Gardner. I had only 40 cents on me, so I could
not wait a day. I must walk.

The others were wandering up and down the
streets at 7 a.m.—over thirty of them and the town
was very small. But shopkeepers, many out of pity,
others for policy, gave them liverwurst and others
food—some were lucky—others not—and they departed to their jungle to eat what they had and then
go East. I said good-bye to Tom and Jack and
buying a little food prepared to start out for Gardner
alone and on foot.

CHAPTER XII

IT'S THE ALTITUDE

I was now in the country where dude ranches abound—but I was not to see a real one for a few days—in the meantime I was to watch the typical Eastern tourist motoring through Yellowstone Park, fully primed by the sensational press for any emergency with bandits and more than once pointing revolvers at quite innocent passers-by.

I was hardly outside Livingstone on my 40-mile trek to Yellowstone when a fellow hobo told me cheerily I hadn't an earthly chance of a lift in those clothes. He was right and I got behind a bridge and put on my lucky grey flannels.

At first they were unlucky. For 11 miles I tramped in a boiling sun, along a road that gave no shelter from trees and showed but scant signs of that mountainous area that I had hoped to find near Yellowstone and to cheer me on the way. My bundle seemed heavy, my arms and face were already smarting under the burn of the sun, and the only trio that had offered me a lift were a girl and two men who said they would lift me to Gardner if I paid for the petrol—as they were penniless and short of gasoline. As I was in the same boat it did not help and it was early afternoon before a dilapidated vehicle stopped and took me in.

There were three inhabitants—cowboys—and they were out for a spree in Gardner. For 33 miles I motored with them in boiling heat and we had no less than seven punctures and bravely we mended the punctures each time. As I was the free guest I had to do most of the pumping in a heat that almost overcame me—and once we were only able to get gasoline by the proprietor of the station accepting their cheque. We talked of the state of the country and my friends felt certain that soon the workers would unite, as have the business-heads, and so get work or food.

At long last we reached Gardner in time for me to go to the post office and get out my money. Never was money so welcome.

I got a room at the so-called hotel in this one-horse town, had a shave and shampoo, and my sun-burnt face and arms rubbed with some cooling lotion and then proceeded to the local speak-easy. The room on the street looked most innocent and you could buy ginger-beer and cigarettes and coffee. Across the centre was a large wooden partition—but the counter extended into the other side of the partition where there seemed to be more activity. I informed the man behind the counter that the barber had sent me along and that I wanted a drink. He pulled a cord, the door in the partition opened and I walked into the other half of the same room. Here to recover from my journey I drank a good many whiskies—straight—with a chaser or two of water afterwards. The whisky cost me 25 cents a drink and if I took three, the bar tender stood me a fourth free—I also tried some of his own brew of beer and felt better. While I drank, others came in to drink also, and we were cheered on by a harpist and a fiddler in the corner playing repeatedly "When Irish Eyes are Smiling."

Next morning early I started off to walk through Yellowstone Park—one of Nature's wonders and one of America's prides. A national Park that in no way has been spoilt, as it so easily might have been had it been in Europe, by trippers and tourists.

I had hardly entered the Park gates where one

has to give one's name and address in case one gets lost, than a motor stopped and a Cockney London voice asked me if by any chance I was the young Englishman whom the Montana newspapers had recently been describing as a former President of the Oxford Union. I never had been anything of the sort, but the papers had, I know, been saying it the week before, and I confessed my identity.

Imagine my surprise when I found these two youths were from English Universities travelling through America on Commonwealth Fund Scholarships through the munificence of Mr. Harkness, and that with them was one Molyneux, himself in fact a President of the Oxford Union, and of course quite convinced I was yet another of those English impersonators, of whom not a few are to be found in the West. Working in separate Universities they all joined together during the vacation for this Western tour and it made them understand America as so few of our people do. They took me as far as Norris Junction, from which I walked through wooded country to Canyon Junction where I decided to spend the night —on free parking space where you can sleep in your own tents or in cars as you like.

I put up my tarpaulin next to a motor containing four Chicago "gangsters" as they called themselves, which on the whole was unwise. For the first part of the night all went well, and rangers passed constantly, flashing torches in every direction and so keeping off the bears. But by 2 a.m. the rangers had retired and the bears came out. Unfortunately my gangsters had left food about and they came all round the car, putting in their paws and prowling and sniffing in every direction. The night was dark and it seemed more than likely they would not see me and might put a paw on my face by mistake. Such

SPOUTING GEYSER, YELLOWSTONE PARK

a thought banished sleep and I spent a miserable time half sitting, half lying, and all the time beating a tattoo with my stick.

Dawn came and I turned to sleep—but now the gangsters awoke and began to prepare to move on. I gave up the attempt and sleepily walked on to the Park's hotel, a luxurious wooden building where I got a shave and a needed wash and where I was told there was another Englishman. He came from Sydney, Australia, and they were surprised when I said he would hardly be considered or consider himself a fellow-countryman.

From there I went to see the Canyon—one of the most gorgeous sights of the West, and spent all that day travelling through scenery as varied as it was gorgeous. The beauty and majesty of the Canyon, the reflections on the red-brown walls and terraces that seemed to mount up around it—then the miles of forest land, the hills, the boiling lakes, the sizzling geysers with Old Faithful especially prominent—and last of all the huge lake that is one of the greatest beauties of the Park. It was a real fairyland.

Having read in Kipling's book and a hundred others of the wonders of the Park, I asked what had happened to the fountain where you could wash and dry your pocket handkerchief. But they told me a couple of years ago a woman had brought all her washing and it had dammed up the spouting geyser for all time. Old Faithful is now closely guarded for fear someone put something in too big to be belched forth in its hourly eruption and so cause the stoppage of Yellowstone's most famous sight.

I had more than one lift that day as I went from Canyon Junction to Madison Junction, to Old Faithful, and on to Thrums.

My first was with a man from Detroit—taking a

holiday to Seattle, Vancouver and back, because times were so bad—if they had been better he could not have spent the time for a holiday which sounded to me good, if new reasoning. Another, though he had plenty of room in the back of the car, would not let me in for fear presumably I hit him or his wife over the head, and so I had to stand on the running-board for a few miles, and yet again I was rescued just as I met a mother bear with her cubs, by a lorry-load of Boy Scouts on their annual camping expedition.

In spite of all precautions people will play with the numerous bears and the casualties each year run into the hundreds.

At Thrums I took a cabin for $1 and after sitting round a camp fire with the ranger who told us of the beauties of the Tetons which he said were not excelled by the Matterhorn—in which statement I now almost agree, and after listening to the experiences of the other travellers, as varied a crowd as one usually finds in such places, I slept, and next morning ate well in the cafeteria before continuing out of the Park.

I found again my English friends, and the President of the Union was sitting under a bridge on the edge of the lake, and after a few minutes I continued with them—three car-loads down into the valley of the Tetons to the village of Moran, a village of wooden shacks and houses, and from there I went on to the Three River Ranch where I was to be the guest of my friend at Montana University.

I walked now with blistered feet the length of the mile drive to a group of cabins—but I did not know which housed my host and I asked a half-naked boy sun-bathing near a pond and he pointed and went away to tell his own parent that "the Burt's Irish Dude" had arrived. My host was out—but his wife was in bed with a cold, and I came to her door and she asked how I had come, and I said I had walked, and so the first part of my tramp life was over.

For three weeks I remained on this ranch and led what I suppose is the equivalent life in America of the life of the people who in England go each year to Scotland. At almost every turn I was reminded of September at home. When I went to the rodeo I felt I was at any games or gathering. As we went fishing or riding or shooting, it was all the same yet with the distinctive differences that made it such fun.

The ranch was big and it was owned by six different friends. They each had their own cabins and their own guests and they came together for meals and whenever else they wanted. Fairly often they took it turn about to give cocktail parties in their cabins, strictly reserved to inhabitants of the ranch. Outsiders only came to lunch or dinner. What with guests and hosts we were sometimes over twenty in number and I gather included names well known in America if not in Europe.

From Philadelphia there were Burts, Newlins, Pages, Reeds, Collins, Harris, and Bisphams; from Connecticut, Merritts; from New York, Carharts, Auchinclosses, Sloanes, and Malones; and from Boston, Hubbards and Amorys; and for me, instead of being the guest of one I seemed the guest of all, and everybody went out of their way to give me a good time.

I had a log cabin to myself—well furnished with rugs on the floor and the wall—a little stream beside my window and hot water brought me each morning by a youth "making good," who made me sit up my first morning by asking me how Victor of Chez Victor fame in London was getting on in Paris, and by talking of nearly every expensive night club and hotel in London and Paris.

After my tin tub wash in the morning, breakfast, and tons of it with waffles, maple syrup and English dishes as well, was to be found for us all in the central cabin, served by a Mormon maid and a grinning Filipino cook. In the morning we rode—each host had his own string of horses, and we rode on western saddles that I felt unpleasant, but for the sort of handle in front, meant for cowboys' ropes, and used by me as leverage when feeling uncomfortably sore. After lunch we would read or sleep or work—and later ride again and then perhaps a cocktail and after that dinner, and we all sat about for an hour in the central cabin's drawing-room and then dispersed to bed or bridge in the different cabins.

These days were varied by visits to other ranches, some over the Great Divide, others along the lake that is at the foot of the Tetons and many of them dude ranches.

A dude ranch, as yet unknown in England, is where the wealthy city man goes in the West to lead the life of the West at considerable expense. The train journey is not cheap, and on the ranch he will pay anything from $11 a day. None of this includes the expense of pack trips into the mountains or big-game shooting—but it includes living in a series of small cottages and eating communal meals and then all getting together for gambling or games or music or just talk. To try and sit alone in the drawing-room after dinner is impossible.

A good ranch will have at least thirty dudes on it—all recommended by friends of the owner—a dude being the Eastern gentleman or lady playing at being a Westerner and dressed to suit the part. At first you may hate it, but the life soon grows on you and it becomes the greatest and the healthiest fun—you do the most amazing things and you call it "The Altitude." You try, as I did, to do your ordinary daily walk and you are soon puffing and panting, for it certainly is the Altitude. That altitude is a delightful strain and an excuse for everything at 6,000 feet above the sea.

I was shy when I was taken to dude ranches and could hardly hear myself in the row of talking voices. Sometimes we went out under the moon to look over the lakes to the Teton Mountains that no Swiss scenery could beat, and then with lights out we sat round a fire in a cabin and the ranch doctor, himself a dude from the East, sang us to guitar accompaniment some of the best songs of the West—and a few too from Ireland. And in the evenings in the cold air we would motor home through forests and prairie land and mountains lit up by a full moon in a starlit sky. They were three weeks of complete joy—and if Ireland and Scotland give you on similar nights a feeling of romance for the past, here too must you feel the full glamour of the West, the Indian, the pioneer, the lumberjack, the cowboy and to-day the forest rangers.

With the rangers I went out in a Government launch on the lake and we had horses to meet us the other side and we climbed the mountains, and another time we lunched with a senator from Philadelphia and his wife, two of America's richest citizens, and they lived with their family in tents "squatting" on the side of a lonely lake, and we lunched on handmade wooden chairs and mine pinched me so much that a large lady noticed it next me, and seeing her danger, got up and snatched the only cushion and put it beneath her, and I thought "thy need is greater than mine," and knew that only the very rich can enjoy poverty. We talked of Augustus John and the Alingtons and the Lygons and Senator Gogarty's hotel in the West of Ireland and it seemed incongruous there.

Another time I dined with some senators from Washington that were touring the West studying the parks, and with them were the representatives of the Rockefeller Foundation which at that time was causing great excitement in the State.

The Foundation had decided to buy up all the land around the Tetons and offer it as a National Park to the Federal Government and the State was not certain that it wanted it. But what was amusing was that in buying up all the land, the Foundation would not allow anyone living on it to have wayside shops or gasoline stations for motors. One man applied to keep round his house just one half-acre where are buried his wife and his children and for sentimental reasons the Foundation allowed him his little graveyard. To their amazement he has now erected on his wife's grave a gasoline station with pumps and it is too late to prevent him. He is the only one within miles and he should make money. The neighbours call it "The Ghost Station."

One day one of the younger members of our party asked me to go into Jackson's Hole, the big town of the district, for the rodeo and to see the fun. I had seen the quiet life of the more middle-aged people that one might find at home. Now I was to see another type of person one may find on the dude ranches—but that is wise in that he gets beneath the skin of the real and rougher westerner.

The rodeo was held on a piece of ground outside the town of Jackson's Hole, at the foot of a mountain and on the edge of prairie. There were stands erected and the seats were occupied by the house parties from the different ranches. All the ladies and nearly all the men were in some form of Western cowboy or cowgirl dress, and on the railings opposite next the pens, where were kept the horses, sat many visitors from the dude ranches and from the farms. In the rows in front of me were females busy reading the fashion notes of Harpers Bazaar and whether Lady Howe or Lady Milford Haven in England used to best advantage a certain face cream—with their photographs attached—whilst in front of them local crack riders and amateurs from the East competed in hair-raising attempts to sit on bucking bronchos for given periods of one or two minutes between revolver shots that seemed to be eternally cracking —and then again other experts dashed past lassooing and pinning resisting steer again within a given time.

All this was exciting enough and everybody watched it dutifully, but with, I felt, an urge for something else. Someone came round to chat with our party and told us that when one horse bucked too near the railings on the other side, several female dudes in multi-coloured silk skirts had fallen backwards into the open motor of a dozing drunk. The latter woke up and murmured joyfully: "I think this wild West is most exciting." It was too much for my friends—the urge had won. We left the rodeo and proceeded into the town—in Prohibition U.S.A.

Our first stopping-place was the best of five speakeasies—or pubs—on the main street. Outside sat a few who had not the wherewithal to buy their drinks, and then inside under the advertisement, "Ginger Ale and Soft Drinks" in a bar that had no door and was open on to the streets we were duly served our whiskies, our gins and our beer, and then we moved into the room behind where were croupiers and roulette and the wheel of chance and the cage and

we lost money, and I was introduced to the two pro-
prietors—one of them a famous bootlegger throughout Wyoming, just visiting this one of his many resorts,
and the other a local inhabitant. They cashed for me
my traveller's cheques and we drank and gambled
peacefully.

In amongst us walked the Sheriff, dressed like the
rest with yellow shirt and a sort of ten-gallon hat—
his only distinguishing mark, his star of office on
his breast, and our bootlegger host could be distinguished by his Elk Chain—a sign of a fraternity
of some importance in that part of the world.

From there I was brought round to the tourist
auto camp—where there were some forty cabins, and
in a double cabin I found myself greeted by a group
of dudes who had hired it for the evening and had
christened it The Ritz. Here almost everyone I had
met in Wyoming, and a host more besides, tried to
fit themselves in on two beds, a few chairs and
tables and the floor. In a corner a student from an
Eastern University and an assistant editor of one of
the world's most famous newspapers mixed the drinks
and dispersed the hospitality. The men paid and
"stood" the women and the noise was deafening.

In one corner stood a rather toothless gentleman
known as Charley to his friends and he sang with
a guitar and was ridiculously drunk. He carried two
revolvers, being wanted for at least two known murders
—one before the war. But he had escaped and served
in the Foreign Legion and been through the war and
much was now forgiven him. And there was many
another tough Western character in the room.

Eventually many of us adjourned to a drug store
where an Eastern lady had rashly invited us to eat
—some twenty in all. Next me on the left sat a
youth whom I was asked to keep from drinking more,

and on the right was Charley, now and then attempting to sing the most vulgar songs, but luckily too drunk to remember much beyond the first lines. His guitar strings burst and the middle-aged son-in-law of one of the most famous modern bankers—known the world over—sitting on his other side pretended to mend it all through dinner and so kept Charley quiet.

Later we adjourned to drink more at the speakeasy but found a crowd outside. I noticed Charley's shirt was hanging out and started to tuck it in to the back of his trousers—but feeling his revolvers there I thought best to leave it, less he think I was taking them and turn nasty.

Mingling with the crowd we discovered it was a raid on the speak-easy by the Federal Officer and the Sheriff—both of whom greeted the owner as an old friend. Charley now became noisy and the Federal Officers arrested him and put him into the car into which they were already loading large quantities of beer and whisky bottles—amounting to over $200 worth. While they were also in the gambling den taking away the roulette wheel, and while the croupiers were lined up, the bar-tender continued hastily to serve liquor at 50 cents a drink—liquor that had been overlooked, and then a friend persuaded the Federal Officers to let Charley off, and the latter came forth from the car, chastened but yet with his pockets full of bottles he had pinched while in the car.

The Federal Officer before going told the bootlegger he was leaving the district next morning—in other words things could carry on then safely. For the moment there was quiet and so The Ritz became fuller and more popular than ever, and a rather pleasant film actor from Hollywood who was consumptive and in Jackson's Hole for his health sang for us, and the hat was passed round and we all grew merrier and merrier, and at last Charley had to be ejected, and it was impossible to tell who was cowboy always from the West, who student from an Eastern University, who millionaire city man from the East and who store-keeper in the town, or character with a past, on one of the ranches, and with them in many cases were their wives.

Within an hour we were back at the raided speakeasy where drinks flourished as before and gambling, and we eventually moved on to a dance in a local barn, and by 3 a.m. we were starting the long ride home to the ranches. It was fun in its way, it went on for several days—the altitude no doubt was responsible—and the rodeo took at least fifth place behind the orgy of drinking that made a "swell evening." A few days later I was again on a dude ranch and I learnt something of its equipment—and how difficult, so seemingly slapdash an organisation is to run.

The average dude ranch, with a central log hut, holding kitchens, living-rooms and dining-rooms, and various cottages—log cabins, consisting of either single or double bedrooms, needs about fifty dudes to pay. For this it will require about twenty-five hands to run it. There will be two cooks, one dishwasher, two waitresses, two cabin girls—who are usually local girls—one housekeeper, two laundresses, one rastabout, one carpenter, a rastabout's help, two house wranglers —day and night—the latter a "night hawk," one teamster, one foreman, two dude wranglers (Eastern College men usually), one truck driver, two guides, two camp-house wranglers, two camp cooks and three partners to run the show, one for the dudes—who can be very tiresome at times—one for the staff— who can easily have rows with the dudes, one to do the housekeeping.

Branding Cattle in Wyoming

Usually the dudes are young men, or flappers, often whole families and occasionally more elderly bachelors and unmarried women. They pay about $11 a day. There is only one sport common to all, away there in the wilds, and that is dancing. Distances are great and one must have a horse for every person and be ready for pack trips that keep on coming in and going out, and the food has usually to last a week. As for dudes they are not encouraged unless they are coming for a stay of a fortnight at least and it is almost essential that they have a special kit.

Such life is, I think, peculiar to North America—certainly it has reached in the Western States to a fine art and must be seen to understand the healthy type of American not often seen on the Riviera nor in London drawing-rooms.

This is the Scotland of America and the people that live its life are the people that prefer the West to Europe just as our lovers of the moors prefer Scotland to the Continent. To know more about the type and the atmosphere and surroundings there is no better book than the *Diary of a Dude Wrangler*, by Struthers Burt. And if the life includes people fond of heavy drinking and gambling, no matter, that is only a part of the people that go there.

I was one evening on another ranch and it was a night with a clear moon and we sat around a camp fire and the wood crackled. We had a case of beer given by the local bootlegger and he with his Elk Chain and his friend, the more important bootlegger, was with us, and there were owners of Eastern newspapers and famous lawyers and their children, and the Mormon keeper of the ranch and the Mormon groom or cowboy and his wife, and the singer from Hollywood and his wife, and the servants who were college boys from the East, and one at least the son of a millionaire and many others, and we all sang Western songs in tune and out of tune and we told ghost stories; and the cayotes came down into the woods that were near us and howled and our cowboys howled in reply, and the cayotes came nearer to see the fire and the fire died down when night became cold, for the altitude was over 6,000 feet and in the distance were the peaks of the Teton Mountains; now and then there was a rustling in the pines and the elk herds were probably near. That too was Wyoming and the West.

The next day I was in the wooden town of Moran and I saw some old papers. I saw that Ramsay MacDonald had resigned, that our King had asked him to form a National Government—that we were borrowing money from the United States and France, and my neighbours said: "Why not," but I was frightened at the news. It was time to get near a railway and I must leave Wyoming where time was forgotten and news did not matter.

CHAPTER XIII

THE MORMONS AND THE ENGLISH

FEW people realise that since about 1880 over 160,000 English people have gone out from England, Scotland and Wales to Salt Lake City to become Mormons.

It is a disgrace in the Mormon Church for a woman not to marry and not to have as many children as possible—and the result must be that there are many times that number of once Britishers, now Mormons and citizens of those five States around Salt Lake City into which Mormonism is gradually and systematically spreading and in which it is gaining political control bit by bit—Utah, which it actually controls, Idaho, which it almost controls, Wyoming, Colorado and New Mexico, in which it is daily becoming stronger. Actually there are about one million Mormons in the United States, of which over a quarter are probably Britishers by birth or immediate descent, and so it was a disappointment to me when I arrived in this the biggest city in an area five or six times the size of Great Britain, worried first at the national crisis in England and next while I was there at our going off the gold standard, to look in the telephone book and find no British Consulate.

By dint of enquiry I found there was a Vice-Consul, who transacted our business in his own office— I think an insurance office, a man who had left Wales at the age of two, was a citizen of the United States and a Mormon to boot. It was not unnatural that though he was pleased to see me, he was much more interested in his own coming election to a municipal office, than in any question of whether there would be a revolution in England or what might become of some of the Britishers interested in what was happening.

But I suppose our Foreign Office has some very good reason why in the city and country that is actually the most British in the whole of the United States, instead of having a representative who was 100 per cent British, knew his own country and could keep alive an interest in it, as do the Germans, the Italians and every other nationality in the United States—they have a charming old gentleman whose parents left England to become citizens of the United States, who in twenty years had only visited England once and then to hear the Eisteddfod and Mr. Lloyd George speak, and who is a Mormon and a man busy about many other things.

To reach Salt Lake City from Wyoming I chose a new means of travel. In those far-away parts men came out from Salt Lake City three or four hundred miles in large vans with vegetables and fruit, once a week, which they sold to their clients on the ranches *en route*. The day after I had read of the crisis in England, came the truck gardener with his van to pay his weekly visit, and with him at eight o'clock that morning I started off for Salt Lake City.

We travelled all day, selling vegetables and fruit on the way. Ranchers came out, more often than their wives, and did the purchasing themselves, and we passed through Jackson's Hole and over the Pass in the Teton Mountains that is 10,000 feet up and down into Idaho, and when we had sold nearly everything, we looked for orchards where we could purchase apples and pears cheaply that might be sold again the next week.

That night we spent at Rigby, he sleeping in his cart with the vegetables outside the town and I in the hotel nearby. Next morning we continued our

Salt Lake City, Utah

journey through the flat plains of Idaho and over the barren mountains, that are bleak in summer and covered in snow in winter, and the life of the farmers there must be lonely and monotonous—for they live miles from each other—they are mostly Mormons and mostly Scandinavians.

The country is poor and not well kept up, and the coal-mines are not used because the railway companies have bought them up and use others further away to get the freight. We lunched at Idaho Falls and passed through Pocatello, and so on to Utah—pronounced You-Taw—where the State badge to be seen on every sign is a Beehive—to show presumably the industry of this State that is 90 per cent Mormon and where you see every sign of real progress and real care and much irrigation.

In the evening we came to Logan, the first town with a Mormon Temple in it, and then we motored on through Brigham to Ogden, the great railway centre where I bade good-bye to my driver, himself a Mormon. On the way he had tried to convert me, and he told me that he was Presbyterian and German by origin, that he lived near Ogden and grew sweet cherries. This is a rare crop and you can sell it in New York at 75 cents a pound. The cherries are only ripe to pick for a fortnight in July and five acres would hold about 100 pickers. The Old Salt Lake in the dim ages past left layers of land on which these sweet cherries are grown. He told me he felt certain that if the Democrats were returned they must do something to recognise Russia or else in eighteen months there would surely be a revolution, as discontent was growing that capital should be in so few hands.

He was quite definite that Mormons had given up polygamy—as he said—recently. But as we passed through one town he pointed out the house of one man who still kept three wives—though he only lived with one—he still keeps them in separate houses; and he told me of another who had just been officially turned out of the Church because he had had a vision that he should have more than one wife. He was really a good Mormon and as my friend added: "If you say you have had a vision it's very difficult for anyone to prove you haven't."

He also told me how strict in all the outlying districts was the supervision of the Mormon Bishop and how he always found when he did not give his 10 per cent of all his profits each year to the Church he did not do so well next year. And so I left this hard-working steady farmer who believed sincerely in his religion if he did not practise it in full, and next day I came to Salt Lake City and found it the cleanest, best planned and in many ways most lovely city of the West.

The streets were broad and at night beautifully lighted, a sight not to be forgotten as one looked down from the Capitol hill, down Main Street or State Street, or as one stood at the Temple, a magnificent nineteenth-century building round which are concentrated all the Mormon offices.

At first they let the town grow haphazard and let the Gentiles—in which term they include Jews—build and develop where they pleased—but for themselves they held tight to the real estate that was near the Temple—what they called the Temple blocks, and they built round it, and now they are encouraging the bus company and the outsider to develop property near it and so enhance its value—on one side of the block they have the magnificent Utah Hotel, there is no better in the Middle West,—on the others lesser hotels and stores, and railway and other offices.

With a letter of introduction to their President which I had received from the Mormons in Canada, I went first to the Information Bureau which is beside the Temple and the Tabernacle and there I was recommended to go to a Mormon hotel, Roberts Hotel across the road, the owner being asked as "Dear Brother" to look after me.

I had also a short talk with one of the guides showing people round the Temple—he was a former Captain in the Royal Fusiliers and was interested to hear of all that was happening in England. He told me to be sure and wait in Salt Lake for the Mormon Convention to be held around the 6th of October. The 6th he pointed out was always a sort of sacred date in his Church because they believe that Christ was born, not on the 25th of December, but on the 6th of April.

And that evening after I had settled down in the Mormon hotel which was a commercial hotel and not unlike many another, I went to the ring to see Jack Dempsey knock out four frightened youths. He got a great reception, for it was his first appearance in Salt Lake City—his own home—since his return to the ring. He looked fit and the men had scarce a chance, and the crowd was as big as the building would hold, and Dempsey—William Harrison Dempsey to give him his full name—received 50 per cent of the gate money. A Mormon Bishop informed me Dempsey had given him free tickets, for Dempsey is himself a Mormon, and as soon as he leaves the ring he says he will return to work actively for the Church to which his father and mother belong and of which his brother was a Bishop.

Next morning I visited what is called the Bishop's Office, where I found many Englishmen, and I was taken in to see Bishop Wells, who is in control of relief to necessitous Mormons, and just leaving him were two stalwart farmers over six foot tall and young, and he told me they had come for relief and advice as a Deputation from Southern Utah, for there for the fourth year in succession there was drought and great misery and they must kill their sheep.

Then it was again explained to me, as it had been in Canada, how the Church, with its 10 per cent tithes on all people earn, help their church-goers and put young men in the way of making money and populate the land which they could not do without capital. They then detailed off to look after me whilst in Salt Lake City a Mr. Hawkes as guide. Hawkes was an Englishman from Tottenham and he had been the head priest at the Mormon Mission there at Deseret House all through the war and had looked after the Mormon missionaries escaping from Belgium and Germany in August 1914.

He told me with real pride how he had been a test case in English law for the Mormon Church. He was eventually conscripted but refused to fight because he said he was a Minister of a religion and so immune from conscription by the Act of Parliament. But the War Office said they did not recognise the Mormons as a Church and finally his case came before the Court of Appeal before Lord Reading and before Mr. Justice Avory—and it was decided for all time in his favour, the Government paying the costs, that a Mormon High Priest is a Minister of Religion, and as Lord Reading put it, that the Church of Jesus Christ of Latter Day Saints—the official name—has the beliefs that entitle it to be termed a Christian Church.

And he told me this before Professor Levi Young, a grandson of the famous pioneer Mormon leader Brigham Young, and a great genealogist, Mormon Archivist and History Professor at the Utah University. The Professor sincerely explained "Really English justice is marvellous. It is the admiration of every genuine American." And Hawkes went on to tell how he had been arrested in Hyde Park for obstruction and acquitted at Marlborough Street by Mr. Mead, and he marvelled that that magistrate, now eighty-five, is still functioning.

That evening I dined with Hawkes in his kitchen in his cottage and the wife waited on us after a long grace before the dinner, and in another room lived a young husband and wife aged about 25—Mormon converts who had come out that year from Lewisham in London and who had been ardent supporters of the Junior Imperial League and who were not finding it easy to earn a living but seemed happy.

After dinner we went to a meeting of the Mutual Society, one of the many ward organisations of the Church which are immensely numerous and are so perfectly organised that they keep the Mormons young and old always busy practising their religion. Each ward has a Bishop and I was put next this Bishop, a friend of Jack Dempsey, and we talked of his fight and he also explained to me their meeting.

It was the first of the winter and they had prayers and hymns and then one or two small plays dealing with episodes in Mormon history and much singing and sundry other scenes. In fact a well-organised concert for the younger members. But with rather too much love in it and altogether with just a slightly suggestive touch that made one feel instinctively, but perhaps wrongly, the last thing encouraged in Mormon women would be false modesty.

And afterwards they danced and I was introduced to a young missionary just back from Norwich, where he himself had at one time lived. And he said going back to Norfolk for the first time for twelve years he found the average Englishman much better off than he used to be, that money was better distributed—but he was sorry to see far fewer children, which seemed to him a sign of the growing selfishness and greed that he noticed now in England.

It was on the next day, Wednesday, that I was to meet the President of the Mormon Church—the religious head and more than any other spiritual head of a Western religion, also the business head, of over one million educated and comparatively wealthy people.

With Professor Young I went to see President Heber Grant in the massive stone and concrete building where are his offices. His home is an ordinary private house. We passed into the secretary's office and he told the Professor that the President was free, and so we walked through two more rooms into a large nicely furnished dark room with a lofty ceiling and the walls panelled in very beautiful Caucasian wood. At a table near the middle of the room sat two tall and elderly men. One of them, the President Grant, walked towards me and shook hands. He was a man of about 6 foot 3 inches, well over 70 years of age, with a slight stoop and a little beard or tuft that I would call an "Uncle Sam" beard. He had a kindly smile, and when he spoke there was only the slightest suspicion of an American accent—though the voice was rather harsh and rasping; and with him was the second President of the Church, President Nibley, a dour-looking, tall, elderly Scot, also with a small beard—a man over 80 years of age who told me he had come out from Scotland when still a boy. During the conversation he occasionally prompted President Grant—but on the whole the latter carried on the conversation entirely by himself and described to me the organisation of the Church.

The Mormon Temple, Salt Lake City

At the head is one President assisted by two other Presidents, making the ruling Trinity, and next to them came the twelve apostles of the Church, then the Council of Seventy and so on. On the death of a ruling President the successor is not one of the other two Presidents—who are themselves two of the Twelve Apostles—but whoever is the senior of the Twelve Apostles—that is senior in appointment.

When President Grant dies, his successor is a man about his own age—but next to him comes the most active of the Twelve Apostles, Senator Smoot, then a Republican Senator at Washington and one of ex-President Hoover's right-hand men. He will soon then be head of the Mormon Church in the United States, and he is likely to make it be very much heard about in the near future. He is the Mormons' greatest asset.

The Church is divided up into Missions abroad and Wards—over which a Bishop presides and almost all the young men are priests of the Church.

President Grant talked to me of the great work they did in Canada and Hawaii and of the unemployment situation. He pointed out they are not trying to find work for the unemployed—that they leave to the State—but they see to it that their own members do not starve.

They are solidly on the side of Capital, and he quoted from the *Book of Mormon* "Subject to Rulers, etc.," and he stressed the influence they use in the United States to keep law and order. He felt bitterly the former propaganda used against the Church in Europe, and especially in the old days, when he was a Missionary, by the press in England, and he added proudly that their numbers were steadily increasing.

Later he walked me all over the building and told me how much Woodrow Wilson had admired the panelling when as President of the United States he had visited him, and he took me up to the Historical and Genealogical Department and explained how one of the strongest beliefs of their religion is that they must be able to convert their dead ancestors to the Mormon religion, and this they can only do in the Temple—but no one can ever enter the Temple unless he or she is a practising Mormon. He regretted deeply his family tree did not go back far enough, but he could at any rate claim 150 ancestors, including collaterals, all of whom presumably he had converted.

He seemed intensely keen on the Boy Scout Movement and showed me photographs of the Liverpool Jamboree when the United States contingent had been led by a Utah Mormon boy. He himself had spent his youth running a horse ranch, and later he had taken up insurance, and to-day he told me actuaries show the lease of life of the Mormon who abstains from tea, coffee and smoking, as well as alcohol, is much longer than that of the ordinary mortal.

Later in the day I went out to the famous Salt Lake and bathed and could not sink—but I swallowed some water which was so salty it made me quite ill, and as I did not take a shower on getting out of the Lake, the salt crystals stuck to my back and I returned to the city feeling very uncomfortable.

That night I went to a meeting of the Mexican colony in the Mormon Chapel in their own district. It was a gala night and they were celebrating the anniversary of Emancipation from Spain. They had songs and speeches and dances and almost all in Spanish, and there were many in national costumes and near me sat swarthy superbly built half Indians, and on the platform sat the Mexican Consul, the Governor of the State, the Mayor of the City and President

Ivins, the third President of the Mormon Church, himself by origin a Scandinavian.

Next afternoon Hawkes took me down to the station to see the departure of some sixty missionaries. These were boys and girls leaving home for the first time perhaps in their lives to be away three years without a break and at the expense of their families, thinking it the greatest honour in the world—and ready to meet all opposition—and they are often tarred and feathered —in the cause of their religion in which they firmly believed.

These boys and girls were going some to different parts of the United States, but the majority to England, and others were going to Germany and to France and to Holland and to Denmark. There was much crying and some forced merriment, there were over 300 people on the platform, and as the train steamed out all uncovered and all sang a Mormon hymn.

These boys and girls who will preach at street corners and give to their Church the years that many Europeans give to conscription, spend first a fortnight in the Mission House before leaving, where they are taught their arguments, and they are chosen the sons of Germans for German Missions, and of Danes for Danish Missions, and so they can all speak the language, and when they leave the Mission House others go in so that every fifteen days some fifty or sixty go out across the world to preach and there are usually about 2,000 out at a time. It was explained to me that when they come back the Church often, with its funds, helps them start work, and the actual Relief Fund is only used to help those in dire need.

This Relief Fund is probably one of the oldest forms of insurance in existence for unemployment, and oddly enough in a country where such a system is bitterly resisted even in the present difficult times. The practising Mormon family will go without food from the first Saturday to the first Sunday of each month for twenty-four hours, and the amount of money saved by the family in those uneaten meals is given to the local branch of the Relief Society—administered by the women of the Mormon Church, and they distribute such money for those in need and to help bury and dress the dead and in other charitable works.

As we walked up from the station to visit Brigham Young's tomb over the town, surrounded by five of his wives and the widow of Joseph Smith, we passed the house where Brigham Young had kept most of his nineteen wives, and the Church, without, I felt, a great sense of humour, have now converted the building into the Beehive Home for unmarried girls.

My guide explained to me here something of the religion—but he would not discuss polygamy, and he pointed out that no negro could be a member of the Church, for they were considered the cursed of Cain, and I remembered again that this was the only really flourishing religion that had been born on American soil and it seemed appropriate that it should bar the negro—but it does not bar the Red Indian.

The religion is contained in the *Book of Mormon* which explains that the Mormons first came out of Asia across to South America and up to the Pacific coast of the United States. They however lost their faith and were turned into Red men and so to-day the present Mormons do what they can to bring back the Red Indian—but without much success.

In 1830 one, Joseph Smith, saw visions, and from tablets shown him translated this *Book of Mormon* and started up the Mormon Church—the Church of Jesus Christ of Latter Day Saints—the only Christian Church using the name of Jesus in its title. And when he was murdered there was a split in the Church

184

and Brigham Young was elected leader of the branch that moved out to Utah in the pioneer days and their journey makes an epic tale.

In their Temples, which are sacred to practising Mormons and where much goes on that is akin to Freemasonry, they marry and convert the dead, and they believe the end of the world and the thousand years of peace will not come till all the next world has had the chance of being converted. Their prophecies tell them that within the next twenty years they should return out of Utah to Independence, Missouri, where is to be the centre of their religion, and so there are many that say the Church is trying to make more valuable the sights of their Temple Blocks—that they may eventually sell and transfer their headquarters back to where they belong.

We went up to the Mormon hospital and I spoke with a former W.A.A.C. from London and walked back with two girls from Darlington, one of whom used to teach singing, and we stopped at a Ward Chapel and one played the organ and the other sang to me very beautifully, and later as I sat facing the Temple with a man whom we will call Cooper he told me a story in all seriousness which I thought funny.

Coming from London he felt short of ancestors and he needed them to convert and so he heard there was an old Miss Cooper, a lady of position in one of the midland counties who had spent all her life getting together a history of the Coopers, and she worshipped her family with a great reverence and she was a true member of the Church of England. He wrote her that he was interested to trace his family and she was thrilled and thought she had found the long lost wealthy American branch; she sent him the book and he found his link with the family and so converted them all in the Temple to the Mormon Church, over

185

300 of them—and I wondered what poor old prim Miss Cooper would have thought in her pleasant English cottage had she known her life's work had gone to making over 300 ancestors, once doughty champions of the Church of England, become Mormons, and who knows, perhaps polygamists, in the next world. Poor Miss Cooper!

If a mere gentile like myself could not visit the Temple, we could at least enter the Tabernacle next door, which housed one of the most perfect organs in America—broadcasting each day superb music from the Pacific to the Atlantic—and there I would often sit and listen to the music and on Sundays to the choir practice and the service, and one Sunday I heard Dr. Talmadge give a lecture on the Constitution of the States, after which the choir rose to sing the " Star Spangled Banner."

But the day before had come the news that England had gone off the gold standard and nobody seemed to understand what would happen—except that every English-born person in Salt Lake City seemed to take it for granted that the Old Country, as they called it, would weather the storm, and all that day I felt for the first time a longing to be at home, and first thing on Monday morning I went to see the manager of the leading newspaper of these five States.

He told me as we talked over the latest news that on Sunday had come through such alarmist headlines from the Chicago papers' "leaders," from which they obtained much of their copy—such as Pillars of the Bank of England collapsing—that he had been sent for when he was in the country, and when he came in he cut all this out and he refused to allow anything to be put in his papers that was more than the mere facts and that could do harm to England, and so throughout a large part of America this quick action of FitzPatrick, the manager of the *Salt Lake Tribune*, saved English-born people from worry and humiliation and probably stopped the seeds of doubt as to Britain's stability from taking root in the minds of many hundreds of thousands.

On his advice I went up next to have a talk with Senator Smoot in his rooms in the Utah Hotel. I found him alone in his sitting-room. A tall, thin, Nonconformist type, hard but just, would be a good description of him, I think, and in every way a simple man. He was head of the Finance Committee of the Senate and had held that position for fourteen years, since 1918—the Committee that has a power over American Governmental finance, that has no equivalent in England, and in this way he was wielding a tremendous influence. Senators wanting money advantage for their separate States had to come to him, and as above all else he is an ardent Mormon they would think twice before allowing anything to be said about the Mormon Church that might offend him.

Not unnaturally our chief subject of conversation was the English financial crisis. He told me straight away that England had exhausted her credit and could not have borrowed another penny—she had come to the end of her resources. In a way he admired her for her pluck—but he thought her Government should have faced facts a little earlier and he had for some time been convinced she must come off the gold standard. It should have happened at least two months earlier and would have saved England a lot of expense. Incidentally he thought the repudiation an excellent move and was very pleased at it.

He then settled down to explain to me how there was nothing like enough gold in the world to go round, and how bimetallism was required. He pointed out how in his opinion this would help India especially, and he felt certain that it would be an important factor in stopping the unrest there.

Allowing for the fact that he was Senator for Utah, a silver-producing State, it was still an interesting statement from a supremely honest man, in touch with the world's financial politics since 1918—but he would not answer me when I asked if the United States would give a lead about bimetallism. He considered now England had faced the question of the gold standard, she must next face the question of silver and bimetallism, and he ended up by telling me with complete conviction that the whole cause of England's trouble was the dole.

He knew, he said, that it had sapped the energy of the English and he spoke with a fervour on this subject that made me think how near he was to the hard narrowness of the noncomformist pioneers his parents surely were. Perhaps he was right in his conclusions, but as he spoke I felt he knew really but little about the working of the unemployment insurance he was muddling up with the dole, that he was speaking from hearsay and I felt depressed that our own crisis should be largely due to lack of confidence by foreigners in our stability—lack of confidence of people like Senator Smoot and those who followed his advice—people who were busy with their own affairs and had not the time to study fairly a system from which they themselves in the long run cannot get away. And as I went away he said "England will never collapse, none of us could let her, anyway—if she went, the world would go too."

While in Salt Lake City I spoke with many non-Mormons—Gentiles they call them—people of import-ance in many parts of the West who happened to be there at the time—Archbishops of the Catholic Church, United States Senators, heads of railways, etc., and I was interested that some of the most important were convinced that Senator Smoot, as head of the Finance Committee, would do all possible to help England with regard to our debt because he was fond of England— but that there was no doubt he was first and foremost a Mormon, and nothing would please him more than that the British Government should do something to stop the beating, the tarring and feathering of Mormon preachers that still sometimes goes on when they come to speak in England.

The worst side of Mormonism was shown to me by them all, but I will leave that until I describe later my visit to the centre of the rival Mormon Church with over 160,000 members, concentrated round Independence, Missouri, and holding great power in Kansas City nearby.

I had still a week to wait until the Mormon Conference, and I went wandering through Southern Utah.

The day I left I found the two hotel maids writing me a note in my room. It was to the effect that they thought I would like to know they "were of English descent and connected with the gentry class in England." I was duly impressed and rather liked them for it. Everywhere there was this affection for England —but oddly enough everywhere a growing dislike for France. The editor of a leading western paper about this time told me the feeling was so strong in the mountain states that he was certain in future the majority of American tourists would only pass through Paris and would make England or Germany, and Berlin or Scandinavia their centres while in Europe.

As soon as I got back, I was taken straight to a rally of all the English Mission and I found some 600 people grouped together in a hall with large signs in different corners—Cardiff, Newcastle, Hull, Manchester and so on, and under these grouped all the people who came from them. We danced and processed up and down and I talked to them, and one wealthy Mormon woman from London, out visiting her children, said: "It's all exaggerated out here, England's not going to break up," and she looked up rather fiercely, I thought, and said: "If the Old Country really was in need I'd hand over every penny I had. After all, I gave them my son."

And when the Conference met in the Tabernacle there were over 10,000 Mormons present, with missionaries back from Canada, Australia, China, Sweden, and all over the world. Amongst the many speakers, there were several that referred to England, and the venerable President Nibley prayed, in his old Scottish accent, that such a thing as the mutiny in the British Navy should never happen again or else indeed, said he, the end of civilisation must be near.

There was no doubt that here I was amongst friends, though they were quite simple farmer stock, and it struck me they were rather hard, and a little too worldly in their religion. Yet they looked to England for stability and for religious tolerance and for level-headedness. And they spoke, especially Senator Smoot, of the growing lack of religion in the United States, as they saw it, and in the growing disrespect for law and order, and one prominent speaker made an attack on the American Legion for openly using drink at their annual meeting, and when they had all spoken, during the three days that the Convention lasted, President Grant in the middle and his twelve Apostles around him—on a dais with the Council of Seventy just below and the organ, and the great choir at their back—I felt that here at any rate was a State that would always vote dry and would always be for prohibition. It was a State and a body that knew what it wanted—so that its influence would be greater and out of all proportion to what the numbers warranted.

What struck me as unique was the interest in genealogy and during the Conference I attended the genealogical meeting. President Ivins told us how the Anglo-Saxons were descended from Ephraim—how the daughter of the King of Babylon had been taken to Ireland to marry an Irish King and be buried at Tara, and how she was ancestress of the Stuarts and "that great English King, George V."

And then they took me to their genealogical building and I met the daughter of Brigham Young—his fifty-sixth and youngest child by his nineteenth wife, and when I showed her my own name in a book of pedigree she was very thrilled, for though they have every genealogical book issued—including the *Almanach de Gotha*—they seldom find their Mormon friends or other visitors in them, and as I looked at the books there was a farmer from Armagh next me looking at the Dublin Parish register for births and deaths. "It's well to be you," said he. "I'm called McCarthy and there are hundreds of McCarthy's, but I can't find which were me grandparents, and sure I know they would want to be converted in the next world."

And next day, before I left, I motored out with the grandson of a famous Mormon Church President to the Brigham Copper Mine—a wonderful sight—an open mountain, and they were blasting it with ease for copper and the town nearby was just one narrow street in a canyon, and as we motored back I spoke to the President's grandson—a man of about forty—about polygamy, and he said, "Surely polygamy is better than mistresses and divorce"—but it was too late to argue, and that day I left for the Eastern States.

CHAPTER XIV

HITCH-HIKING

My preliminary trip as a hitch-hiker was to see if I could bear it for an eighteen-hundred mile walk across to Chicago, and most important of all—to see if I could, on the road, meet those people who are the salt of the Middle West, those that are still in all but name frontiers men, and yet are the smaller middle class of other countries. To them letters of introduction would be futile—and in any case where would I get enough of them?—and an occasional lift on the road, with that quick life story the Middle-Westerner so loves to tell and hear, might be all I wanted. It was and I enjoyed it.

One afternoon, in a grey flannel suit, with some dollars in my pocket, a small washing-bag on my back and a letter from the local head of the railway to his friend Mr. Cramton—well-known Republican Congressman, leading dry and friend of President Hoover—were my only assets. Mr. Cramton was in charge of the new Federal city at Las Vegas and it was over 300 miles south, you went all through the gorgeous scenery of Utah, touching New Mexico across the desert into Nevada, always becoming a little warmer, the scenery a little more barren, and the sunsets a little redder, a little more lovely. Yes!—I was a tramp and a tramp that was happy.

Out the long streets of Salt Lake City I walked in the early afternoon, and it was many miles before I was given a lift. Hiking we all know, Hitch is the addition for the man that takes a lift when he gets one and occasionally stands, hopefully jerking his thumb in the direction he wants to go. By 9 p.m. I had reached Provo, a distance of 44 miles, and nineteen of them I had walked.

It was as the sun was setting over the almost barren hills, with on the other side the shimmering waters of Salt Lake, that I was given a lift in a truck. After a bit my friend left me, for he turned aside to the local farm for which he worked, bringing fruit to Salt Lake City almost daily and occasionally taking greater loads to Los Angeles—and again an hour or so later as I walked along in the dark—for I had not yet learnt how difficult it is to get a lift in the dark, and how much easier to be run over, the same youth in his lorry, but now with three friends, came again and stopped, recognising me, and took me into Provo where he and his friends were going to dance for the evening.

There I slept the night and next morning would have moved on but was nearly run over by Monsignor Hunt, the Catholic Bishop's assistant, who broadcasts across the mountain States on Catholicism, and had recently forcefully defended England's rule in India against the doctrines of Gandhi. He had said that Christianity must still be preached by missionaries in India, for Christ had said: "Go ye and teach all nations even to the uttermost ends of the earth," and Gandhi would have no more missionaries, and this "man of peace" had said he would gain his ends if even by bloodshed.

The Monsignor stopped me and told me that that day in Provo they would unveil a tablet to Fra Escalante, the monk who had come preaching a year before the Mormons through what to-day is Utah. And I joined the group and the Catholic choir sang hymns. The children had paid with their pennies for the monument and a Mormon opened the ceremony with prayer, a Mormon professor gave us an historical sketch, the Catholic Bishop Mitty gave a fine address, and then a Franciscan gave the blessing as the plaque was unveiled. I went away rather proud of my Church, and also not a little pleased at the courtly behaviour of the Mormons, who after all completely rule that country.

My lifts now became more frequent, and I passed quickly through Springville, through Payson and on to Santaguin—all through country that farms apples and peaches and grapes, and sends them for sale or to be shipped to Los Angeles and so through the Panama Canal. It was a rich country and my hosts were prosperous farmers. And then I went on in a dilapidated Dodge truck to Nephi, and the driver seemed very depressed. That morning for the first time for eighteen years, by mutual consent, he had left his wife in Salt Lake City, for she preferred another man who paid for them to live *à trois*, and he did not enjoy it, and in the truck behind were his piano and a bed and a small wardrobe and a trunk, for he was going to his brother who lived in the mountains near Nephi, and to console himself he ate peppermints by the dozen. At Nephi I left him and wished him luck, but he just murmured: "Yeah—I left her at ten o'clock this morning and she's keeping the kids."

Soon another truck took me on, but outside Levan he let me down, for his boss did not allow him to give people lifts. By now I had got a good way south, and all these towns were called after characters in the *Book of Mormon*—and there was scarcely a Gentile within miles—but I forgot to look at the map and I walked on out of the town for over 5 miles before it got dark and there was no sign of a car that would give me a lift. Another town I thought must be near, but that was not so, and the land grew bleaker and bleaker.

194

It was open country between the Rocky Mountains or Wasatch Range, and the oncoming Nevada Desert—over the hills soon came a clear moon which made walking a little easier—but even so along the pebbled road it was hard going and it began to get cold, and now and then along the long distant road I could see the lights of a car. I would try to look as little like a criminal as possible—nearer the lights would come and as quickly would they pass me by, and then for perhaps another hour nothing would appear.

Finally, 20 miles from Levan and near midnight, giving up any hope of a lift and realising of how little use dollars in your pocket sometimes can be, I lay down near a swamp by the side of the road and tried to sleep.

But sea-gulls screamed through the night, the ground was hard and the night was bitter, and as that moon moved slowly across, letting itself be constantly defeated by faster moving clouds, I became more and more depressed; as dawn came I shook myself all frozen and feeling filthy, and took to the road again. That experience I would never repeat, but it was seven o'clock before I got another lift,—a coal-truck driver, and he took me into Scipio.

The day before, going had been so good ; I had only bought chocolates in Nephi, thinking to have a good dinner somewhere, and so since Provo—where at ten o'clock I had had hot cakes and syrup—I had, during a strenuous twenty-four hours, eaten nothing. As I walked into the drug store in tiny Scipio—looking none too clean, I nonplussed the woman there by ordering all that I had got to like in America. I had grapenuts first, then I had eggs and small sausages, I even had waffles and syrup, and I ended up, admittedly all wrongly, with a chocolate malted milk, and now feeling none too well, and the waitress certain I had waylaid someone for the money the night before, I departed to get my next lift to Holden 14 miles on. The driver and his father had motored all night, having taken his mother to hospital in Salt Lake City, and they had only enough money to get them home, and they left me wondering just what complaint I might have caught, sitting there with pillows and a mattress on which the sick woman had been that night.

It was then that I went 28 miles with a typical black-coated Mormon family of a husband and two women— were they both wives ? I never found out—but they were going to Kanosh to the Mormon Quarterly Conference, and they had a brother in Calgary, who was in oil, and another in Lethbridge, Alberta, who farmed, and they showed me Fillmore, the former capital of Utah, and the rather Georgian house that was the Capitol and is to-day a museum, and smilingly they showed me a meadow where the Mormons massacred the Gentile emigrants years ago, about which the driver told me his mother never let him speak for his father had taken part.

In Kanosh I had a long talk with a fellow tramp wending his way towards Las Vegas—but he slept out every night, and he told me, what luckily I had the night before forgotten, of tarantuli, big spiders that bite, and you quickly die, and of the snakes from whom death comes as certainly but more slowly, and then I was glad to get a lift in a fast-moving army lorry. It was a Ford Air Force waggon, with a cheerful driver, and he took me at great speed all the way to Beaver, which was nearly 50 miles, and we passed over hills that were 6,500 feet high, and through fascinating desert scenery, through thickets of sage bush and through occasional wooded country, and then past Cove Fort that had been a Mormon Fort in olden times against the Indians, and so on to Beaver. It was getting late, and determined to sleep that night in bed, I stopped at the nearest approach to an hotel where I paid what I liked and that was one dollar—for the landlady told me times were very bad and the hotel was nearly empty; but my feet were beginning to hurt a great deal, and so I did not leave till quite late the next morning.

From Beaver I hiked many sore miles out into the hills that always threatened this desert which never seemed fully to materialise, and at last a Government land surveyor gave me a lift into Cedar City. On the way we passed many other tramps, and it rained, and they included my snake friend of the day before, who, like in a game of leap-frog, must have got past Beaver and beyond me while I slept, and I now was getting ahead of him. I never saw him again. The land surveyor told me that the Federal Government does not sell its land but it will homestead people up to about 620 acres, and I remembered Struthers Burt describing this process to me of one for the Government of heads they win, tails you lose. To take up a homestead you must live seven months of the year for three to five years on the land and each year you must do $1·20 worth of reclamation or improvement per acre.

Now there is very little good land left, and as on Federal land not yet homesteaded you can graze free, the land has already been ruined. The result has been the vast areas that I thought were the famous desert—once good lands, now hardly fit for sheep. In the hills they are using the land in the same way and it too will soon be worthless. The Government, it is true, is beginning to take notice—but like everywhere else in every country the Government is just too late.

From Cedar City I had many small uninteresting lifts and one was with a family where I sat behind with

the children and we read the previous Sunday papers—
they the comic bits, I the Wall Street news—and so on
again into the dark, and I was afraid I would have
another night out.

But, about ten o'clock a smart Buick passed me;
then pulled up. Imagine the joy for me of those
squeaking brakes that meant a lift! The owner,
young, well-dressed and good-looking, was very cheerful about everything. He told me so far when he
gave lifts nobody had hit him, so I promised also to
leave him alone and we talked first about his work.

He had made his own business and for the last five
nights he had worked all day and driven all night.
He is head of a truck company and has no patience
with the railways ; they, he thought, are trying to keep
their customers without facing modern improvements
—and here he was the typical Westerner—they don't
want to see new methods that put them out of date
and so he had no sympathy for them. Technically,
he has been arrested in several neighbouring States
at the instigation of the railways—for carrying too
high freightage on his trucks. Utah only allows five
tons per truck—but in California he has carried as
much as thirty-four tons. He adds a trailer to his
truck and so gets round the laws.

He was convinced the Mormon Church is the
largest stock holder in the Union Pacific Railway, and
then he asked me about England and Europe. Yes,
he wanted awfully to go there—he'd love to see the
world—but first he must make his fortune—he looked
about thirty-six—and he was intensely earnest and
keen and interested in everything, and asked me when
we parted in St. George to meet him at seven o'clock
next morning and go on across the desert.

But at seven o'clock I was still in bed, for my feet
were hurting, and the night before as we came down

the hill into St. George I had noticed the fine white Mormon Temple all lit up by electric flood-lights and hand made, and I went there and looked at it, for it is one of the only six in North America, and no Gentile can enter, and the hotel where I had stopped the night was no longer an hotel, for the owner was being sold up and ejected next morning, and she had already closed for good; but for a dollar I slept there.

I next got a lift to Santa Clara on the edge of the desert, and having been warned not to start across it on foot for fear of winds and heat and animals and desperate men, and having refused a lift from un-pleasant-looking Indians, I sat by the side of the road with a boiling sun over our heads with a shell-shocked Army veteran, and I feared he would have a stroke, and he told me what America does for her war veterans and I was amazed at the generosity.

This man was returning to the Veterans' Home near Santa Monica, near Hollywood, near the sea and in the warmth of Southern California, where for a slight disablement he would live for the rest of his life, and his wife would be nearby at Long Beach, and he could go to stay with her at intervals—and they gave him $40.00 a month. Then another friend I met was a pedlar with a yellow box-like contraption on one wheel which he peddles round and calls a mowing machine.

Soon after this came two youths in a Star Model of 1923 packed high with belongings—they had motored all the way from Des Moines in Illinois, and on reaching Los Angeles hoped to get a job for the winter. They were cheerful, and a quarter way over the desert we burst a tyre—later we had four punctures and we found the water was leaking. So we had to stop at the many service stations dotted across the desert and fill up with water. This water, which at much expense the stations get hauled across the desert to them, they must give free to their clients. But we could not afford to get petrol and yet they gave us the water, laughing, and once at a station we saw a tarantulus crawling across the road, and I remembered my night out and shuddered.

The desert is 130 miles long and is an amazing hot wilderness in the midst of rocky mountains with one or two long flat desert plains. The colourings changed almost every minute, and were often red, as often brown, grey and green-grey, and then black hills, and sometimes too they were a dark blue, and then again you seemed to pass through canyons around which everything was a vivid red sand—both the hills and the plains. And once towards the middle we were thirsty and drank iced water at a service station, but the water cost us 5 cents a pitcher.

It was ten-thirty before we reached Las Vegas—it was now Pacific time and so only nine-thirty, and for the last hour we had driven against oncoming lights, and as René the driver was nearly blind, he took the afternoon and evening to drive and so save the glare of the sun—which alarmed me; and Jim drove in the morning and they went on to a car park to sleep and I started to look around the town for a room.

Las Vegas, Nevada, is like Reno, Nevada—as wide open, as full of criminals—but not as smart. It too suffers from publicity but of another sort, for near here is Boulder City, where the Hoover Dam is being built, and all through America amongst those out of work runs the rumour—"There is work to be had at Las Vegas," and these so-called slackers, to whom it would be criminal to give a dole, travel a whole continent in dire discomfort—some on freight trains, some by road—that they may find work on the Hoover Dam. The

At work on the Hoover Dam

The New Hoover Dam

result is inevitable. It is now forbidden to go within a mile of where the dam is being constructed without a work pass, and this you get in Las Vegas, and so in Las Vegas, a town of 3,000 inhabitants, are standing more than a thousand unemployed.

As I walked through the streets that night I found doss-houses that were as expensive as the hotels of Southern Utah, and hotels, so called, that equalled big cities in price, and they were all full, and the food in the restaurants was dearer than elsewhere, and yet there was more life, more poverty and more crime here than in any city I had yet visited.

The women came out of the houses in streets where you saw little in the dark, and they tried to drag you in, and here and there there were groups, and they were grouped round fighting men, and one man yelled to another, "You're a stool-pigeon"—and there may have been police, but I did not see them. There must have been, because next day I was told by a responsible inhabitant there were six people in prison awaiting trial for murder.

I walked into one wide-open gambling den. Yes, some men were playing at the tables, but the largest number were lying about the room and some were huddled in chairs—they did not seem drunk, they were just tired men—men who perhaps had not had much food. And at two tables some men were playing and threw their money in amongst what looked like wax figures—figures of other men who had nowhere else to sleep and were at corners of the table; asleep with their heads on their folded arms on the table; and then I went back to the hotel where I had found a room, but on the way I passed the green patches in front of the station and they were covered with bodies of men that were sleeping out, for here it was not very cold.

I only lay stress on this town because it struck me

forcibly as typical of the wrong side of *laissez faire*
methods as against organised unemployment relief
by a state or nation. Here had congregated thousands
of men—not criminals like so many are supposed to
be who go to Washington in protest processions—for
they had nothing else to gain but work—they were
presumably genuine unemployed. And had there
been some registration system throughout the nation,
before leaving wherever they were registered to go to
Las Vegas—or indeed by asking at any employment
office along the line—they could have been told what
everyone in Las Vegas knew—that there was no work
for them at Hoover Dam and that those that are taken
on must come with some introduction from someone
already there, and that they prefer single to married
men. Instead of which they came hopefully to this
minute city, a city with no means of supporting them—
no Community Chest or charitable organisation at all,
and equally with no means of controlling them or
force to turn them away.

It was just chaos and they suffered undeserved
misery, and stopped on, hoping, hoping for a job that
no one could give them. Of course there were
employment brokers—there and everywhere else, and
sometimes they found the men jobs and took a percentage, and as often as not they took the men's last
dollars, found no work, and themselves decamped.
But that, I suppose, is pioneer life—all right in normal
times but inconceivably ghastly in times of widespread
distress.

And next morning at eight o'clock, passing the
station green where the men lying down had not yet
woken up, I went to the Reclamation Office to see Mr.
Cramton, who had been well known in the House of
Representatives and who on defeat had been given
by President Hoover the post of the head of the

Government land organisation at Boulder City and Hoover Dam.

He told me I was lucky in my day because he had a bad toothache, and so would not stop in the office but would himself motor me out and show me the dam. On the way out—it was about 2 miles—he explained it all to me.

For ten years the present plan has been mooted, meeting with constant opposition. It is to harness the Colorado River at a place to be known as Hoover Dam. The scheme should be finished by 1938, and therefore to carry it out, for they are employing 1,800 men and will eventually employ 2,500 men, they have had to build a town. This dam will necessitate a lake, and they are constructing a huge lake out of a plain between the hills that will be 115 miles long and will swamp two villages, which villages were amongst those "vested interests" opposing the scheme, and they will make this a Federal pleasure resort, a sort of National Park with boating, etc., and a magnificent hotel—and so the city that is to be built to house the workmen is to remain on as a city beside the lake, and it is being planned for permanency and is being called Boulder City—and 2 miles away remains Las Vegas, which is trying, while it has the time, to make what money it can out of the builders; and so Mr. Cramton is in charge, with very extensive powers.

The object of the dam is grandiose enough, for it will save the Imperial Valley of California from floods —which are frequent and were the first cause of the mooting of a dam. It will give power for industry in Arizona, in California, in Nevada, and perhaps in New Mexico; it will help irrigation is this desert land, and especially in the fruit lands of the Imperial Valley; and lastly it will enable water to be brought by aqueduct hundreds of miles to that growing city, Los

Angeles, which only voted in favour of the scheme, already well advanced, the day I was at Hoover Dam.

Before we started out they showed me the Government office in Las Vegas where the men are taken on, and in the Reclamation office we first spent an hour, where all and every type of person came about their businesses at Boulder City.

There was a man to talk about his ice-cream shop, and Mr. Cramton, looking at the plans, told him where it was to be; and another applied for a concession to have a theatre, and there were those that had come to enquire about stores and about clothes shops, and they were filing their application, for the Government would control this city and none could buy real estate, and shops were only to be had on leases.

And with us to Boulder City to examine it at first hand, came a middle-aged slightly military-looking man in a blue suit. He intended making money with his daughter in opening up a recreation hall, and he laughed a little grimly as he told me of how he had run them before in mining towns all the way from Alaska to New Mexico, and Mr. Cramton told me he was a well-known man in frontier life—Yes, he was still in frontier life—it is not dead in America, nor will be the type it breeds for another generation at least.

As we motored out along a road that was not fully completed and that gave us many a bump, we passed through a rather flat scenery, but gradually approached to a gorge and then to the site of the new city. Here we were joined by the head of the police and the visiting Ranger of the Petrified Forests in New Mexico —both dressed in broad-brimmed hats, light khaki and green shirts respectively, knicker-bockers and high-laced boots. They took us through the collection of huts that was to be the city and up over a hill to look down on the plain that was to be a lake and then to the top of the cliff looking straight down to the muddy waters of the Colorado where slowly the dam was being constructed.

Our mining town recreation promoter stopped a little back, for he did not like heights—and this was so high that it was on this point the year before that "Ma" Kennedy—the mother of the famous Hot Gospeller, Aimée McPherson—had been joined by a clergyman, with photographers present, to "What a Man" Hudson, and the head of the police explained to me that as they were short of a name for this Point, they have almost decided to call it "What a Man Point."

When we got back into the city, Mr. Cramton said I must meet the head of the athletics for the men— and he was called Moran, the Boxer, who boxed Beckett in London, and he asked me if I knew any of the "Bachelor Club Boys" in London, and I in my old grey flannel suit just off the road confessed I was one myself, and we talked of the boxing of Lord Clydesdale, of Eddy Eagan and of a dozen others.

It seemed strange just here to meet this man, and we all went in to lunch in a canteen where food is kept regularly all day for nearly 800 men to eat at a time, and my host passed me some marmalade with my potatoes, saying: "I know Englishmen like marmalade," and Moran came to my rescue and said scornfully: "Yes, sir, but with their breakfast, not with their lunch."

I motored back to Las Vegas with the nicest host I had had for a long time and Moran seemed sad to say good-bye to such a brief link with the London he had enjoyed, the fights, the nights at the National Sporting Club, and the training he had given many a London young hopeful at the request of worried mothers to keep their sons healthy and perhaps away from drink. And by four o'clock I was on the road again back to Salt Lake City to be in time for the Mormon Conference.

I got one lift that took me to the edge of the desert and there I slept in a cabin, and at seven-thirty next morning got a lift of 360 miles in a Franklin car with a type of American that is like a tonic. He was a former "Grievance" man for the Union Pacific Railway—that is to say he used to settle disputes with the men and so had to have their confidence and be a friendly sort of being. Now he lived in Los Angeles and had a fruit farm of seven acres and two motor-cars.

He told me it was impossible for a man to get a job picking fruit even for his keep; it did not pay now to pick fruit—it was just left to rot on the trees. This year he too felt poorer by receiving no dividends, and he felt the whole thing was engineered by Wall Street and the millionaires. He gave me as he thought a good proof.

During the war he sold Bonds to the railway men for the Government. Everybody, including all the poor, were supposed to subscribe, and for that reason they were to be tax free. After the war they went down to 75, and there was a slump, and so the working man, having nothing to fall back upon, had to sell. The millionaires bought and then they went up to over 100 and paid no tax, and so he felt that was a good stunt for the millionaire, who on a large part of his income paid no tax—like the French Noble, just before the French Revolution, and he felt to-day was largely another millionaire drive; but he felt now the middle classes, that before had been with the millionaires, were being ruined too, and they were joining the working man and that might spell revolution. And his remedy was also typical.

Now was the time for those that could, to buy every-thing—the millionaire would not dare to go too far—else there would be revolution, and there must be still higher tariffs to keep away from this depressing out-side world and there must be a minimum price.   Then there must be temporary works—but for permanent improvement—the U.S.A. must cut working hours and keep up wages.   Such was his creed and that of half the States as well, and with faith they say all things are possible, and his faith in America was quite wonderful and in Los Angeles above all—it would be the New York of the Pacific—and as Detroit is the centre for motors, so will Los Angeles be for aeroplanes.

People from Kansas and Iowa were settling at Long Beach near Los Angeles; it was a good sign, for the Middle Westerner was a go-ahead type, but he had a great contempt for the Easterner—though he pre-ferred him socially.   And I left him at Nephi.   We had come through scenery that I had passed through before by night when I had been picked up in the Black Canyon, and we had gone up from St. George through red clay hills and sage green that for all the world looked like beef and spinach, until finally we reached cultivated valleys and passed mountains covered in gorgeous golden shrubs.

From Nephi to Provo I travelled with a youth who, married at eighteen, was now keeping a mistress at twenty-two, and next day I went to Salt Lake City with Mormon farmers coming up for the Conference, and they smilingly assured to me that they had no horns on their heads as the English thought; we talked of new methods of selling cheaply and making quick profits, I rested a few days in Salt Lake City, and then started out East, for this roadside experience was the best insight I had yet had into the backbone type of American.

CHAPTER XV

MOUNTAINS AND PLAINS

ONE evening I went to the Salvation Army Hostel in Salt Lake City where I found those hoboes who could afford a 25-cent bed, and I asked hints from the men on how to hobo, and one told me "never sleep in other people's newspapers"—for obvious reasons—but he strongly recommended my taking newspapers with me for warmth, and he told me of a town where there was a "Bull"—that is to say a railway policeman—who hates hoboes, for his brother was once killed by a hobo; and another man told me it was difficult to leave Salt Lake City by train, for a Bull walks on the top of the freights looking for hoboes, and a fellow Bull drives in a motor-car along the road that is beside the train and sees any hoboes that are underneath. They take them off to the county jail and the police often raid the jungles and take people to jail just to get their finger-prints.

Then a girl in gaiters, riding-breeches, blouse and cap told me how she sometimes got food. "I went into a shop to-day and said, 'I'm a girl and I'm hungry. I'll do any work you like if you'll give me some food.' And he said, 'Sit down.'" She told me to get food you must have gumption, and she complained the woman upstairs with the baby had no gumption. She made her also go in and tell him she'd got a baby and was hungry—and then she had gone in and got milk and a few biscuits.

I could not help but ask myself on whom was this fair—the woman with the baby or the shopkeeper? Neither, I felt, and went on down to the jungle to talk to the less well-off hoboes who were sitting round a fire they had just made, and it was dark;

but they were friendly, just twenty of them—and I heard one speaking: "Say, boy, the freight stopped, they got off and got ten heads of cabbage and near a sack of rosy potatoes"; and another was saying, "Christ, he was like the President of the line—he got on that freight right in the station." And then they turned to me. "Where are you heading, partner?"—and I told them, East.

They told me food was cheap in Denver, but it was getting cold going that way. Some had just come from there, one having even bummed a lift on an aeroplane part of the way from the East, and they told me Soldiers Summit was the dangerous spot— everyone always got arrested, as the Bull had a gun, and the only thing to do was to scatter.

They advised me not to go to Texas in winter— it was cold; and one told me that his friend had been thrown off the Santa Fé by the Bulls near Pueblo while the train was moving, and his face was terribly cut. And nearly all that were there had been in prison the night before—for they were stopped when walking in the street, and having no money, made to go to the police station, where they were put on a floor and some in bunks of iron—they got no mattress but two blankets each and a mush break-fast. The police told them they each cost the State $1.50, but they thought it more like twenty cents.

They advised me to keep to the roads, and when I said I was afraid if arrested I would be deported, they replied: "You say you were born in San Francisco. All the registers were burnt there in 1906, they can't prove you weren't. We all do. And then you can say you were in England—why you might have been at Oxford—no one would know you hadn't." But as I had, I thought things were getting too warm, and I moved off, and while going

they advised me again—"You keep with the decent
bums, don't get in with the lousy ones, they'll biff
you," and I remembered what they said and next
afternoon started East.

My first lift was with an undertaker, who told me
business was bad—people were living through the
slump, and he had only five deaths in ten days. But
he had a fine car, and we went 30 miles through
Parley Canyon—a beautiful drive taking us to nearly
10,000 feet at the summit—through the Canyon
where the Mormon Pioneers first marched. This
lift was followed by one with a Mormon farmer,
who was all in favour of the use of silver dollars
rather than paper "green backs" in the Eastern States
—it would help the Utah mines, for in the mountain States you never see a dollar bill of less than
five dollars, but the silver becomes heavy; and later
I went 40 miles in a big car through Echo to Evans-
town, and there were three other hoboes given lifts,
and one was a father with his small son of whom
he took the greatest care; nobody talked, and we
drove through lands where the sheep were being
brought down from the mountains for the winter.
And here I spent the night. Next morning it was
cold, and there was a biting wind; we were high up
in the hills and I travelled 40 miles to Lyman on a
truck with a three-and-a-half-ton load of bran for
the sheep. The driver spoke slowly and seldom.
We never went faster than 20 miles an hour and up
hills at about 2 miles per hour. But he told me
not only was this country snowed up in winter, but
often aeroplanes had to come in to feed the inhabitants, and it seemed to me no different from Canada.

By midday there was near a hurricane blowing,
and a freezing blast at that; but I walked along miles
of pebbled road that made a hole in my shoe, until

eventually there came an odd vehicle that was covered in belongings, and inside sat a young man and his wife and child, and they too were nearly frozen, for it had only a hood and they had come from Vancouver, British Columbia, and they were going to New York. I sat up behind on a tent and bedding and heard their tale of adventure, shouted back to me as we motored on nearly 50 miles to Green River.

There I could stand it no longer and travelled through that night without them to Rock Spring, a depressing mining town and a big coal centre, where they pay the miners a minimum wage of $6.75 a day and are keeping the men on by only working them three days a week. We passed through Fort Bridger where the Army had been posted to keep an eye on the Mormons in the olden days, and on along the Oregon Trail, and the route the Hudson Bay and Astor fur trackers took when long ago they were followed by the Red Indians.

And having had a lucky day, I thought I would risk a night in a real doss-house; so for 50 cents I got a "room" to myself—it was a cubicle and there was plenty of draught—the building was an old barn refurnished, and in the office there was a stove and above my head a blue-green ceiling. The thermometer said 44°—the day before they said it had been 70°—and we chatted about a new Hoover Scheme out that day and about people on the road—of boys of sixteen and even one of only twelve years who, having spent the money his father gave him for something else on malted milks, had passed through Rock Springs on the bum the day before.

That night I slept little and I came away the next day, which was warmer, with a feeling of regret for my rashness that I was not to shake off until I had been in Denver and some luxury.

That day I had many lifts, and one man, who told me the price of sheep was $3 to $5, also explained to me in Wyoming—where we now were—the law ordained that the man who gives the tramp a lift is arrested—not the hobo. And another man did not believe in the Hoover Scheme, and thought no matter what plans were made, nothing good could come to the country until there was a change of government —it was the psychological effect that was needed, and so talking we covered a good deal of country.

It was rolling country with much sage bush and uninteresting—it was good only for sheep and cattle, and there was no water—the winter snow being the only substitute—and we were all the time on a plateau at least 6,000 feet up. But it was prettier as we covered the road from Rawlins to Rock Springs. I travelled first, with an hotel chef who took a fancy to me and told me if I got no more lifts, to come back to his hotel and he would feed me in the kitchen; and then on a truck with another hobo who had only four cents left and had come from Portland. The owner of the hotel where I spent the night—it was also a Pool room—had just lost all his money in the local bank failure, and the town was full with a gang repairing roads.

Next morning I got a lift of 195 miles straight through to Denver in a Buick belonging to a commercial traveller doing the whole Pacific and mountain States for a Philadelphia curtain firm. He told me Denver was a coming city—a city of 320,000 people which had increased by 100,000 in the last ten years; it was mainly a mining and a tourist centre. As we passed through the country, he showed me a lot of sugar beet farms that made a profit, but only with the aid of Japanese labour and of Mexican labour that has spread north for this purpose through

Utah and up to Idaho—for they alone can bear the strain to the back in picking. We passed a famous mushroom factory *en route*, and so descended into Denver, a great centre for consumptive patients, passing from Laramish through parts of the mountains to Fort Collins and then through a fertile plain with the Rocky Mountains stretching away to the right until we reached Denver.

As we came near, my driver told me how he disliked selling curtains in Canada—for they take the patterns, send them back to Scotland, and next year he finds the Scotch are selling the curtains cheaper than he ever can. He said he gets his cottons from Tahiti and the South Sea Islands and I suppose the Southern States.

Two things struck me this day—the heat, which they called an Indian Summer, saying it might all the same soon be as much as 28° below zero, and the number of carcases of dead rabbits and the skeletons of cows and sheep and even horses I saw along the road.

I stopped two days in Denver in comfort, getting out my trunk that I had sent on, and some clothes, and I interviewed the city officials and visited the parks and museums of which there were plenty. Then I concentrated on the unemployed. They told me at the Community Chest that they were organising for over 30,000 unemployed that winter—it was now October the 10th—they were building a new Mission House to be ready for homeless men about November 1st—and it would have all the modern conveniences, including compulsory baths and a fumigator for clothes, and I understood the Community Chest were looking after the overflow from the City Council who have already two "hotels." After all, Denver is mainly a tourist centre without a heavy

213

pay roll and so they have no very heavy unemployment of their own.

Yet that night I was to witness a rally that one could not help but admire. It was in the auditorium, and the city had been summoned by the Mayor. They gave me a good seat, and I listened to the opening of a drive against the city's unemployment that was to last a week. The organ played—5,000 people listened—all the Churches, all the Parties were represented. A Roman Catholic priest first prayed and he chose the Our Father, for no better prayer exists in which all Churches can agree; and then the Chairman, then the Mayor, who told us crime would soon be banished from Denver; next the head of the Community Chest, who pointed out what many forget.

Before giving to the fund to help the newly unemployed and stop starvation, you must give as you gave before to the ordinary charities in the Community Chest—now strained for finance more than ever—for if the unemployed are not to starve, the lunatics, the orphans, the cripples and the blind, they too must be looked after as before—and yet the incomes of those that keep them have often sunk to nothing and the invested funds of these charities, they too have fallen low. And as I sat there and as I sat later at half a dozen other luncheons and appeals, I marvelled at the unbelievably wonderful courage of these workers and these givers, and I thought again how grossly unfair that, through lack of taxation, those others who are less charitable get off almost unscathed, while others "give until it hurts."

Then spoke a Socialist, who talked of the Bill of Rights and the right to work, and after him came the Commander of the Army—against unemployment. Then we sang songs, and then we went home. Here in Denver they were making an effort which impressed on my mind how much the individualistic American in times of stress or uncertainty likes to get into a group and work in communities, and how much he always dearly loves a parade, a badge, a uniform, or a secret society. Here are some extracts from the pamphlet showing how the city was to carry out its first drive against unemployment.

"INSTRUCTIONS

to the Denver Employment Army for the Week of October 12th to October 17th."

*****

1. The Army

The Citizens Employment Committee, under its Chairman, J. F. Welborn (hereinafter called the Committee), has assigned only a limited objective to the Army. That objective is to canvass the homes and dwelling places of the entire city for work wanted and work offered, arouse a civic consciousness, try to place all the people possible in the positions offered by their respective districts, and then turn over all cards and records to the Committee, which will thereupon assume the responsibility for the relief of our unemployed. Consequently, except for doing our utmost in our respective blocks until the crisis is past, the main work of the Army will be completed by October 17th, by which time all records should have been delivered to the Committee.

2. District Majors

Each District has a headquarters, which is directed by the District Major and his Staff. These District headquarters will be open from 9:00 a.m., Monday, October 12th, to 5:00 p.m., Saturday, October 17th. The clerical work at these headquarters will be done by volunteers from the Women's Clubs, who will handle the cards turned in by the Precinct Captains. These volunteers will be responsible to the Majors but will receive their instructions from Mrs. Frank McLister, Assistant Chief of Staff, and will be on duty at each District Headquarters from Tuesday, October 13th, through Saturday, October 17th.

The District Headquarters are the working offices of the Districts, for clerical purposes only, but are not assembly places for those seeking employment.

The District Majors have the responsibility for the organisation of their districts, for the complete canvassing of their sections for work wanted and work offered, for the placement of all possible jobs in their own districts and, as soon as this work is finished, for the delivery of the record cards to the Committee at 324 Colorado National Bank Building to Mr. Harmon L. Thompson. Commencing Tuesday, October 13th, the Majors will also fill out and return the daily district reports and consolidated reports to Philip S. Van Cise on forms to be furnished. Before delivery of the cards to Mr. Thompson the Majors will make proper notations on all cards showing what dispositions have been made of applicants for work wanted and work offered.

3. Precinct Captains

The Precinct Captains will check all cards and countersign Lieutenants' reports before turning them over to the District Headquarters, and will see that the cards and reports are properly filled out according to the instructions to the Lieutenants. The Captains will keep a duplicate copy of the Lieutenants' reports, and upon completion of their precinct, will deliver a consolidated Precinct Report to the District Major. As fast as the Lieutenants' reports are checked by the Captains they should be delivered to District Headquarters. Each Block set of cards, together with the Block Lieutenant's report, must be tied in a separate bundle.

If Precinct Captains can award work offered to needy persons in their precincts, they will do so, making notations on the cards to that effect.

4. Block Lieutenants

The Lieutenants are the backbone of the Army. They are *the ones who go over the top and carry the work of the Army into the homes and hearts of Denver.* They can make the campaign a real success by the careful manner in which they prepare their cards. They are being given a form for their report, which they are asked to fill out, then tie all the Block cards

216

in one package, with the report card on top, and deliver it to the Precinct Captain as soon as the Block is finished. Do not deliver any cards until the entire Block is completed.

Our cards should have been printed to show more information, and we want this to be supplied by you and added to the printed form.

White "Employment Wanted" Cards.

On the top of each white card, above the printing, write, in ink or indelible pencil, the District, Precinct, Classification, whether Male (M) or Female (F), and if the need is urgent put a cross in the upper left-hand corner.

Example: A needy male garment worker in District A, Precinct 4, would be marked this way:

"X Dist. A Pct. 4 Class 9 M."

If the person wanting work has been in Denver less than one year, write on the bottom of the card "New Citizen."

Where the person seeking employment is employed part time but not full time, state the facts thereof under "remarks" by the words "Part time."

CLASSIFICATIONS OF EMPLOYMENT WANTED

On the white "employment wanted" cards, on the line "Kind of work capable of doing" write what the applicant is—viz: clerk, barber, waitress, etc., then add what kind of work the applicant will take. Then at the top of this card put the number of that person's classification before turning in your cards to the Precinct Captains. A clerk in an office would be an office worker and marked as No. 6; a clerk in a store would be a store worker and marked as No. 7; a barber would be Miscellaneous and marked as No. 5.

Such were the instructions for raising $755,000 for over 30,000 unemployed and for the ordinary Community Chest Budget, and there were to be 400 men and 700 women collecting the money. Other towns did not differ much in their methods.

And that night before I slept, I read in the local

papers a strong complaint against the States on the Pacific Coast in favour of their own inland country —it read:

"Why raise freight rates? rather, put a levy on the Panama Canal Tolls—the boats are bringing goods round to the Pacific Coast at cut rate fares and the railways cannot compete — Result—Denver, which gets over $3,500,000, spent by the Union Pacific Railway in the district, suffers."

Only too true; in so vast a continent—an empire —it is not possible for even major interests to be the same; and to-day, there seemed only three things uniting the majority of the people: solving the unemployment problem; high tariffs as a remedy; and as much isolation from the rest of the world, especially Europe, as possible.

Next day I moved off, and I had many lifts on my three days' journey to Kansas City. One man told me that east of Denver the people go in mostly for dairy farms—as truck gardening for fruit and vegetables is in the hands of the Italian colony to the other side of Denver, with whom it is no use competing, for they have large families to work, whilst the husband drives the truck; and they told me that Denver was most noted for its large Catholic population, and for its being the biggest centre of Federal Government officials in the West.

All this first day took me over flat uninteresting country, and the road was so straight that when it is complete, it will be known as the Air Road to Kansas—for people will be able to drive along it at incredible speed. Next day I left Burlington in Colorado and I was in the State of Kansas.

I drove first with a strange but typical character, an elderly man who had first been a miner in Canada, then a real estate man, and finally a loan man in

Colorado. He had just lost his last $1,500 in Burlington's Bank failure the previous Monday. He was left with $3 and he was motoring into Goodland to borrow money to pay off his taxes. Yes, if he did not pay, the Government would sell him up eventually, though they do not press, and he and others did not see why we in England should be let off our debt to America by the same Government —nor could he, nor others, understand why if our Parliament had passed an Act putting England on the Gold Standard, we could ever go off it again. And it was not easy to explain the intricacies of the Gold Standard to Kansas farmers, nor were they much interested—though they thought a world of Ramsay MacDonald, the only English statesman, bar Lloyd George, they had ever heard about.

They knew a lot about the Middle West and the prairies, and my friend told me seven local banks had failed within the last week and there was misery in the district. The Burlington Bank had failed on a run for $55,000—and many of the loans were bad. He had lost his all twice before—once in an Arkansas bank and once again in Burlington in the bank failure and slump of 1921. Money he made in the future he would always keep in the safe— and it will be difficult to persuade many another like him to do otherwise, after two such failures in ten years.

He told me of the fear of Kansas farmers, who for the last ten years have been persuaded by big mortgage companies to borrow and improve and again to borrow when they did not really need it, and now, with a slump, they cannot pay, and the mortgages are being foreclosed by the big companies, who will run them at a greater profit and on the lines, he thinks, of English estates. He thought nearly 75 per cent of the Kansas farms are mortgaged, and one Omaha company already owns 10,000 acres.

Then I travelled with a traveller for a building company in his new Chrysler, and he told me how once an English lord—called Lord Kutz—had lived on him for three months in San Francisco. Oh yes, he was a real lord—he had his crest on his cards, and frankly my friend said he was not surprised that I, a hobo, had never heard of him, and I realised a hobo perhaps might not; and then he told me how he himself can always make money—a dollar or so if necessary—for he once was a magician; and he would go in the old days on freight trains as a hobo in a suit of overalls and then at a town he would take them off and underneath he wore dress clothes, and he would go into an hotel and do some tricks and pass the hat and make $5, and so he kept himself for two winters.

No, he did not want a dole for the U.S.A.; the people wanted to be independent. He dropped me at Colby, the only town in the U.S.A. that has no municipal taxes, living on electricity returns. It now was pouring with rain and muddy and we skidded in other cars until I came to Wakeeney. Once we forced the stage bus into the ditch through skidding, and it was there some hours with its indignant passengers.

Soon I passed houses that were all built of mud and look shaky—but they are warm. They turn cows round and round in the mud until it makes thick lumps and is ready for building; and a driver told me in those parts banking was very bad—the Nation and the State seemed to compete—one would make the Federal laws easier to get the business, and then the State would make still easier laws and so came many failures. Yet Chain Banking would never be popular there in the prairies—for people liked the personal touch.

Next as I stood on the road, a car came up, slowed down, the driver had a look at me and quickly put on the accelerator. "There," thought I, "goes insult number one—as if I'm not good enough for him." And my next host told me how Kansas City is growing as a great distributing centre for agriculture and for tractors and combines, much used in Kansas State, and that St. Louis is the distributing centre for the south-east and depends more on cotton; and another that he sells bucking horses for rodeos, normally getting $200 or $300, and hiring them out at $20 to $25 a day—but now he can buy back those same horses he sold, at no more than $40— and he always spends his winters in California for the warmth.

As I went to bed in Wakeeney, I listened in the hotel to the old miners from the North talking of their old-time tales, and I was told I was in the centre of 50 miles of large Catholic Churches, of settlers from East Prussia and Poland with buildings on their farms that looked Russian.

Next day, on a road that was nothing but mud, I continued looking at farms that were very much scattered—for it was not like Utah where the farmers, for fear of Indians, lived closely together and in villages. Here they lived on their own, and one showed me an article from *The Nation* which told much of the plight of farmers and spoke in terms of barter which in many places was taking the place of money. With wheat, then at 25 cents a bushel, and oats at 12 cents a bushel, the following values in Kansas are of interest:

1 bushel (60 pounds) (wheat) buys less than three 10-cent loaves of bread.

5 bushels (wheat) = enough petrol (with State tax) to drive 100 miles in an automobile.

1 bushel ,, = one 5-cent ice-cream cone each for a family of five.

1 bushel ,, = one thick plug of Drummond tobacco to chew a day.

1 bushel ,, = one package of cigarettes and one package of chewing gum.

16 bushels ,, = one $4 pair of shoes.
(more than average for one whole acre)

120 bushels (7 acres) = $30 suit of clothes.

25 pounds of butter fat = 1 $5 hat.

1 dozen eggs = 3 spools of thread.

And in all cases it has cost the farmers more than 25 cents, sometimes twice as much, to produce that bushel.

Such is the happy life of the wealthy farmer. Then one farmer and his son gave me a lift to Hayes, but they had not money enough to get petrol and go further. And afterwards, I drove with an old man from St. Louis to Salina. He was in a model T. Ford so packed that my legs were left perched on the bucket filled with water which every ten minutes we poured into the car, and he had been for his rheumatism to a hot spring in Idaho where his brother lived, and now he had only enough money to get to St. Louis if he travelled by night, and the lights of his car were flickering and finally went out and we drove in the dark; and with other cars coming, I got so frightened that I got off at Salina, and the old man said I was better than the rest of them, for five hoboes had refused lifts in his car that day, for they said it looked too uncomfortable.

And he was a cheery old soul and told me how St. Louis had once been half Irish and half German, but that to-day the Negro vote could turn any election—the city was too conservative to be progressive. And that day, what had most gladdened my heart was the sight of a few trees. There began —500 miles from Denver—to be some sign of green, of water and of clumps of trees—it seemed more like the country I knew and I felt I was almost coming home.

Next day, I drove to Kansas City—first on a truck where we were joined by a man of 35 and his sister, and later on, along the road, we passed a crippled old man of 70 and his wife about 60, and they were their father and mother, and we gave them also a lift, and the whole family had come in fifteen days from California *en route* for St. Louis, and then on the truck came a man from Oklahoma and another from nowhere in particular and so we wandered on.

Later I joined a man motoring from Los Angeles to Kansas City, and we bought apple cider in jars by the roadside to bring to his relations in Kansas City, and we were there by five o'clock. The scenery had been pretty, for now there were plenty of valleys well wooded, and more than one river, and as we approached Kansas City, I realised that there were two Kansas Cities—one in Missouri, the big one with sky-scrapers—and the other in Kansas State with a bridge across the Missouri river to join them; but they were as separate as London and Paris, for they were in two different States, with different laws, taxes, unemployment problems in the State, and ambitions, and I felt that the Missouri river meant leaving the prairies, their problems and ideas—the freedom of their beliefs and opinions, and entering into States almost totally different, with other problems and with their friends and relations more often working on the Pacific Coast than in the prairies or the mountain States that intervened. Geographically it was yet another part of a loosely knit Empire.

CHAPTER XVI

THE BIBLE-BELT

"You can't have a room over the week-end. We don't take guests Saturday to Monday and we don't serve food on Sundays."

It was a Communist hotel in a Communist village in the heart of Iowa. The hotel-keeper was civil—and his explanation on the whole logical. Week-ends were my holiday, so also were they his, and his family objected to cooking for extra people on Sunday. Eventually, however, he let me in after much argument and I joined the four regular inhabitants. They were all old men and they scarcely ever spoke; when they did, it was in German. They smoked clay pipes and walked up and down the room, occasionally stopping to swat a fly. It was dark early and they continued their walk by the light of gas lamps. Sometimes they rested and read the latest German newspaper from St. Louis. I never found out anything about them and nobody seemed to know about them, least of all themselves, even when I spoke to them in German.

My bedroom was upstairs, the mattress was straw but comfortable, the price of the room was reasonable, 50 cents. The breakfast was 50 cents, the lunch was 50 cents, and the dinner was 50 cents; some meals seemed of more value, some of less, on the whole I think the greatest profit was the bedroom. But I forget, there was no profit—the money went into the village community fund. A large rope was attached to my window with Fire Escape written over it, and the wash-basin, for everybody was in the sitting-room downstairs; communal washing took place most mornings early, for breakfast was not served after 7.30 a.m.

and dinner was at 6 p.m. We were in bed by nine o'clock. Swatting flies with an elderly silent German became monotonous after that hour.

The chief interest about this community—I left the road from Kansas to Chicago to visit—is that it is both a religious organisation as well as a communist organisation. It has been in existence as a religious body since 1714, but only as a communist group since its advent to America in 1842—ninety years ago.

As a communist organisation, it has grown, flourished considerably, and then gradually sunk, until to-day it has at last decided to break away from communism, as impracticable, and to turn its attentions to the old religious framework, leaving the worldly gains in the possession of the members in the form of stocks and bonds in a new company. In short it is one of the last of those literally hundreds of religious groups that once lived and experimented in Iowa and Indiana, that helped give the area the name of Bible Belt, and that gradually have given way before twentieth-century materialism. But this one is making a last effort in serving God and Mammon to see if by giving Mammon a bigger service, it might still do its duty to God.

In 1842 a much persecuted German religious sect came to America. They purchased land near Buffalo, 5,000 acres at $10 per acre. Everybody seemed pleased to see them except the Indians, who until then had thought they owned that land, and yet they were not the people who got the $10 per acre. Eventually, the religious Germans got rid of them—but it was more difficult to keep away the oncoming civilisation. The Ebenezer Society, for so they called themselves, did not feel their new communism needed the outside world. They sold their lands at a profit, and in 1854

A Village in the Amana Colony

moved west to 20 miles west of Iowa City. Land was cheap there, and there they remained.

They now changed their name to the Amana Colony —meaning "Be Truthful"—and settled down to communism. Religiously, they might be termed Lutherans. In each of their villages they have small meeting houses where they pray each evening for thirty minutes under the auspices of an Elder. Each member says aloud what prayer pleases him for two or three minutes and then the Elder finishes up with a longer prayer. On Sundays they all come together to the main village of Amana to the big Prayer house, and sit, the men one side, the women the other. Facing them, an Elder presides, and to his right and left fifty other Elders flank the wall. Everything is plain and simple —the women dressed in long dark dresses without jewellery, the men in ordinary dark suits.

Of their many religious regulations, the most unusual is that on marriage. Until quite recently, they considered marriage a failing rather than an asset and certainly nothing to boast about. The bachelor and the virgin were definitely purer and should be encouraged. Now they consider marriage has got to be faced, but they still do not encourage it too much. No girl must marry before she is 19 and no man before he is 23. Their engagement must be approved by the Trustees of the community, and they cannot marry until they have been engaged at least one year.

With seven villages, nearly fourteen hundred members, over 26,000 acres of land, and a woollen blanket factory, it is difficult to say whether all this was built up by religious enthusiasm or by the communist mode of life. The membership has never increased much, nor has proselytising been encouraged. The services are held in German, and everyone speaks German, and nobody is wanted who is not a German. Undoubtedly the Government of the community has been thoroughly organised, in true German style—but its communism is not much excelled in Russia.

In each house live from one to two families. The houses are large and well built, and each person over the age of 16 is entitled to a separate room. There are no kitchens in the houses, only communal ones at certain vantage points in the village. Where there is a kitchen, there is also an eating-room. Here come the villagers, and they either eat in community or take away with them the food to eat in their own houses. The latter practice is gradually becoming more popular. The women are detailed off to do the cooking, each village has its bakery as well as a communal vegetable patch. The bread is remarkably good— so much so that one old member recently dying in California—for you are free to leave the community if you will—decided he must have one more bite of the bread before he died. A loaf was eventually sent him, but whether he was then too weak to bite, or the loaf, on arrival, too stale to be bitten, history does not relate—the old man soon died. The food is healthy and comes mostly from the community lands. The furniture is very well made—by the local carpenters of the colony, in a Victorian style, and the clothes and other necessaries can be obtained at the village store—obtained, not purchased with money, for such a thing is not in use.

The members of the colony all originally pooled their resources, and guaranteed only to demand back what they or their ancestors had put in, should they desire to leave the colony for good. They could then only take out what they had put in—regardless of interest or possible appreciation in value of their investment. In return for this, each member was guaranteed board and lodging and free care when sick for the rest of his life. This is what has eventually proved the undoing of the community. It made life certain, and it made life too easy.

The members undertook to obey their leaders, and the community started off. No wages for work were to be recognised, and each year the rulers of the colony decided how much credit—a sort of pocket money—was to be allowed each individual member per week for the ensuing year. The amount was usually based on the applicant's needs, behaviour the previous year, and the type of goods on which he had spent this credit. The credit varied between $5 to $10 a week and took the form of credit at the local store, where he could obtain tobacco, clothes, more food, etc. If a member wanted to visit a neighbouring town—and this was not encouraged—he must first apply to the Elders for the use of the Communal Fords, and if these were already in use, say on a Sunday for visiting other villages, then he could use one of the old carriages. To obtain money for any journey or contact with the outside world, he also had to apply to the Elder-Trustee.

Certain contacts with the outside world are however inevitable, and are met logically. Take for example teachers and the schools. The teachers are all themselves community members. They are never women—that the community forbids. In order to teach, these men are themselves sent at the expense of the community to the University, and when they return they teach the whole year round. First the ordinary nine months for which they are paid a salary by the State. This salary they turn into the common pool. Then the next three months they teach for nothing. The community does not recognise holidays, other than Sundays. For nine months the lessons are in

English. Then the extra three months everything is taught in German.

The result is interesting. The whole colony speaks German almost all the time, only English when strangers are about. That English, even after ninety years and three generations, is very broken, just as the German is a patois dialect with many mongrel American expressions, not easy to understand. The whole atmosphere is Germanic. Yet of their religion, not one practising member remains in Germany, and there are only two members of the colony who have ever been to Germany. One, because his children, who left the colony, went to Germany and having made money, sent him the price of a holiday there. The colony allowed him to go and when the old man returned, plied him excitedly with a thousand questions. The other was one of the community's four doctors who was sent there to study medicine.

I'm not sure I would like to be an Amana boy. No holidays and twelve months school each year, no dancing, and at first no games. Now youth is rebelling and games such as baseball are allowed. Equally are the girls rebelling, and they no longer have to wear long dark dresses all day long—but dancing and jewellery are still forbidden.

The farm lands and their capital value are undoubtedly additions to the wealth of the community —but the main source of income comes from the woollen factory. Amana blankets have quite a market in the Middle West, and the work put into this factory has, in the past, been a work of love as much as profit. But of recent years the members of the colony have worked less hard, they have never stuck to even an eight-hour day, and certain that they will never lose their board and lodging, they have put, both into the factory work and the farm work, only the minimum amount required. The result is that, as the brochure on the colony by its leaders admits, "several hundred hired labourers are employed for the heavier work." In the woollen factory alone over seventy outsiders are now employed. With prices as low as the present, this does not pay, and the colony has at last had to face facts, and the leaders to take action.

The nucleus of the government of the community is formed by the Church Elders. Of these there are sixty, and they are elected for life. They are however not elected by the community, but by the board of thirteen Trustees. These thirteen Trustees are themselves elected annually, and are the actual rulers of the colony. The thirteen Trustees are elected directly by the whole community, but the only candidates for the office that are eligible are the sixty Elders. From them must come the Trustees and as each Elder dies off, these Trustees appoint from the community someone else to replace the dead man, among the Elders. Over the Trustees presides the President—but he is only a figure-head and as President has no particular power. The present one is actually 88 years of age. In practice, the same Trustees are appointed each year. Each of the seven villages has in addition a head man and a committee to run the more everyday detail work of the village.

As 1930 and finally 1931 put the Amana woollen factory and the whole colony more and more into financial uncertainties, and as gradually the youth of the villages discussed with more earnestness the advantages and disadvantages of their present life, the Trustees decided it was time to make a change in the organisation.

The colony owed its foundation and ideals to religion. Communism had only been accepted on landing in America, as the best way to stop jealousies in a new country between rich and poor members, and to give all an equal start. The Trustees will tell you now that communism never has succeeded anywhere, and never will succeed, for more than at most two generations. They will tell you, and tell you from experience, that to practise communism at all, all members must be enthusiastic about it. It is not a natural form of life, and unless those practising it are all buoyed up with a genuine enthusiasm, it is apt to become a degenerating influence. It cuts out natural competition, it makes life too easy, and as the dead body is eaten up by worms, so is the communistic colony, deprived of its enlivening spark of enthusiasm, eaten up with the worm of decay and laziness.

Their first settlers were all enthusiasts, both religious and communistic. The next generation was less keen but still quite steady-going. The present generation has ceased to feel the spirit of disinterested affection for neighbours, and the ideal, and only remembers that one need not work very hard as somehow board and lodging is assured for life, and if you become sick, you will be cared for. The colonists have lacked a spark that would make them work and like the ancient Greeks, they are getting in hired men to do the harder work. To stop this rot, the Trustees have decided from 1932 on to get rid of communism and to turn the whole colony into a stock-holding company.

It is all to be worked out gradually. The actuaries have been at work, trying to apportion the value of the farm lands, the villages, and the woollen factory. The shares are then to be divided up amongst the members of the colony. Those who have been there longest, the older members, are to receive the largest number of shares, and they will all be perfectly at liberty to sell or bequeath those shares to whomsoever they will. The purchase of such shares, however, will not carry with it any voting rights in regard to the government of the colony. It will still remain as difficult for a non-German or anybody else to become a member, and the mode of election of Trustees and Elders will remain the same.

All it means is that money is to be introduced into the colony; there is to be no further communal division of property, and everyone is to be free to better himself or herself and to make money. No longer will there be security of tenure, free board, and free care for the sick. It will all have to be paid for out of the dividends of the new company, out of whatever extra money the colonists may make, and until dividends are paid, out of the sale of their stock. This means the younger people will have to wake up, turn away those outside hirelings, do the work for themselves, and put the colony back on its feet again.

Already can be noticed a quickening interest amongst the youth. They are going to work to better themselves as well as everyone else. They are interested, they are keen. For them it makes all the difference—this difference between dull deadening communism, and vital active competition.

As you walk down the village streets of Amana, High Amana, Middle Amana, South Amana, West Amana, East Amana, and Homestead, the seven villages of the colony, all within 3 to 4 miles of each other, you find more or less the same streets, the communal bakery, communal store, the watchmakers, the carpenters, the hotel, in a few villages, the doctor's house in others, the Prayer house, and the kitchen, the village pump, and the village meeting-place on the green, the barns, and the communal vegetable plots. They are all there. The first village was built in 1854, the last, Middle Amana, in 1862. No paint was used on the houses for economy sake, and to-day they look

233

all the pleasanter without it. The atmosphere may be Victorian, but it is also German. There is a little colour where the window frames are painted green. There are plenty of well-kept gardens and in true German style at many corners, on long poles, are small dovecots. The Iowa River flows in and out between the villages, and a canal, running through the biggest village Amana, passes under the walls of the up-to-date woollen factory.

All this is a monument to the enthusiasm of the first founders—since when the deadening hand of security and comfort has lain hold of the place and you feel you are walking through the sleepiest of mediaeval districts. Here is every advantage, here every opportunity for the youth of the colony to develop priceless assets. Will they succeed, or will this new wine of capitalism break up the old bottles, and make the religious side too weak a link to hold the colony together? It is an interesting experiment for themselves and also for their fellow Americans as well. No need to go to Russia and see there the breaking up of forced communism. Here they have, in the State of Iowa, only a few miles from the Lincoln Highway, a proof of how far and no farther enthusiastic voluntary communism can go—and how even the hereditary communism has become in a sense forced, has completely failed, and in order to save the whole edifice from falling to pieces the old competition and the old uncertainty and insecurity of life has got to be resuscitated. Communism, it seems, cannot last even under the most favourable circumstances.

I was glad I had visited that settlement; I had made it a goal from the day I left Kansas City. There, in Kansas, I had studied the unemployed, and I had found that this city too was attempting a house-to-house canvass, but it was to be undertaken by the students of the University, and the majority of the homeless men were well taken care of in the Helping Hand Institute, where every effort was made to find men work, suitable work, and to keep them until their morale had been recovered and some attempt made to put them on their feet.

Next I had gone out a few miles to Independence, Missouri, where the Mormons by prophecy believe their eventual centre and temple will exist, and where that actual spot is held on to tenaciously by a small sect of dissatisfied Mormons, the Hedonites—about 700 in number—and until they die out or are financially unable any longer to hold on to this piece of land, the Mormons must "wait and see." Nearby is the rival Mormon Church—the Reorganised Church of Latter Day Saints—a Church with about 160,000 members —of whom over 110,000 live in Kansas City. This Church is almost unique in western Christianity in that it has an hereditary family headship. The Prophet Smith was head of all the Mormons over one hundred years ago. After his murder, they say, Brigham Young had no right to make himself head and with his supporters marched off towards Utah, and some therefore remained and recognised the Prophet's son as their head. To-day his grandson, the only ruling Smith in the world, reigns at Independence, near Kansas City.

His branch have never practised polygamy, and they have many bitter things to say about the million followers of Brigham Young. They say he practised atonement by blood—and made people commit suicide for crimes; that he arranged divorces and other laws for sums of money and so made wealthy himself and his fifty-nine children; that refusal to take tea, to smoke or drink strong drinks, was due not to divine inspiration, but difficulty in procuring such things while crossing the Utah Desert; and that polygamy was enforced first to make up for the shortage of men, conscripted to fight the Mexicans, and secondly to provide, as wives and children, cheap labour on the farms without paying wages.

There is no love lost between the elective Mormons of Salt Lake City, and the hereditary Mormons of Kansas City—but though the former may never mention the latter, yet the Kansas Mormons are powerful enough in the Middle West around Kansas City, and are building a colossal auditorium, which I visited, begun five years ago but not yet completed, that will have eventually cost $1,500,000.

From there, I started out on the road to Amana, and first travelled with a man who was motoring about the country in his own car on the look out for work. This is a type, I think, unique to the United States, and I found many near Los Angeles who were unemployed men being given work by the city to keep them from starving and yet who motored in their own car to work, for you can sell a second-hand car in most of America for almost nothing—the vast number for sale, that are little better than junk, outside nearly every United States town of size, is truly amazing. As I passed through St. Joseph, I was warned the police were arresting every hobo for "investigation," but I met no one, and soon went riding with a man selling burial plots in cemeteries on the instalment system.

I next drove in great state, for a car, negro chauffeur, limousine and fat man and young wife passed me. I was much too humble to suggest a lift—but the man leant forward and the car stopped as soon as it could, and I saw the wife protesting that I might easily hold them up, and the negro chauffeur too disapproved and pointed disdainfully to the seat next him, and then the man, just out for a drive, asked me questions, and they both knew London and Paris well, and I was able to tell the lady the Hotel Cecil was no more, but there were no changes in the staff at the Savoy, and I talked of Quaglino's Restaurant and Sovrani in London—how hungry it made me feel on this long road in Missouri!—and when they left me, the man wished me good luck, and wished he was my age, the woman shook hands and wished, she said, they could have taken me on to Chicago, and the negro chauffeur, at whom I grinned, looked as if he would have loved to have killed me, liar that he was sure I was.

Next lift was not so pleasant, for it was in the back of a farm motor with a cow that did not like my red handkerchief or me, and at last I was left in the dark, 7 miles from a village. As I passed farms out came the dogs barking alarmingly, and there was no noise re-echoing through the dark, along the lanes, but the tramp of my feet—the preparation of the dog at the next farm, perhaps to pounce as I came along, and then the burr of a car and soon its passing on. I began to despair—but just then round the corner appeared the glaring headlights of an Auburn. Its brakes went on and it came to a standstill.

"Jump in," said the man, "I hate to drive alone," and he took me 140 miles through the dark to Des Moines—and he would have taken me further, but he was going north to Albert Lea to shoot next day at midday; he would drive all through the night—I wondered if he really thought he could shoot next day. He was young—about 30 and worked in St. Paul—and we talked first of how he would make money quickly and then of the Bible. He was in the winebrick business that might do better without prohibition and in the meantime he gambled in real estate. He made a quick turnover and through agents would purchase farms anywhere—in Florida or Oregon—and re-sell them as quickly or trade them for other properties elsewhere, and if possible he would get rid of them before taxes were due. He had a fruit farm in California, a farm in Florida, something in Texas, and he had just been to Kansas City to look at his houses. "I am not rich," said he, "but I'm going to be. If a man can't make money in the States, it's his fault." Duluth, he was convinced, is a town of the future if the St. Lawrence is opened up, as the head city of the Lakes, and then the Mississippi would be made navigable from the north, so helping Iowa and Minnesota.

All these were things that made me realise how America is only beginning in her powers of development. Then we talked of cars and how the Auburn had only been used by the negroes until a man called Chord, aged 32, came along and pushed the car up from thirtieth to thirteenth place in car-land.

And immediately we switched to religion and he showed me an amazing knowledge of the Bible and its prophecies which he maintained included Mussolini, the second Roman Empire and the Millennium; he advised me strongly to read Schofield's Bible and to visit the English youths at Mudie's Bible School in Chicago, and then he left me at Des Moines that night—this tall, rich, very earnest, good-looking young man that combined a business sharpness with intimate Bible knowledge.

Next day, a driver complained that the States were getting into the hands of Trusts for everything, including Universities, and that Chicago University made the laws for the other Universities—and another farmer told me he saw a bigger future for Canada than for the United States, and that he had farms of his own in Saskatchewan, and much admired Canadian justice —in the States, he said, "a judge is like an umpire at a ball game." My next driver took me through to the Amana Colony for which I had been searching.

When I left the colony my drivers told me, one that Iowa was the centre of the cotton belt, chock full of graft and only "talked poor," with farmers wealthy and prices cheap, and in 1928 he made $10,000. He was a traveller in electricity getting $250 a month—but for this he had to find his own petrol, and worked by day, travelling by night and hardly ever seeing his wife. A lot of American middle-class business men hardly ever do seem to see their wives. Another was a German who came to America with five brothers after the war, and in spite of all, they are doing well, and he felt happy as do most of the Germans living in this part around Davenport. There that night, I walked to the bridge and for the first time looked at the Mississippi—Ol' Man River—vast and silent in the darkness of the night—this river that once divided a continent, and has inspired endless writers—but in Davenport there was nothing of particular interest, and next day I continued to Chicago.

I had one interesting lift—it was with an ex-South-Western Mounted Policeman—who had also been in the Secret Service, and now he was a journalist. His worst troubles had been with Red Indians when drunk, but next in difficulty had come the large number of American outlaws who used to take part in pre-war gold rushes and booms in Texas and Oklahoma. To-day he assured me, his main interest was in the Bible and Bible prophecies, and he spent some time quoting me proof that the world is about to end, and he informed me he could never become a Roman Catholic because the Catholics had changed the Sabbath from Saturday to Sunday, and this led to a long dissertation on the advantages of the Seventh Day Adventist creed and a final summing up that people were getting every

day more interested in religion and in the Bible prophecies, and that he was determined to "make a good
thing" out of it in writing.

And so that night I left him on Chicago Heights and
took a bus the last few miles to Chicago. I had come
1,850 miles hitch-hiking all the way and I had had
enough. I had passed through what seems to me the
real America of to-morrow, and I had got to know, I
think, a representative crowd I could never else have
met of the 40,000,000 people that there complain the
East lets them be ruined while the East lends money
to Europe.

And part of that journey had been through that
Bible Belt, that influences America so much, that takes
no old maxim unless they prove it themselves—least
of all the one that "You cannot serve God and Mammon," and the resulting *mélange* with Mammon only
slightly winning is unique and fascinating.

It brought me to Chicago, the last few hundred
miles through cultivated but uninteresting country,
and I arrived with shoes nearly gone, suit in a worse
condition and needing a haircut badly. To no decent
hotel could I go that night, so I stopped at the
Y.M.C.A., an odd *mélange* again of religion and
business. The next morning I rushed off to get some
suitcases and out of them respectable clothes.

My well-tried grey flannels and my shoes retired
to the waste-paper basket—and I sallied forth, armed
with letters gathered in the West, to find a good hotel
on the Lake front—Michigan Drive, to have a haircut and to be just in time to lunch at a Woman's Club
—gloriously modern, and have delicious wine again,
and meet there ladies of Chicago.

One of them was Mrs. Rockefeller McCormack,
supposed once to have been the world's richest woman,
and daughter of the old Mr. Rockefeller. I think

these ladies only half believed my tale of where I'd been the day before—but they showed me in the next few days all I wanted to see of Chicago—and as I left them and walked along the Lake Shore Drive, and later amidst the skyscrapers of that marvellous Lake front, I smiled and thought it a funny ending to my ten days' tramp over nearly 2,000 miles of land.

CHAPTER XVII

AMERICA'S GREATEST PROBLEM

WHEN I was a child, a dear old priest used to cheer me up immensely by saying in sepulchral tones, "My boy, turn the searchlight of death upon your soul every evening." And nearly every morning and every evening at one time the world turned the searchlight of publicity on Chicago.

If the same searchlight had been as conscientiously turned on Paris or Marseilles or many another city, it is to be doubted if as the leading crime centre, Chicago would have held the reputation it holds to-day. A reputation largely gained by the go-ahead enterprise of its own newspapers, apt to dismiss quickly any reporter who does not bring in enough sensational tales for its extremely sensational headlines. And so perhaps we forget that Chicago has only one policeman for every 900 citizens, whereas London has one policeman for every 175 citizens.

And yet when all is said in its favour, the city has got to live down that in 1929, in its streets and houses, were exploded no less than 115 bombs with an average loss per bomb of $1,713 value—and there were no convictions; and in 1928, the city boasted 376 murders, of which 129 were unsolved, 37 resulted in acquittals, 39 jail sentences ensued, 16 murderers were declared insane and another 16 committed suicide, and in the eliminating gangster process so popular in Chicago and New York, 11 murderers were themselves killed—but in any case nobody was executed. Add to this the more material troubles that in 1930 the Municipality was on the verge of bankruptcy—40,123 public employees including police, firemen, school teachers, janitors and clerks were unpaid, back salaries aggregating $11,000,000, and over 1,643 widowed mothers were destitute with unpaid pensions, and you will feel that political graft has reached its zenith in this city with a future that probably is yet unrealised.

Here is the net result of allowing literally millions of foreigners—mostly of Latin or Slav races—to enter and swamp the country. Here is what a professor from Boston rightly described to me as: "America's India and Egypt—you English have to try and instil order in chaotic empires outside your own country— but we few with Anglo-Saxon traditions have a much more uphill battle to impress ourselves on the jumble of races that stretch from Philadelphia via Pittsburgh to Chicago."

And we in England can take a lesson from the chaos that is in many parts of Eastern America and remember it when we offer the thousand and one races, creeds, and traditions of a geographic name— India—the opportunity to govern themselves.

It is undoubtedly political graft that has put Chicago and other cities back, and it is as true that Prohibition has given political graft an amazing impetus. When then Al Capone was sentenced for only tax evasion, it was not so incongruous as it seemed at first sight. After gangster illegality has come tax evasion in the United States, and this has reached such alarming heights that the senior citizens, in the know, have been more worried over that than over anything else. They trace it to drink law evasions first—and that has done more than anything to make them—former ardent Dries—decide to vote Wet in future.

Needless to say for a stranger in the States for only a few months, to poke his nose into the intricacies of gangster life, would have taught him nothing and probably ended in an accident, and so I contented

243

myself with hearing from others, and seeing what I could.

Of Chicago, I shall never forget the memory of the glorious line of skycrapers along the lake front unequalled I think even by New York, nor shall I forget both there and in New York the shabbiness and sordidness of the slum streets often just behind the skyscrapers. There may not be ten people asleep in one room as in London, but as I went through those streets, as I visited Hull House in Chicago, and other settlements in New York, I never felt any more uplifted or in a better atmosphere there, amongst the Greeks and the Sicilians and the Irish, than in Canning Town, or Tidal Basin, or Poplar, Limehouse, or Whitechapel—and politics seemed to be very much on the same lines in both worlds.

They took me to a Republican meeting in Chicago down in the slums, the Halstead 43rd ward, and a little woman next me, when the Chairman said: "You can't blame them in England for not finding work, they haven't got the funds"—turned to me and said: "Do you think things are as bad in England as they say in the papers here?" and I answered: "No, I know they're not, I'm English." "Oh dear," said the little woman, "I wish my mother had heard you say that— she died last week and just before she died she sat up and she said, 'I'm worried about England.' She didn't speak again—she came from Putney forty years ago—we all did. I hope what you say is true."

And then we heard many speeches to cheer the audience—but the most sensible was from an Indian chief, who said many to-day were begging who didn't need a cent; and then got up an Italian orator who could only speak in broken English and he told us, in a fiery harangue, about Lincoln and the wonders of the eighteenth-century colonial patriots, and with him were many other foreign types. And after that I walked into a well-known ballroom to have supper, and there was not one solitary soul eating or dancing, and the band told me how they longed to come to the Kit-Cat in London.

Another day I motored to the University, where the President is only 32, and later to a luncheon of twelve fairly youthful rich Republicans who are trying to get the graft out of Chicago politics, and they included District Attorneys and State Senators.

There the head of Mayor Cermak's Unemployment Relief Committee told me Chicago has no Community Chest, for it is too big to group together all its charities, and that there were then at least 500,000 unemployed out of a population of 3,000,000 people in Chicago. "But," said he, "this year people are not sleeping under arches with hotels sending them out food— things are being better organised." He confessed the measures to be only temporary, as when improvement takes place, his group felt the majority of unemployed would be absorbed and then the Government would work out plans later to deal with the question more permanently—but many doubt if the Government will ever do this, should times get normal once again.

At the lunch, it was suggested as 400,000 citizens had lost money in the recent Chicago Bank failures— failures if we include amalgamations, which amounted to 150 banks in the city and county—some more prosecutions ought to be undertaken, but this was immediately hotly opposed by the District Attorney representing the banks, and they turned to discuss the position of the Republican Governor of the State— Illinois—who the Saturday before at the Races had been publicly booed by 15,000 people. They all admitted the present unpopularity of Republicanism, and realised the party needed reorganisation from top to bottom.

And they impressed me a lot with their earnestness, this body of youngish men who, as they said, wished to bring into politics the type that worked for their country in England without too much ulterior motive, and that afternoon I went to the voluntary Relief Organisation, which, backing the Civic Efforts, was in the hands of Samuel Insull, Jnr. Then the Insulls were the heroes of Chicago and working hard to help the unemployed—less than a year after, they were chased through Europe by the self-same city. Then they were raising $8,800,000 by Drives, Charity Race Meetings and Wrestling Matches for the poor, and in their office I met the famous Strangler Lewis. One of their most remunerative schemes was to get employees of different firms to give up one day's pay a month for the unemployed.

That night I left for Detroit—left a city racked by graft and in the slums by lawlessness, but a city where if that is put down, a future remains that is dazzling in its possibilities; and if the St. Lawrence, and the Lakes, and the Mississippi are all to become navigable right through, there are many who say Chicago will quickly take the place of New York as the American centre of America, just as to-day it is in many ways the most American city, and one, unless you are looking for gangsters, in which you can be as comfortable and as peaceful as in Cheltenham or Bath.

Detroit offered me little but a wet day and a sad drabness. Of all the cities of America, this, the fourth largest, is I understand the most communistically inclined. Its bonds stand lowest and here the more serious of this winter's riots took place. Nearby is the Ford Factory—but it is outside the city limits and does not pay towards the taxes that support the city's unemployed, many of whom were former Ford work-men. The company on the road—for I had travelled by stage bus to see the country which train-travel makes almost impossible—included some hoboes who had just their fare to Detroit—they enlivened us with a song called "Allelujah! I'm a Bum," and told me of the real difficulty now for anyone to get into Canada to get work, or if a foreigner, once in Canada to get back to America.

I visited the Windsor-Detroit Tunnel and was told how since the depreciation in value of the Canadian dollar, much fewer Canadians came to Detroit to do their shopping, finding prices too high, so that cross-river traffic was considerably lower than had been estimated when the tunnel was completed the year before. At the Employment Exchange, they told me that Packard and a few other motor companies are looking after their own unemployed, but that the Community Chest had still to raise over $3,000,000 and was finding it none too easy.

From Detroit I motored through attractive scenery along the shores of Lake Ontario, through Toledo —the city with the biggest number of bank failures in the United States—and so to Cleveland. Here over 1,000,000 people live in a gorgeous setting on the side of the lake looking across to the horizon over the water, beyond which is Toronto and Canada. Near to factory centres and such places as Akron, where the giant airship was built, and Youngstown, the steel centre—Cleveland has a large unemployment problem to tackle, no small part of which is Negro— and here they told me they hoped soon to adopt the Pittsburgh method whereby charitably inclined people buy a book of food tickets, and if a man asks you for money for food you give him the ticket, so that he cannot descend on the local speak-easy.

Eventually I passed on, occasionally seeing a factory, but mostly concentrating on unemployment, for the other sides of this part of the United States have been all too frequently seen, written about, and criticised before. I felt I knew them and I felt that at any rate there was nothing that was truly an American spirit here that I had not seen elsewhere.

It was a pretty drive to Pittsburgh through the autumn woods, and nobody could say that we were in a "Black Country" as around Birmingham, or Wolverhampton, or Durham in England. The approach even to Pittsburgh itself, a centre of cosmopolitan poverty and wealth in the United States, was pretty, along a river, and below the road above the water were still the chimneys of the factories. That night I walked amongst the few skyscrapers, passed the Mellon Bank, and so to the Grant Building from the top of which, thirty-seven stories up, I looked down at night on this city of Italians, Greeks, Jews and Negroes. Around me were hills, and furnaces could be seen blasting all along the river. The rivers converged, three of them, making the Ohio River that later joins the Mississippi, and moored along the river were the Show Boats and the night clubs of the city.

Next morning, I visited the Chamber of Commerce and talked with the Secretary of the Emergency Relief Fund. Every city seems to work its unemployment problem differently, and here everything was done voluntarily. It was a business organisation of wealthy citizens that controlled everything. They were trying to raise funds to pay the labour on any scheme the taxing authorities in the country might decide on, to help their unemployed, and they hoped to raise for this $3,000,000 which would employ 15,000 men, but there were 125,000 unemployed in their population of nearly 1,300,000.

Over and above this $3,000,000 they would try and raise another $2,900,000 to cover the other unemployed and their problems. But the secretary admitted that would probably not be enough and that the situation was extremely grave. Work first, then relief was to be the watchword, but officially the city was doing nothing other than to ask their employees to give three days' wages in six months to help the others.

It was not until I got to a large city in the Southern States, that I found a place where the civic authorities were compulsorily docking their employees' wages and giving that sum and that alone to help the unemployed —the taxpayers being asked to contribute nothing.

The secretary told me the committee was also studying the social problems of the future—though he felt (unlike the gentlemen in Chicago) that if all goes well—Big Business, and that means the Government, will feel it no longer incumbent to go on with social experiments. A disaster this, for slumps will recur frequently in the future, and he pointed out the National Social Services Survey for 1928–29 before the crisis had shown that machinery was fast supplanting manual labour, and that a goodly proportion of those unemployed to-day will remain permanently so, and already what seemed most serious was that the standard of living so proudly fostered in the States is fast disappearing, and all that could possibly be said for the present drift and lack of Federal legislation, was that the voluntary business stops fool legislation, and gives experience on which to work for future legislation, should it ever be brought in—as well as a body with which to function.

He finds many in Pittsburgh, not yet officially unemployed, are only doing three days a week or one week in two. And I remembered towns where I found the canvassers put down men as being in "Part time employment" who had only had one day's work within the last month. And there were many families too living on the generosity of the one member still working, and should that one lose his or her job, then, not one more, but perhaps seven or eight, would come on the generosity of the city's more charitable citizens.

It might not be so bad, this bad enough situation in districts where the people were all themselves native born and patriotic, but in areas like this part of America it was different, for the people had come there as to an Eldorado to make money and grow rich, and their affections for the others that were already rich, the country's traditions and its future could not be certain.

This still seems to me America's greatest problem— the foreign poor in the East and their care in times of stress—they make a festering wound that breeds poison.

This struck me forcibly when I next visited the Citizen's Class office, and was shown the papers new citizens get. They go to night classes and after five years' residence, and at least two years after filing their first papers, they take an examination in United States citizenship. You find the Jews the most active to naturalise themselves, and their brethren; and they themselves, those already citizens, have their own "field workers" who get together the legally required number—twenty women of Jewish origin, and then they can demand a teacher for themselves and so become citizens quicker through being better coached. For easy though the exam. may be, the intellect of the candidate is not often brilliant. The most illiterate, it seems, are the Southern Italians, and the Italian newspapers use every effort in Pittsburgh to make the Italian-born parents learn a bit more and so try and live up to the standards of their own children, educated in Pittsburgh.

Later, I turned to another side, and I walked on the golf links, passed the house of Mr. Mellon, almost the richest man in America, and from there down to the Carnegie Library and Gallery filled with beautiful things—through the exhibition of International Painting held annually with Carnegie funds, and then scattered through the States before returning to Europe.

For this purpose, a Director goes annually to Europe, collects the year's best pictures, brings them to show the Pittsburgh citizens, and sends them eventually back—insured all the way. And here I saw Laverys and Orpens, pictures from the United States, from France, Belgium and Austria, from Scandinavia, Germany, Spain and Italy, from Hungary and from Czecho-Slovakia, and also from Poland, and a room that was filled with pictures, mostly industrial scenes from Pittsburgh's new rivals—the Soviet Republics of Russia.

And as I came out, I looked across the street towards the huge skyscraper being built at the Pittsburgh University by Mr. Mellon, and to be called the Cathedral of Learning, and to cost over $3,000,000. And who could not but wonder at this unnatural difference between the foreign element, the poverty of this city, and its huge monuments to the wealthy bankers and steel magnates famed throughout the world.

That day I left for Harrisburg, over hills and through beautiful wooded scenery—I might have been in the heart of England, in Buckinghamshire or again in Derbyshire. Harrisburg was yet again something totally different. The capital of this vast state of Pennsylvania, that includes Pittsburgh and Philadelphia, it is little more than an old English town like Aylesbury or Thame.

The hotel might have had post-horses and a coach outside its yellow walls instead of stage buses, and round about the squares were red-brick Georgian houses with white porticoes and so along the drives to the river and the gorgeous Capitol, with trees along the roads, all dimly lit at night. Here were the Anglo-Saxon elements again fighting bravely with the aid of tradition against their India, their Egypt, that was Pittsburgh and Philadelphia.

And so I continued over the Alleghany Mountains, until next night, having passed Lancaster County and the Mennonites and those darkly garbed men and women of strange and old German sects, I came to that city that is the greatest blend of antiquity and modernity in America, Philadelphia, founded by old secret societies of Europe in the seventeenth and eighteenth centuries, and planned in parts to-day to rival Paris in its gorgeous width and the magnificence of its buildings.

CHAPTER XVIII

THE QUAKER CITY

IN Philadelphia I was again welcomed by friends from Wyoming and I received a hospitality that was American—American as one had heard of it before.

A bedroom, bathroom and sitting-room were mine —the use of a car and a chauffeur; and should I ever prefer the train, a season ticket into the heart of Philadelphia—for we were just outside as were most others of the Philadelphia families.

That night I listened in on the radio to a voice that came across the sea from London, and I heard the first results of our General Election. I heard of friends that were now M.P.'s, and I heard my former opponent Miss Susan Lawrence was defeated. Then, I, too, had I been at home, would have been in Parliament. For a moment, and indeed for several days, after all this hitch-hiking across a continent which had been a strain, it seemed a bit too much that I should also have missed an opportunity at home, an opportunity that might not recur again.

But in the meantime, there was a new city to see, and to see under the best of auspices. First was I taken to the museum, of unparalleled magnificence, and I saw whole rooms taken bodily from Sutton Scarsdale, and the living quarters of the Tower of London—whole chapels from Spain and Renaissance Rooms from Italy, huge carpets from the East and almost entire houses from the Pennsylvania Dutch— those half Quakers, half German Mennonites that still people the farm lands of Pennsylvania. From there we went on to the building of the Curtis Publications, and here we entered the sacred precincts of the

Saturday Evening Post and its Editor, and the man who made it so powerful an influence in America, Mr. Lorimer.

To see this great man, one had to get a ticket, and once admitted we went through offices and rooms that were elaborate in their modern frescoes and their panelling, and at the end we found Mr. Lorimer—a small man who, perched on the window-sill, did all the talking and told me all about British politics, and made himself really pleasant. Later I was shown over all the plant—the plant that produces weekly over three million copies of the *Saturday Evening Post*, nearly one and a half million copies of the *Woman's Home Journal*, and also a large edition of the *Country Gentleman*.

That evening I talked with the servants and found the outdoor ones were all English and Scotch, and the indoor ones German, and later we went to see Raymond Massey act "Hamlet" in an elaborate Bel Geddes production.

Next day I concentrated on the Community Chest and was a guest at a big lunch the Chest gave in the Bellevue Stratford Hotel. This was to inaugurate the preparations for their coming drive to raise $9,000,000 to help over a quarter of a million unemployed. I talked a long time with Mr. Bookman, who is the head of the Welfare organisations of Cincinnati, a city that like the others had grouped all its Charities together into a Community Chest to make one joint annual appeal. They told me on all sides, at this lunch where were gathered together all the social and religious workers of the city, as well as some of the business men and the society leaders, that Cincinnati had the reputation of being the most go-ahead city for social work in America.

But Mr. Bookman told me that he and his fellow

workers were far from happy at the effect the English sweeping national majority would have on the reactionary elements in the United States. He was certain—and you could already see it in the newspapers—that they would interpret their victory as one that meant death to the dole and death to unemployment insurance. Such was the opinion, no matter how much we denied it, and Bookman felt sure it meant the further postponement on the part of the Government of any effort in America to work out a permanent scheme for unemployment. And I could not help but be amused that the only four opinions extensively quoted in the American papers on the result of the English elections as serious, were those of Lloyd George, Ramsay MacDonald, Stanley Baldwin—and Bernard Shaw!

My next day was spent in Germantown—just outside Philadelphia, and historically one of the most interesting suburbs in the world. You simply cannot understand anything of America and its Puritanism unless you see something of the religious sects that have been, and still are, all over the country. Their influence, direct and indirect, has all along been momentous, and if they seem strange, crude and eccentric, a large proportion of the saner Americans to-day are themselves descended from such strange, crude and eccentric ancestors.

In Germantown you find the chapels and the tombs of those earlier seventeenth- and eighteenth-century Mennonites—that, mixed up with societies such as the Rosaecrucians—made Pennsylvania strong—invented much that was valuable, started up the strange houses of Ephreta and Wissahikon—and spread right across America and into Canada and Central America, and to-day are still bringing out their brethren from Southern Russia.

Only a few months ago they spent $25,000 to form a colony in Paraguay on the borders of Bolivia where these people, who are Pacifists and Conscientious Objectors, were unlucky enough to be the first to be bombed in the recent dispute between these two Southern States.

But there are a dozen other sects that started from this suburb, and I spent a long time in the chapel of one—the Dunkards—or, to give them their more official title, the "Church of the Brethren."

As I entered the chapel, I was interested in some of the notices on the walls—homilies one should call them, and two read as follows:

"The Ladder of Life is full of Splinters—but they always prick the hardest when we're sliding down."

and:

"If you want to be Satisfied with your lot—build a Service Station on it."

For the benefit of English readers, a Service Station in America is where you get petrol on the road.

In the vestibule of the chapel are hangers where the women leave their hats and put on veils—whilst in more conservative districts the women do not ever wear hats, but only black bonnets.   And in the chapel, the pews were so built that they pull down, forming a table, and twice a year the Lord's Supper is served here as they believe it was served in the time of Our Lord.

Underneath the chapel is a kitchen where the supper is cooked, and above the men sit together and the women together. They have a tablecloth and knives and forks, and they wash each other's feet, and then they have soup—which is a meat one—and a meat dish which must always be lamb, and unleavened bread, and they still use wine, that is now plain grape juice and is poured into glass cups, and while eating they read the Scriptures.

But in Chicago, they are more up to date, they have abolished the kitchen and instead of having a lamb dish for the Lord's Supper, they have lamb sandwiches.

That afternoon I went to hear the famous Philadelphia Philharmonic Symphony Orchestra, and the theatre was crowded to capacity, and later I dined with the Senator and his wife whom I had met in Wyoming. They were leading Quakers, and they gave me two volumes to read on the old-time Quakers and Pennsylvanian religious sects that abounded around Philadelphia, and in my honour, as an Irishman, they had placed a pot of shamrock in front of each guest and afterwards we went to see Henry IV given by the Stratford Players.

I went behind to see a friend and he told me that a foreign actor in America, after he has had one part, cannot accept another contract part for six months— so that it becomes a gamble when an actor crosses the Atlantic if his play will be a success or not, and if not, and he wishes to stay on, he is stranded workless for six months.

Next evening I was again taken to the theatre, by my hostess with a party of twelve, and we went on to the Saturday Evening Club at the Bellevue Stratford Hotel where all Philadelphia seemed to have forgotten the slump, and champagne and whisky flowed freely— but mostly the latter, for everybody had brought their own, and the men of our and other parties could be seen arriving with huge paper bundles of bottles.

Next day I watched a Swedenborgian Service in the Swedenborgian Cathedral outside Philadelphia. Not unlike the new Buckfast Abbey in England, it is

257   R

impressively large and beautiful—built, and not yet finished, almost regardless of cost, by the richest Swedenborgian families who have started this wealthy colony on the outskirts of the city with their own schools, houses for less wealthy members, and other buildings. The colony, largely Scandinavian, and also largely English, is now the chief centre of the followers of Swedenborg throughout the world.

As I stood at the great door of the cathedral, I looked at the length of the nave to the altar and the beautiful windows above it, and over all was a Swedish crown of gold lit in a faintly blue tint, and the choir, male and female, were in black and white, whilst the tall clergymen in this lofty Gothic church wore long flowing white garments with red albs that added brilliantly to the colour.

The verger, who showed me so many of the best works of the cathedral, came himself, as did his wife, from Colchester in Essex, where there are many Swedenborgians—and after talking of the mysticism of their old-time founder, we discoursed about the Colchester Oyster Feast and their former Member of Parliament, Sir Laming Worthington-Evans, and of the outings in Colchester to which I used to bring the Conservative women from my own Essex constituency, West Ham, and this man told me he had gone from Philadelphia to Canada during the war and joined the Canadian Army and later returned to America.

Soon after, I was taken to a meeting of the Republican Women's Club with Mrs. Lorimer presiding. I was the only male guest present, and all the ladies, ranging from old age to newly married, were there to listen, like all good American women, to a lecture.

The lecturer was the head of the Police of Phila-

The Swedenborgian Cathedral near Philadelphia

delphia—Major Schofield—and he had succeeded
General Butler who was lecturing in Denver when I
had passed through, and General Butler had then
advocated a National Police Force to be drafted here
and there throughout America and so avoid local
graft and bribery. But Major Schofield told the ladies
the days of graft in the Philadelphia Police were over,
that he had had to enforce many reforms and get rid
of old policemen who could not have run a hundred
yards, and who had been accustomed for years to be
on one beat, and he assured them he knew of no boot-
legging now in the city, and this statement was much
clapped.

Unfortunately I could not wait to have tea with this
gentleman as I had to leave for a house where I was
to meet the head of the Philadelphia bootleggers, the
leading gangster, and the local rival of Al Capone. The
man was small and shy, Jewish yet with a round, rather
decadent face—mild-looking and kind. He wore a
brown suit and there was a large diamond in his gold
ring. He was amused when I told him what Major
Schofield had said and he replied: "Yes, I saw his car
to-day, and I noticed he has changed his number
plate." He could not, he said, let me go with the
bootleggers, for once with them you can never leave
them. Their secrets are too precious. And those
noises of guns going off after dark—just one shot in a
silent night—that I sometimes heard from my room
out there in the country near Philadelphia—those he
told me were the signals of men on the main roads
hearing the police and warning the cartloads of drink
that might be coming by the lanes.

Drink he said was motored in quite often across the
border from Canada and again in the South from
Mexico—but more often the drink came in from the
sea. He spoke of those boats waiting outside the

limit, from which motor-boats run in to shore and play hide and seek with the Customs' pinnaces.

But he said the worst risk to him was from sea pirates—for now there were many pirates that themselves held up the bootleggers smuggling along the coast, and he told me of fights out at sea that were as exciting as those of eighteenth-century corsairs. In the early days, if one load out of every four got through, it paid you to be a bootlegger, but now it must be three out of every four, for the graft-middlemen of the trade are so numerous and the bribes that have to be paid so heavy, a profit is difficult to obtain. He told me that more than one of the biggest business men in Philadelphia had offered him large sums to join their staffs—for his flaire for business organisation one could see, was little short of brilliant, but he had refused—and it was obvious why—he dare not quit— he was with the bootleggers for good or for bad to the end; and another business man told me that evening that a bootlegger had that day offered him for a tenth their value the accounts of once rich men in the city who owed him money for drink—but could not pay and he had no power to collect.

To-day the bootlegger's job is not an easy or very profitable one—yet they vote regularly for Prohibition, and my gangster friend told me he had tried to penetrate the Chicago and the Florida ring, but he was frozen out by Al Capone—and he also found the New York hotel keepers were frightened to deal with other than New York bootleggers.

All through these big cities there is a racket in almost every phase of industry. You cannot carry on business in this trade or in that without paying tribute to some group of racketeers who else will burn down or blow up your office or otherwise ruin you, and in New York, besides a milk racket, there is even a cloak-room racket, and in all the hotels and night clubs a cloak-room girl cannot hold her job unless she pays tribute to the ring—so that your tips must be big to be appreciated and to make it possible for her to live. And he left us, this well-mannered, quiet gangster, in a taxi, but he first gave the friend I was with a present of half a dozen expensive handkerchiefs.

And for all I know to-day, he may be dead and another reigning in his stead—but if he is alive, he could prove to the world there is still excitement and romance for the Dick Turpins of the twentieth century.

Next I went out, after a lunch in a delightful Georgian house in the eighteenth-century quarter of Philadelphia, with a hostess who writes well and keeps a literary salon both here and in New York, to the studio of Mr. Wyeth the mural painter, near Wilmington, and on to the house of John Hempel—who stood last for the Governorship of Pennsylvania—a house that reminded me of early Georgian days with its high red-brick wall on the village green, and its low ceilings and attractive stairs—and then again on to West Chester to visit a writer I had often longed to meet, a writer of those early days in America—Joseph Hergesheimer.

We found him in his small converted Pennsylvania Dutch farm-house—which he calls the Dower House. And at first no one was sure how the meeting would go, for if he does not like you, he says so—but we brought with us a deaf lady, and so everybody had to shout and that broke the ice. There was much noise in the small dining-room as we all sat round the shining mahogany table, with good coloured German and Dutch glass along the walls, panelled and painted white, and we drank a potent whisky cocktail that Mr. Hergesheimer himself prepared.

His wife talked to all while he told me quietly how he had lectured and told his audience of an author who never existed, and how a bookseller in San Francisco had told one of his audience that he was sold out of that author's work.

Mr. Hergesheimer is a man of medium stature with shaggy eyebrows, and his picture in another small room painted by Wyeth, made him look exactly like the Cardinal, Archbishop of Westminster. He told me that he had just spent three months in Berlin, and that he was sure it will eventually take the place of Paris for gaiety, and he advised me there were only two ways of describing a country, when he heard I was writing about America. One way is to describe it economically—impossible for me after so short a visit—and the other just exactly as you see it yourself, and if I did that, he strongly advised me whatever else I described, not to forget the all-important religious sects, the backbone of modern American history.

He has another cottage in the village where he goes to work and where none may disturb him, and in the evenings he goes down to the village and plays poker or backgammon with the villagers in the inn.

When we left him, we talked of the religious sects of Pennsylvania, and they told me of the origin of the word "Sacking."

In those olden days, 150 years ago, when a young farmer went to visit other farmers, usually the distance was too great for him to return the same night. But the houses then were small and spare bedrooms, even spare beds, were usually unknown, so the guest would have to sleep in the same room and often bed as a daughter of the house; both guest and daughter would be put in sacks, tied at the top, and both carried to bed and left there safely for the night—this was in Pennsylvania with the Quakers, and not so long ago.

Next I concentrated on the unemployed of Philadelphia and dined one evening at the leading Settlement. There were about twenty of us at table, and they included one or two people who had studied Social Service at Toynbee Hall in London, and others came from Settlements in other parts of America. Afterwards they showed me their plans for a theatre run in connection with the nation-wide group of Settlements, and I saw the house where they made pottery, the boys and the girls, and their gymnasium, their clinic, and their playrooms, and afterwards I left this Greek—Italian—Irish poor quarter, where also there were negroes, and went to see the Municipal Lodging House, an old converted factory or may be it was a garage, where Philadelphia could house over 4,000 men, homeless men and many of them transient hoboes.

At the door stood the janitors—tall, strong, themselves unemployed now working for their keep. On the next floor and in a big hall the men registered, gave their names, the address of their nearest relative, how long they had been in the States, their former work, and so on. Three nights was the limit they could stay if they came from other cities—but the local men—for them some work might be found in the building—they could cook perhaps, or be waiters, or run the showers, the fumigating plant, the concerts, be janitors, or just clean out the rooms each morning.

They took me up to the top, to the floor first where the whites were lodged, then to the floor of the negroes. In each, the rules were the same. Below the men had been given a bed ticket. They reached their beds, undressed, hung their clothes on a hook in regulation order with shirts beneath and coats on top, and half a hundred always got it wrong. Their clothes were passed through the fumigator if they were new men, and they moved to the shower.

Here, washing, were negroes, men well over six foot tall, stallions of a healthy breed you might well call them—fine long shiny silk-like backs, muscles standing out, but workless, powerless in all their strength against the havoc of modern machinery. And then they went before the doctor—the examination was reasonably efficient, and on to a row of benches. Here a little ridiculous, they sat stark naked, those tall finely built negroes, and beside them white-haired older negroes, many bent and thin, ribs showing, and others looking vacantly into space, just wondering where and why they were, and after the regulation five minutes—through the door would come their clothes and they went and hung them up where they were told and went into the beds most of them naked—or else they took their vests or shirts, if they preferred it, and putting them on, retired warmer to sleep.

Down below on the next floor the whites looked much the same—ex-soldiers many, but somehow their physique did not seem to be just quite so good. It was not until ten o'clock that all need go to bed; before that time, they could, and did, stay in the recreation room—one huge room a whole floor long, and negroes and whites mixed here indiscriminately, and it was the habitual laugh, the cheerfulness that nothing can damp that is always in the negro, that made towards the noise and the gaiety of this room.

Rightly the city had decided that to save the men's morale was all-important, and games and concerts had been organised in that recreation hall. On Mondays and Thursdays whites and blacks joined in boxing bouts, on Tuesdays and Fridays there was music, and the negro jazz urged all to cheer up once again. Wednes-

days and Saturdays there were pool games, and there
was a cinema show given for those 4,000 men, and on
Sundays there was Church and a few less exciting
games. Such was the life they lived.

The city recognised, it seems, no dole, but they
were reasonable enough to realise something must be
done to keep away starvation and worse than that,
depression. The citizens did not interest themselves
notably in the work, and only a few visited the lodging-
house—but the city officials were conscientious about
it and the Mayor of Philadelphia went himself incog-
nito, got a bed, a shower bath, and a general fumiga-
tion—and when I heard it my mind travelled back to
the Lord Mayor of London, and I thought of his
being fumigated.

But it was a big effort for the city, and their voluntary
effort to raise that 9 million dollars began also about
this time. It was ushered in with a huge dinner and
huge subscriptions. The money, and more was raised
in a month, and on that first evening sirens blew in the
river, and all through the city as on New Year's Eve,
and the Mayor's appeal and that of the Commander
of their Drive were broadcast to every home, and
from then on, daughters of different big houses went
about canvassing their neighbours and their neighbours' servants and everyone was supposed "to give
until it hurt."

The next Sunday brought me to the Catholic Old
Cathedral. Outside it was a plaque to Barry, the
Naval Commander against the British in the War of
Independence and an Irishman, and there was a
reference to the Service there for a Republic on July 4,
1779, and on another plaque was recorded that on
November 4, 1781, there had been a Te Deum offered
here attended by the American and French troops in
the presence of the French and Spanish Ambassadors,

and the English flags captured in battle had been lain upon the altar.

And I looked round, and just opposite all this, on the other side of the street, to-day stands the British Consulate, proudly displaying the British shield. I walked in and it was to attend the 150 Years Mass to celebrate Yorktown Battle.

The Cardinal presided, and there was much pomp and ceremony and a brilliant preacher told us how no Revolution would have been successful had not the French religious orders at the critical moment lent money to the armies fighting the English, and the celebrant of the Mass was a Father Washington, great-great-nephew of George Washington. The church was packed, and I was an interested spectator, and later visited Franklin's tomb, the Hall of Liberty, and Christ Church where Washington and others had worshipped.

Then, just before I left Philadelphia, I dined with some of those really wealthy Philadelphians one often reads about, and next morning early they were all off to the Whitney racecourse where the Aintree Grand National Course is being rivalled, and they hope later will be outdone. Like in the Kentucky Derby, though for tradition's sake they thank God they left us, many of these people still love us for our sport and copy our traditions whenever they can.

But in their cheerfulness at the prospects of this race, I knew that for some it was forced, for one man had told me if by the following week he could not raise an almost impossible sum, his family's business for forty years must close down and he be virtually ruined. And my hostess had that morning told me she knew of now seven friends in their own little district who had recently committed suicide—penniless, and their nerves frayed or gone, and one only that morning had been found dead in his garage in his car.

Such was the Philadelphia of the early nineteen-thirties, facing some bravely, some hysterically, a crisis the citizens could not rightly understand.

CHAPTER XIX

SEEN IN NEW YORK

In New York I next spent six weeks—almost exactly one year after my first arrival—and my most interesting experience was as guest of the police.

One morning before 8.45, I was at the police headquarters—down towards the Wall Street section of the city, and a police-sergeant took me up, as arranged, to see "the line up." This is the mildest form of the American third-degree—it is the questioning by spot-light of all those accused of more serious crimes, and arrested the night before. There was a large hall filled with rows of seats, and alternately half the detectives of New York come here every morning. They looked fat, healthy, ordinary citizens as they sat there all around me, men and women, waiting. I was in the third row, and in front of me, in their uniforms, sat the more important heads of the police. Then still further in front were three more chairs.

We all stood up as their occupants entered—for it was Mulroony, the head of the police, and his assistants. Slowly in driblets of twos and threes, dishevelled, some after an unpleasant night in the cells, men criminals and also women, negroes, foreigners, and American whites, they were brought in, some from one police station, some from others.

In front of all was a large raised dais—a sort of stage, and behind it was a huge white board with coloured lines that showed men's heights. And then they called out names. First one man was pushed forward and he mounted the steps. All lights were out except the spot-light burning down fiercely on him, and in the audience sat half a hundred detectives or more waiting to see if they recognised him for some crimes of the past. Just in front of him was a microphone through which his voice could be heard, and behind him were the lines against which came his uncovered head showing that he was just under six feet tall.

Straight in front of him, on a block of wood four steps up with a microphone and controlling the spotlight, stood a police officer with a voice that was none too soft. He asked the man his name, and told him of what he was accused. He had taken a small girl to his room. He denied it. The officer, in a gruffer tone, told him how the landlady and others had sworn evidence that he had done so. He began to hedge. It was enough. The officer read out his past history. The man had done it before, and it made one feel ill. He saw the game was up and remained silent. They took him away.

Then came three men, receivers of stolen goods and thieves. Under a strenuous and clever cross-questioning, the whole story came out. Before this crowd—looking at the light and into the darkness beyond—the men were frightened and became confused. Others came, one would not confess. For half an hour he stood there on the stand while yet others were tried, and between each case he was brought forward again, and at last he confessed.

And then a man accused of murder. He, too, finally gave in, and the moment seemed to me the most dramatic one of all. Then later came two boys. They had robbed with violence in a tunnel. And one had only known the other a week, and he had been told the other had never done it before. "Never before," laughed the officer, and read out half a dozen convictions and sentences for this boy that seemed scarce twenty. And as each conviction was read out, the other lad looked more surprised and more disgusted so that it was a comedy to see, and I laughed for my own nerves were completely on edge.

And then the last case. Two men, Filipinos or perhaps Japanese—they had attacked a man—they did not know he was dead and they listened with cold interest as the officer told them of their murder. For all these cases there was no counsel for defence and these creatures, scared as they mostly were, were one against one hundred.

And yet there is much in favour of the methods that make the third degree. A few, even many cases, there may be where grave injustice is done, where even death ensues, and yet against it all, we must remember these police have got to deal with criminals that are the toughest in the world—murderers and blackmailers that are of European nationalities—and they have known no other police methods; if these police of New York and other cities did not sometimes put the fear of God into these people, the crime statistics of the United States would be a thousand times worse—but perhaps they would not—for crimes would never be discovered.

Next they took me down to the finger-print room, where they promised me they would give me the only impression taken. I had myself finger-printed and took away the result. Near me were those already sentenced, and they were finger-printed one by one, and they took me into the developing room where they kept and classified finger-prints that could be telegraphed all over America in a few hours, and I met their specialists who could classify types, and they showed me their criminals' portrait gallery that included Al Capone and Legs Diamond at different stages of their careers.

From there I went with a guide to the other end

of New York to the Armoury, where the police students were in training doing their final intensive course before becoming patrolmen—a course that lasts for ninety days. Here they were doing the physical courses, and some were preparing for a boxing match they would have that week in Brooklyn with the local inhabitants, all part of the programme to make the police more popular with the people. And in a room downstairs, in groups of ten, the doctor from the nearby hospital was giving them a strenuous test that was mental as well as physical, for recently there had come up cases of policemen that were epileptics. They allowed me to go and sit with the doctor and I stopped with him for over an hour.

One by one the young men, nearly all of them six feet tall, and one or two negroes that would become policemen in Harlem, came in and were questioned minutely about their relations, their own antecedents, their hobbies, their family's health and the reason why they wished to join the police force. In many cases they gave as reason that they wanted steady employment, and I was interested at the large number that had already been taxi-drivers. They were in age between 24 and 30, as well as I remember. Next they undressed and all ten came in together naked and in a row. They were told to close their eyes and then stand on one leg, put out their hands, move them backwards and forwards before their noses, open and close their fingers, and so on, and to me it was amusing to see those well-built and also fat negroes, Irishmen, Germans and pure Americans tottering naked from side to side and themselves not knowing any reason for these absurd contortions, whilst the doctor explained it quietly to me.

Then I went back to their classes at police head-

271

quarters and they let me attend them, sitting as a student, sharing the notebooks and the primers of the young policemen.

I went into the museum of the police and their library, where we talked of the Mafia of Sicily and other secret societies whose activities were to-day being repeated in America, and I was shown photographs and relics of famous murderers and various implements, the uses of which are taught these future guardians of the law. Their chief had been born and bred until he was near twenty years of age in the Midlands of England, and they assured me, and I agreed, from what I had already seen, that the actual training of the New York police was as good as that of any police force—the only difficulty came from the top, where political influence often made it impossible for the policemen to carry out their duties as they would have liked—and it was not one police officer that told me this but half a dozen.

They also explained to me their new methods for trying to keep children from surroundings in the slums that breed crime, and they told me of the immense assistance that is given them by the staffs of the local Settlements. Then they showed me their notebooks for the young policemen, and some of the hints for tackling crime intrigued me as a foreigner.

For instance, amongst the different ways of working homicides were the following:

Homicides, having revenge and jealousy as motives, are committed by:
(a) Gangsters.
(b) Bootleggers.
(c) Former Sweethearts, etc.

and again, under "Disposal of body when carted from scene of crime," comes "Dismembering body of

VICTIM often resorted to by perpetrator to make disposal easier."

In these cases:

> (*a*) parts are taken in bundles and dropped at different places.
> (*b*) different members of the body are often deposited around same locality.
> (*c*) body sections may be stuffed into trunk or barrel and transported to outlying section in vehicle and dumped.

And for arsonists, I found they may burn houses by setting on fire baby carriages usually under the wooden stairs in the hall.

For a bank robbery, the criminal is apt to select banks where armoured cars are not provided for transferring the money. And here I must refer to what struck me more in New York than in Chicago—the number of armoured cars used by shops in delivering their goods, to avoid being held up by gangsters. Comments on the bank robbers include:

> If there is any possibility of their identity being known by the bank messenger or guards, they shoot to kill without giving warning.

Burglars in New York it seems carry their tools either

> (*a*) In musical cases such as violin cases, banjo cases, mandolin cases.
> (*b*) In leather brief case.
> (*c*) In suitcase.
> or (*d*) Wrapped in paper.

It also seems that in regard to flat robberies—the burglar who burgles in the evening is usually not armed—whereas the one who burgles after midnight is armed and will shoot to kill; therefore after mid-

273   s

night one would be well advised to resign oneself to one's loss. And in regard to apartment burglars, they are classed as two types—the Supper Man and the Night Man. They have, it seems, two different techniques, and work at supper-time or after midnight.

As regards New York gangsters, "though they are not organised, gangsters are governed by a code of ethics. They will not inform upon one another unless to save themselves, and they generally settle all differences amongst themselves." Further, "The assassins are known as the 'Killers' and hold themselves open for employment as such. They are generally well dressed, and look like clerks." But the notes that interested me most were those on the drug sellers.

The Drug Seller:
Organisation:
    (*a*) The dealer or boss.
    (*b*) The agent.
    (*c*) Look-outs.
    (*d*) Runners.

Operate: Where:
    (*a*) One day of the week the agent will be at a specified corner between the hours of 9 and 11 a.m.
    (*b*) The next day he will be at a different corner, from 11 a.m. to 1 p.m.
    (*c*) The following day he will be at a different corner from 1 p.m. to 3 p.m., and so on.

Operate: How:
    (*a*) The boss has one or two agents on his staff.
    (*b*) The agents obtain the drugs from the boss:
        1. They take their posts on corner as outlined above.
        2. Have what are called "look-outs" who watch for police or Government agents.
        3. The "look-outs" are often schoolboys.

4. When a stranger who appears to be connected with police is observed in the neighbourhood, look-out informs the agent, who

5. Packs up and moves to new location, leaving "look-out" behind to direct addicts.

(c) Agent has quarter-ounce packages at certain locations and half-ounce packages at others, and so forth.

(d) Addict pays the agent, whose station is at a safe distance from where the drug is secreted.

(e) Agent directs him to go to an address and at a particular place, as under the stoop or under mat in hallway he will find drugs.

(f) Sometimes young boys are used as runners to secure the drug from the boss, the agent paying them 10 cents for each package delivered.

(g) Agent sometimes operates from a furnished room.

(h) In this case:

1. He takes money from the addict in the street, and

2. Instructs him to wait on a certain corner in front of a conspicuous object as a sign, water hydrant, store or bank.

3. Informs him that a man will pass him the drug.

4. Agent returns to furnished room, describes addict to a runner, and tells him where he will be found.

5. Gives drug to the runner who delivers it to the addict.

After the police I visited the headquarters of another organisation, the Junior League.

In most countries of the world there is a definite Society with a big S, and usually you can tell when you are in it. You will find it in France in the Faubourg St. Honoré; in Rome in the Blacks and the Whites; in London at Ascot or at the house of a wealthy American; but in America—though the Americans will tell you they can tell themselves instinctively—the foreigner is at sea going from big city to big city—each of which has its own Society, admitting no other to be its better. And there seems only one link across the country, the Junior League.

This organisation was started over thirty years ago by the debutantes of New York to distribute the numerous bouquets they received to the hospitals, and even till to-day all the girls in the different cities of America for whom, shall we say, a "coming out" dance is given—though I do not know if that is necessarily the qualification, it probably is not—join their branch of this league and do very useful social work—learn from lecturers what they want to know, as long as it is not politics, and make clothes for the poor and generally are useful. They have large offices and a club in New York, where I was shown their organisation, and they have annual meetings and conventions—but as their secretary put it to me: "unlike the Kiwanis and Rotarians, we always put in private houses the visiting delegates."

From then on I did very much the same as in other big capitals, seeing little that was typically American, but much that was New York. I was taken to private dance clubs that only meet three or four times a year, such as the Jinks Club, to speakeasies, night clubs, first nights with dramatic critics, and literary clubs like the Coffee House, and literary dinners like the P.E.N. Club Dinner.

On Thanksgiving Day and Christmas Day, New Yorkers were as kind to me as ever, and I lunched with them at their big family lunches, once with the head of the Farm Board, carving appropriately enough the turkey, and quite cheerful after appearing the day before at a Senate Inquisition.

I spent my six week-ends in the country, one in a Connecticut artists' colony where everybody lived

in converted old New England farm-houses, once in
a Connecticut Congressman's home, near his own
factory, and I heard he was likely eventually to be
Republican Governor of that State, and there I met
the famous Colonel Cooper who, with his wife, lives
in Russia and looks after all the many American industries that are busy helping Russia bring her Five
Year Plan to fruition. And I spent a week-end in
the Far Hills, where there were forty people at a
dinner party, plenty of champagne, the men guests
many in red hunt-coats, and not a few English guests,
and a negro band came down from New York that
we might dance afterwards.

Then I spent three week-ends at Tuxedo Park—
which showed me how even the American rich love
to live in community for their enjoyment and not to
do things on their own. Here was a park, so fashionable that the dinner jacket in America has been called
after it as a Tuxedo—a park with 200 inhabitants
and covering over 9,000 acres, of which my host
owned twenty-five acres. You join the club and you
take shares in the park. You have your own land,
and you share communally the roads, the tennis (including a real tennis court), the swimming, the skating,
the taxicabs, the saloon on the train for business men
morning and evening, and the general club life.

Here one night, I sat next the daughter of the
President of one of the lines on which I had ridden
as a hobo. She told her father, and he had no idea
that hoboes went on his train—though sometimes
there were 100 a day; and another day I talked there
to the head of one of the biggest banks of America,
and he was not sorry for this slump, for he felt in
the West it would turn out the new man who had
recently taken to farming and knew nothing about
it; and it would force back from their idle life on the

Pacific Coast those still middle-aged people who had made their pile but knew their business, and they would have to go back and work at what they knew. In short, he felt it a good, if painful, shaking down for the nation.

And there I saw the New Year in at their fancy dress dance—but Tuxedo was depressed, for many of the inhabitants were stockbrokers. Next day, in the snow, we went to Mass in the Catholic Chapel of the village, for many of the inhabitants of Tuxedo are catholics, and later we went to a tea-party where we drank a strange New Year drink called Egg Nogg.

And when I was again in New York I had tea with Colonel House in his small flat on Park Avenue that was full of photographs of President Wilson and his contemporaries. Colonel House seemed depressed at the situation, and he told me how dangerous he felt it was—that if not that winter then by the next there were almost sure to be riots and he only hoped no attempt at revolution.

And he complained to me that people in Europe would not realise that the Americans are most excitable people and more easily roused than in any other country; and after talking much about the States and advising me strongly to see Speaker Garner as the most interesting man in Washington, I left this delicate, polite little man from Texas, whose influence on Europe during and after the years of the war was almost as great as his influence on America.

Next I visited the Settlements and had dinner with Miss Wald at the Henry Street Settlement. Here Ramsay MacDonald and his daughter have been visitors—the latter frequently, and though I was an English Conservative, a thing my hostess disapproved of totally, I was allowed to speak a few words afterwards and to see all their work.

What struck me most here, in Philadelphia and in Chicago, was that Settlements do all the pioneer work in social service in the slums, and when it is successful, they hand over the work to the Municipality, leaving themselves and their money free to start experiments in something else, and so they are not tied down as in England with works that the civic authorities should undertake and with lack of funds for increased development. From there I went to the hostels for the homeless men. Many more thousand than in Philadelphia were to be housed here, down on the river next to the Millionaires' Yacht Club, and no attempt was made to keep them during the day, to find them work, on the premises, or to give them amusements. It was just sheer dole, and all the effort made was to prevent the men stopping more than three days, to keep them clean, and to discover any foreigners that were illegally in the country; so that in the end, one found hundreds more who could not, or would not, go in; and in the cold, and often snow, they tried to live in archways or down by the river and to suffer in silence—for baths they did not appreciate!

I visited the centres for raising relief funds, I heard how foreign artists were giving benefit concerts, and how others, paying a tax for their ordinary profits to the State, would do no more. I heard the complaints of city men, hard hit, who had to give for their firms as largely as those not hard hit—for the sake of advertisement; and if they did not give, people would talk, so that instead they had to dismiss a few more clerks; and I heard at cocktail parties given by the ladies responsible for collecting in whole areas of New York the latest reports on what funds were coming in.

It was not so difficult to raise money in New York,

for here lived all the rich; and many gave in New York where they should have given more in Pittsburgh, Cleveland or Detroit, from which perhaps their millions came, but which they did not visit, and where they neither subscribed nor were taxed.

Then came a ghastly visit to the City Morgue, where a Dickensian character, a cripple, showed me the bodies—those stored and iced and unclaimed, and those packed and embalmed ready for postage to relatives abroad; and my guide informed me smilingly, "Curiosity, you know, killed the cat." Lastly I visited two types of hospital.

First the Bellevue City Hospital, run by the Municipality, untidy, dark and miserable; and then the Rockefeller Institute, where no money is spared to diagnose new types of cases.

From there I went to their other buildings, and I learnt of the functions of the Rockefeller Foundation that since 1913 has given out over £30 million, of which large sums each year are distributed in a thousand ways all over the world and in the British Empire, Oxford and Cambridge and other English Universities, as well as hospitals often receiving large grants. A whole volume could be written of this wonderful work, and to me, one of the American traditions of which America should be proudest is that when you have made vast sums of money—however you have made them—you should distribute them systematically to be of use to the world. Here, in the Rockefeller Foundation, before, in such efforts as the Mellon Cathedral of Learning, the Carnegie Libraries, Technical Schools and Galleries, and the Harkness Fellowship, and later in the John Hopkins Hospital that I was next to visit in Baltimore, and the Rosenwald Fund, I found a unique system of princely donations that were gestures to the world and not just small national or parochial gifts.

And before I left I walked through the Institute where, in a painless way, I saw experiments being made that required 2,000 mice a week, hundreds of monkeys that cost $15 each and were brought from India. In the cages were parakeets, rabbits, rats and chimpanzees, and in other rooms were stalls occupied by goats, by horses, and even by zebras. All these to fight disease, and so far the result is the conquest of hookworm in the South, and yellow fever throughout most of the world—to mention but two outstanding successes.

In the end I climbed the Empire State Building at sunset. It did not exist when I landed a year before—and I looked down on the millions of lights that made New York and its suburbs a city the most international in the world—and yet a city that to me will never mean America or more than its smallest part. The money that is Wall Street and the stage, these are the only two great influences on America that emanate from New York.

CHAPTER XX

WASHINGTON AND THE CATHOLIC CHURCH

WHEN I was in Utah, Senator Smoot told me: "If you want to see the national side of America, you must come to Washington." And in the West, Archbishop Hanna of San Francisco: "If you want to see the work of Catholicism in America, you must come to Washington for the National Catholic Welfare Conference."

And so I went to Washington for the Catholic Conference in November and again in January for the meeting of Congress.

At the Conference that was held in the Catholic University, I found seventy-eight Bishops—so that, as I spoke to the Bishop of Utah, and then to the Bishop of Omaha, to the Bishop of Pittsburgh, and to the new Archbishop of St. Paul—I felt that my time would have been wasted in crossing the Continent, had I only been able to talk quietly with each of these Bishops from every part of the United States.

Probably no set of Ministers are more in touch with the poorer people of the United States—especially that large number of European poor that have come in within the last thirty years—than the priests and Bishops of the Catholic Church. These immigrants coming from a Europe that perhaps has been to them none too kind, and none too generous—to a land where they look principally for the goods of this world—unlike the old settlers who came to obtain religious freedom—sometimes, even often, they feel a nausea that is loneliness; and they have nothing to which to turn that they ever knew before, nothing but the Church—that is the same here as it was there, and that provides these people with priests speaking their own language, and that often prevents them from committing acts of despair. In Canada, too zealous sects frequently persuade the immigrant to change his religion with his land, forgetting often that the northern colder religions will never appeal to the Catholic, and that the latter leaving his old Church, will soon leave the new one too, and then with no sheet anchor in times of misfortune, will develop criminal tendencies.

Such situations I cannot say I ever saw in the United States—perhaps because the Catholic Church is there too well organised, too old, and too powerful. But, just as an American Catholic is not sorry to see flourishing, however strange they may seem to him, the thousand and one sects of the North and West, for he knows at least they mean some religion, badly needed these days, rather than paganism—so it seems to me is there no sense in grudging Catholicism to those that prefer it or have had it before entering the States. For it must be remembered if these people lose their Catholicism, nothing else is likely to appeal to their natures, and drifting into nothing, they will become a dangerous and criminal liability to the State, rather than that asset to organised society that a practising Catholic should always be.

Such, at least it seemed to me, was the position in America, where the twenty million Catholics are far from popular with other creeds, and I was interested, while in Washington, to read, in view of the Washington Centenary and also of criticism as to Catholic loyalty, two interesting quotations.

One was in an order from Washington when he went to Cambridge to take command of the Continental Army:

"As the Commander-in-Chief has been appraised of a design formed for the observance of that ridiculous and childish custom of burning the effigy of the Pope, he cannot help expressing his surprise that there should be officers and soldiers in this army so devoid of common sense as not to see the impropriety of such a step. It is so monstrous as not to be suffered or excused. Indeed, instead of offering the most remote insult, it is our duty to address public thanks to our Catholic brethren, as to them we are indebted for every late success over the common enemy in Canada."

And again, March 12, 1790, in another letter:

"To the Roman Catholics in the United States," he says, "I hope ever to see America among the foremost nations, in examples of justice and liberality, and I presume that your Protestant fellow citizens will not forget the patriotic part you took in the accomplishment of the Revolution and the establishment of the Government, or the important assistance which they received from a nation in which the Roman Catholic faith is professed."

Here naturally he refers to France, and it is interesting further to note that over 2,000, Frenchmen, of Irish descent, a sort of Irish brigade, went out under Count Arthur Dillon from Brest in 1779.

So much for their disloyalty as a Church to the American Republic. To-day they have formed an interesting organisation, the National Catholic Welfare Conference with a membership of over 100 Bishops with offices in Washington. Here they deal with almost every phase of life that could affect a Catholic—tariffs that affect Catholic utensils, laws that affect divorce or birth control, education questions, immigration, publicity, cinemas—in short, every imaginable subject. And once a year the Bishops meet to discuss the general situation.

Now that Cardinal Gibbons is dead, there is no definite Catholic leader in America, and at each of the Conferences, each day, the Senior Cardinal in order of appointment presides. On the first day it is Car-

dinal O'Connell of Boston—and he takes care not
to be there on the other days, so that eventually it
comes to the fourth and Junior Cardinal, Cardinal
Hayes of New York. There are two other Cardinals,
Cardinal Dogherty of Philadelphia, and Cardinal
Mundelein of Chicago. At this particular Conference over $200,000 was voted to help the organisation
and the subjects most discussed were mixed marriages
with non-Catholics and education. In the first
instance, the practice of over 100 outside Bishops
was read, including, I understand, a statement
from Cardinal Bourne in London, who has similar
problems.

There is no doubt that outside the Vatican at Rome
there is no such organised and large group of Catholic
prelates in the world, and it is perhaps because the
German and the Pole, the Italians and the Irish, are
all so jealous of each other that they would never be
likely to form a National Church—that so far Rome
has at least within recent years encouraged the work.
And behind it all, not obtruding his brilliant brain,
but quietly working for a greater understanding all
over the world, works their Secretary, Father Burke.
If ever it would be interesting to hear a man speak of
his experiences, it would be this man—as some told
me—more powerful than any Bishop.

Tall, thin, quiet, white haired, a saintly man, he
spoke to me of Mexico—of what went on there behind
the scenes, of how Prohibition in America meant the
ruin of the onion trade in Egypt, which goes to the
making of whisky, of how no country to-day can isolate
herself in the world, and similarly no Bishoprics in
America. "If the Pope had been better informed,"
said Father Burke, "he would never have sent Philip II
against England, similarly if the Bishops of America
are well informed they will make less mistakes, unlike

the poor Bishops of Mexico who can never meet and knowing nothing of what the others are doing must look to Washington for information."

I left this man having gathered, through what he said and what he left unsaid, more about the inner workings of at least three Governments than in a month of other visits.

And there were those in Washington at that time who told me whereas previously the Irish and the German Catholics had been the main Catholic influence in America—now the Italians and the Poles were coming up level with them. But it was the English Catholic element, that founded Maryland with Lord Baltimore, that had first been the Catholic influence, and it was quite possible that influence will be revived during and after the Maryland Catholic Centenary Celebrations for which preparations are being made for 1934.

And after that I concentrated, on my next visit, on politics, and I also wandered round the city that reminded me of Europe—full of embassies and diplomatic pomp, of politicians, broad boulevards, fine monuments and streets and buildings that are yet unfinished.

I first visited my friend of Las Vegas, the Hon. Louis Cramton, in his offices in an unfinished government building.

He took me to lunch in Congress with a dozen Republican Congressmen of it seems some years' standing, and they got muddled at what he told them about me, and the rumour went round Congress that I was one of Father Cox's Unemployed Army, then encamped outside the Capitol. Next me sat Congressman French from Idaho and he arranged for me an interview next morning with Senator Borah.

Neither Congress nor the President can get anything passed into law unless the Senate agrees, and the Senate divides itself up into Committees that advise it on different subjects. Of whichever side is in power, the Senator who has been longest on that Committee becomes Chairman—whether he knows much about that subject or not, and his influence is as great, and often greater, than the member of the Government responsible. So that when President Wilson went to Versailles, he offended Senator Lodge, then Chairman of the Senate Foreign Affairs Committee, by not taking him with him. And the fact that the Senate never allowed America to join the League of Nations was chiefly due to the influence of the offended Senator Lodge.

When I visited Washington, Senator Borah was Chairman of the Foreign Affairs Committee, and Senator Smoot, Chairman of the Finance Committee. With Reparations so much to the fore in Europe, both these Senators dealt with Committees that have many subjects in common, and though Senator Smoot was much less independent than Senator Borah and much more a friend of President Hoover, yet they both came from and represented adjoining States, with agricultural constituents, largely Mormon—Utah and Idaho respectively, and both States are vitally interested in the question of silver.

Premier Laval of France was foolish a few weeks before to announce in Washington he had come to visit President Hoover and not Senator Borah, for it showed an ignorance of the American Constitution, and I was not surprised one of the first things Senator Borah said to me, was how interested he was at the complete change that had so recently occurred in the United States in their feelings towards France—the feeling had changed from one almost of affection after the War to now definite dislike and distrust, and he added that on the other hand England had never been more respected and popular.

Yet he felt that did not mean that because England backed a country or a movement it would necessarily be any more favourably received in America. He felt convinced that America was extremely keen to get back to her position of isolation before the War, "especially with regard to having no European political entanglements," and he did not seem to think much of Pacts. He pointed out that after all Pacts are only useful for great Powers dealing with weak Powers. They never have been any use when great Power deals with great Power.

And he suggested Manchuria be left to Japan, for after all, all the great Powers are out of it—we would all be most unlikely to go to war about it, and Japan knowing that is quite quietly carrying out her plans as she arranged them, and as she started in 1915.

And then we talked about reparations, and Senator Borah told me, then, in January, what he made public later on, that he was convinced America is for cancellation if—and only if—reparations in Europe, disarmament and general European reconstruction can be arranged. Even if the Presidential Elections went against this, he felt certain it could be arranged.

And he knew that the farmers of Idaho and elsewhere are getting nothing out of the money paid to America. It is a ridiculously small sum compared with the American budget taxation. It reduces no taxes, and if he could tell the farmers that by cancellation, Europe would be in a better economic position to buy from them, and they would benefit—of course then they would vote for it.

After half an hour I left this moderate-sized outspoken Westerner. He had been pleasant and there was a friendly twinkle in his eye. He had a rugged kind face and brown hair parted in the middle, going grey at the temples. He wore a blue suit, seemed comfortably fat, and he came to greet me at the door of his senatorial offices and sat me beside him at the round table where his committee always meets. He may know little of Europe, this farmer from Idaho, for he has never visited it, I believe; but his mind is clear, he is well informed by America's representatives abroad, and though he may be unpopular with the Eastern bankers, and with the Society ladies of Washington, who say he offends their "dear diplomats" who give such excellent parties—yet I think he represents the America that is beginning more and more to matter, and he wishes to be sincerely fair and honest and the result is perhaps a disconcerting frankness.

Through the kindness of Mr. Kent of the *Baltimore Sun*, I was also able to sit in the Press Gallery of the Senate and also of the House of Representatives.

In the latter I watched Speaker Garner take the Chair, and he put down the cigar he was smoking while another Congressman offered up the Prayer, and then this democratic Texan took up again his cigar and the mallet with which he kept order and the day's business began. The women representatives were hatless, but in the Senate I only found one.

Here the debate seemed dignified, the Senators discussed reclamation to the tune of two billions with Vice-President Curtis in the Chair and the Senators sat at desks in a horseshoe shape. The bell boys dashing about the floor of the Senate wore black short jackets and black plus-fours. Later Mr. Cramton took me round the buildings, and I met a woman representative from California, the majority leader, and representatives from Pittsburgh, Louisiana, and Ohio. I visited the Speaker's office, the floor of the House of

Representatives, and finally downstairs I was shown a group of statuary that at first I thought represented some Mormon wives from Utah—but I found it was only suffragettes.

Last, before I left for the South, after speaking at Toc H, I attended the opening of the Democratic Campaign for the Presidential Elections.

It took the form of a dinner, called the Jackson Day Dinner, and there were nearly 2,000 people present. I managed to get in, representing Sir Willmot Lewis, *The Times* Correspondent. And so I sat in the Press Gallery opposite the high table where presided Mr. Raskob and next him sat Mrs. Woodrow Wilson and beside her Mr. Al Smith, and there were others at the high table including a woman Governor, Mrs. Taylour, evidently suffering from the draught, for round her shoulders she insisted on putting the napkin that should normally have been used by her neighbour, Ambassador John W. Davis.

I cannot say that the speeches, broadcast across America, were either inspiring or filled with suggestions for a future brilliant programme; and of all those, including Speaker Garner, who were vociferously cheered, only one seemed to be a man with the personality or dignity that one would imagine in an American President—Governor Ritchie of Maryland; but then Governor Roosevelt was not present that evening. It also struck me that with nearly 15 million negroes in the United States it was a little unwise for the Democrats' future that there was not one single negro present. And that night I left by train for Southern Pines in Northern Carolina.

CHAPTER XXI

THE PROBLEM OF THE NEGRO

Nobody denies that there are at least 10 million negroes in the United States—and the negroes themselves claim 15 millions. It may not be quite such a large total, but it is probably nearer fifteen than ten, and the majority of these negroes are in the South—below the Mason-Dixon line, where they are constantly reminded of their slave origin. And then there are the half-castes—and altogether they might be said fast to be forming a new brown race. You only very seldom see a really coal-black nigger, and almost all are directly descended from at most 750,000 negro slaves that were imported to America as cheap labour, one hundred, two and even three hundred years ago.

It must not be forgotten that for the vast majority, freedom from slavery has only come in their grandfathers' time—and it is already far too soon to state with any reasonable accuracy what their influence is going to be on America and on the world. Their complaint in the South is that in the old days they belonged to the families of gentry and were usually well taken care of, but that always the poor white, the man never rich enough to own slaves, had treated them badly. Now the old gentry are fast dying out or becoming impoverished, and in their place comes this former poor white man, now a small business man, who still looks on the negro as dirt—no matter how much he tries to keep himself in his place—a place very clearly defined in the South. The result has been that as many as possible of the brown or black race have moved North, and you see them working in the factories of New England in Chicago and Cleveland, and enjoying themselves at night in their huge New York Colony, Harlem.

Their power at the moment is almost nil, and some authorities think in fifty years, through their insanitary living, there will be no negro problem, they will die out; others consider they will disappear through white intermarriage—and all these are serious thinkers; but yet others face the fact that to-day their numbers are growing—by how much it is difficult to tell, owing to the unwillingness of whites to allow them to register in many places.

They are not only laughing singers and poets of Harlem—they are already producing fine writers and orators and even millionaires. Their education too has only been comparatively recent, and its fruits are not yet apparent; but the fruits will certainly include a demand on the part of the negro to use the vote to which he is legally entitled.

And even now the negro leaders claim that if all negroes voted as negroes they could elect whom they liked in many States, and they could be the deciding factor in a Presidential Election. They are a fascinating problem, a problem scarcely faced in America —where even to meet a negro is considered often a disgrace.

In New York I visited many of their social service organisations as well as their night clubs where I was the only white. And later in Washington I was taken all through their University—Howard University—which is partly financed by the Federal Government.

Here I was interested to see in the visitors' book above my own name that of a recent visitor—the son of the Home Secretary in the new patriotic English National Government, and he had entered as his home address—"London and Jerusalem."

Later as I went South, I visited the Atlanta School of Social Work, an organisation of negroes that works entirely to train for social work amongst the negro poor of North and South, an efficient group of coloured workers. Negroes came to work there on a two-years' course from many parts of the world and also from such British dependencies and dominions as the West Indies and South Africa. The organisation was made possible by donations from the Rockefeller Funds, as was also partly the more famous Negro Institute farther South, Tuskegee. Here I spent nearly a whole day, being shown around by the son of Booker Washington—himself born a slave, who lived to found this technical institute to teach the negroes first and foremost to be themselves good farmers.

The Institute, which has some extremely fine buildings, is fast growing and has as pupils many negro British subjects who will eventually return home to their own Colonies. It is endowed with over 8 million dollars, and has over 2,000 pupils. White guests are encouraged and are given entirely separate quarters for living and for eating, and behind the Institute, beside the Rockefellers, are the directors of the Rosenwald Fund that has done so very much for the negro. One of the negro professors is already a world-famous scientist and has for years been busy on formulæ that extract rubber from sweet potatoes, and he is still experimenting on pea-nuts.

But I felt a little sorry when later sitting in a bus as we passed the Institute, in front of the students, one elderly professor got into the bus and finding no seat at the back, sat on a vacant one in front. The conductor stopped the bus, turned round and looked at this negro teacher: "What the —— do you think you're doing—get back there to the end, you filthy nigger," was all he politely snarled, and back the man had to go and be squashed and bumped between much less pleasant negroes for nearly 30 miles.

The attitude of the State authorities is, however, not that of the Federal Government, and near Tuskegee the latter have built an extremely fine Negro Veterans' Hospital, with negro doctors, nurses and janitors, where I found over 600 patients, and the very latest equipment, put in regardless of expense, and the negress nurses were loud in their praise of the Government's generosity.

But back in the railway station, there were separate entrances for whites and for blacks; separate waiting-rooms, separate parts of the train, and the coloured people were not allowed to eat at the railway restaurants, nor could they enter most of the restaurants in the cities, whilst to speak to them on the main streets was encouraged by neither side. And so in New Orleans, when I wanted to be taken anywhere by negroes, I had to meet them away from my hotel which they could not enter, and in the trains we had to separate.

Yet willingly they took me to their meetings, and I visited one of the only negro reformatories in the South, where Dickens could well have described the boys' band that played for me, the bare dormitories with the paper peeling off the damp walls, and the man and his wife that were in charge, and the sergeant that taught them to drill. And I was told on good authority that the negro gets his fair share of help, in proportion to the taxes he pays—but not in proportion to the number of negroes that exist.

CHAPTER XXII

THE LIFE OF THE NEGRO

To see the private lives of negroes one must see them at prayer and at play, and in New Orleans I visited two types of Church.

First I went one Sunday evening to the Church of God in Christ on 6th Street, and I was received by the assistant, known as the Rev. Willy, a youth of about 25, and he gave me a seat near the platform. On the platform sat six men, and below them, in a big hall, was a pulpit next a table with two chairs, and then in the front rows sat the women and again on the right of the platform were rows for women, and on the left for men, and at the back could sit the non-members, and the numbers were about 300. First they all knelt in almost silent prayer—for occasionally there was a moan—and then they sang and the Rev. Willy came down to the pulpit and read a little from the Bible—quotations to prove that we should all be happy and dance, so that the piano was now played and the women began to sing and to scream to the Lord, and they all stood up and clapped hands for a long time. One woman had a tambourine and another cymbals, so that there was plenty of noise, and now and then women shouted aloud of their joy in the Lord, and the Pastor and others bellowed forth frequently Amen and Allelujah.

The Pastor indeed was the most impressive figure —for he was coal-black and was dressed in clerical garments; he was massive and his voice was like the roar of a bull—as he opened lips, all red showing white teeth all with a black background. And keeping company with the noise came the shrill stuttering of a woman that sounded like tut-tut-tut-tut, and she rolled her head and body from side to side and seemed about to have a fit—but they told me she was only "getting happy." Then the Pastor ordered a collection for the entertainment fund of their Church brethren from the Southern States who would visit New Orleans during Lent. They collected five dollars, and while they were collecting the Pastor and the congregation sang a spiritual on the subject of giving to the Church and there was much irony in the hymn.

After that the Pastor gave us a half-hour sermon, full of Biblical quotations and accompanied by much roaring and frequent Amens. And the last words were a fierce attack on Voodooism and the ignorance which encouraged it. When he had finished, the women continued to dance step-dances and at last people began to move forward to the table to be received and be baptised in the Holy Spirit. Finally some fifteen people came forward and there was much chanting and hymns, praying over each other and singing; but in the end, only one woman was converted, and she rose up and told us her sins of adultery and vice, and so the meeting came to an end.

A few days later I went to a more primitive religious meeting in a church that was better kept and that looked more flourishing, and it was in the middle of the week. The church was called the Church of Christian Sunset Mission. Before going there I visited the Cracker-Jack Negro Drug Store—where they sell incense, candles, ointments, and crackers, and later I was told I could be taught about Voodooism and given their book if I was willing to pay for it, and they told me of an English woman and her family who are living just outside New Orleans and who practise Voodooism as it was taught them by Mother Katherine—on whose grave in the city people still make signs and invocations. And we must not forget that the negroes always scrub and keep the doorsteps very clean to rub out any Voodoo evil sign that an enemy might make on their doorstep to hurt their house.

So I came to the church and before going in a negress at the door showed me a little bottle of their wonderful oil, and she told me how, through finger-cracking around her, the Pastor had cured her of her most painful corns. Then we went into a church that was crowded to the door with negroes. And the meeting was in full swing—from the altar the preacher, a tall man with a loud voice, dressed in a flowing Japanese kimono with the Rising Sun embroidered in front, shouted, yelled, and gesticulated, and in chorus the men moaned Amen and Allelujah and the women screamed, and suddenly in different parts of the church and one in a pew in front of me, three women, screaming, had seizures, and vergers of great strength held them down while they kicked till they lay still—and they too were "just getting happy"—for now I was at a real meeting of the Holy Rollers. Supporting the Pastor were a choir of eleven women—that were dressed as the choir of Aimée Semple McPherson at Los Angeles in black and white—and like Lyons' waitresses in London, and with them were four men in kimonos.

After a time the lights went out and the attendants' choir moved up and down the aisle singing:

> "Oh come unto Me
> It is all right
> Jesus says—It is all right."

And one by one the congregation moved up to be healed and the attendants stood round each one in a weird subdued lighting, and I watched them crack their fingers up and down and all around them from head to feet, and otherwise there was a deadly silence, just this low cracking, as the people turned first one way and then the other.

Later there was a collection and bottles of yellow liquid were given round, but my negro companion begged me not to take one for I was the only white there and everyone watched me, and he was afraid of the liquid. After this there was a long pause until the choir and attendants began to form a circle before the altar in the dim light.

They held hands and they swayed backwards and forwards and they moaned and then suddenly one of the four men fell down to the ground in a fit, and the others began to sway more ominously still. At last one of the fattest of the women fell over, kicking and foaming at the mouth. Soon she lay still and there was complete silence as the bodies were carried out and the lights went up and another procession was formed. This time, the attendants came down amidst the congregation and they gave us messages from Heaven and mine was uncannily correct, and to see what would happen I denied vigorously the woman's statement and she got into a complete frenzy and swore that what she was saying about me was true, and it was and there was much babbling of voices as the attendants gave the messages all round.

Next I turned to the more educated negroes who were about to celebrate Carnival; I went to two of their balls and again I was the only white man there. And one night, the wife of the Bishop of Louisiana asked me how I had enjoyed the negro ball the night before because her servants had recognised me there, and on another occasion the very lovely debutante Queen of a Carnival Ball told me: "You are seeing

THE NEGRESS DEBUTANTES, 1932-33, AT A NEW ORLEANS NEGRO BALL

a New Orleans we are never allowed to see," and two old ladies who always spoke French and only English with a broken accent, yet had never been to Europe, were amazed when after dinner at eleven o'clock I excused myself as going to a negro ball —this was the ball given by twenty negro bachelors to open the negro carnival season—before the Mardi Gras.

I went to the roof garden on the top of the Pytheas Building, and as I walked into the room and up to the balcony where I was to sit and watch, I was struck by one of the most beautiful sights I have ever seen. Once a year this fancy dress ball is held, and for nearly ten months before, it has been decided what is to be the theme of the ball, so that the negroes that know they will be invited can save and prepare their dresses. In daily life they may be servants, or school teachers, or undertakers, they may have to be segregated in tram-cars, keep out of certain buildings and be humble in the presence of white people, but here they were dressed as princes, and they behaved as ordinary men and women.

The ball was an Arabian Ball, and the room had been so decorated that it might have been a picture from the Arabian Nights. And then the dancers themselves—their dresses were quite beautiful and all of the richest and brightest colours, and there could be nothing incongruous to see the beautiful Eastern headdresses and flowing robes covering the tall black and brown figures of such Ethiopian types. To me it did not seem fancy dress at all. It seemed much more natural than to see the same people by daylight in Western dress.

And I sat there alone for hours to music that was negro jazz and negro spirituals almost at the same time, and before me passed to and fro these gorgeous

Eastern figures and they were neither drunk nor noisy and I was glad I had come.

A little while later, as Mardi Gras drew near, I went again to the same place to another negro ball —the smartest of the season—the ball given by the Illinois Club for the negress debutantes of 1932. This was not fancy dress. It was serious, and as it was explained to me "select." I was there by ten-thirty in my corner in the balcony, and Customs officials and their wives, and undertakers and their wives, and editors of coloured newspapers, and doctors, came and kept me company. Dancing down below to a jazz band that was full of fire, were over 700 people all coloured and the dresses were quite good —those of the debutantes, lovely.

At eleven o'clock a passage was railed off up to the elevated stage and then the curtains went up to clapping and loud noises from the band, and we beheld the Negress Queen of Carnival surrounded by nineteen debutantes of 1932. They were all dressed in white and some had blond hair, and some looked like Italian beauties. Their faces were often very attractive, and I noticed the negroes clapped mostly the fair-haired negresses. Each carried a large bouquet and the stage was elaborately decorated. The Queen, who was a very negroid type, wore a crown and had a long sweeping black and gold embroidered train, and behind her was a large cardboard moon. But alas! in front of her regal throne —this otherwise dignified scene was marred by a three-legged wooden footstool of very ordinary variety.

On each side of the Queen stood a maid of honour, one with a pink train, the other with a blue train. Beside this scene stood the Master of Ceremonies, who was dressed in a tail coat with a black tie, and white flannel trousers with a black stripe. Across his chest he wore a yellow ribbon or order and by his side hung a sword. The other members of the club, who were grouped near him, were similarly dressed and they all held some kind of toy that dangled at their side, either it was a bugle or a violin, or some carried canes.

The Master of Ceremonies, as soon as the clapping died down, started a speech that was pompous and dignified and that was filled with long words. He told us that "this is the original, positively the original Illinois Club, and it has much pleasure in welcoming the distinguished guests to-night. . . . The original Illinois Club feels and realises that it owes a duty to Society and so it has great pleasure in presenting the debutantes of 1932." He explained to us that this was the 34th Annual Ball of the Illinois Club which had been founded in 1896, and it was the most exclusive negro club in the South. But unfortunately, at this moment, he completely forgot his speech and there was much laughter—later with the aid of a paper he called forth singly every one of the debutantes, and told us whose daughters they were, and they were clapped and cheered by the 700 guests, especially the blondes.

The Queen, I gathered, was a daughter of one of the chief Customs officials in the docks. Next, each debutante was given a glass of champagne and the Queen stood forth from her throne—drank her glass to their health, and then hurled it, crashing, to the floor. Immediately the band started up a march and all the wives of the, I think, twenty members of the Illinois Club, walked down and up the middle of the floor. They were well dressed and to distinguish them from the others, they each carried a small open Japanese parasol. Next they were joined by their white-trousered husbands carrying canes under their arms. Then they lined up along the floor forming a guard of honour and in between them marched the Queen, showing off her train, followed by the debutantes in twos. This lasted until midnight and I sat and watched while they ate and drank at a buffet in the corner, later to continue their ordinary dancing.

And their behaviour? It was perhaps better than an ordinary Country Club dance—it was certainly as dignified as any middle-class function, and if there were drunken men, as of course there were, they were treated as at other dances and eventually turned out. And I could not help but think a little seriously on how all this was going on to the complete ignorance of the white people in the town—how different education had made these people from those attending the Holy Roller Meetings of the Church of the Sunset Mission, and how dangerous it is so completely to ignore their growing numbers.

I came away feeling not a little like a dowager who has been to a ball she has very much enjoyed and where she has seen nothing of which she could disapprove, hard though she has looked in every corner—and yet I came away a little frightened at this America's serious and terrible problem—I saw many educated negroes that do not like the whites —and what may be their influence as negro leaders?

CHAPTER XXIII

MORTICIANS' PARLOURS OR FUNERAL HOMES

I visited a negro undertaker's establishment—but
first I will describe a white one seen by me in
a Western city that must remain nameless. They
call it a Funeral Home, or more often a Mortician's
Parlour. Such things are all over America, and they
are, I think, a native product.

In many States it is now compulsory by law that
the dead be embalmed, and in these homes it all
takes place, the body being moved there often on
the day of death. The one I visited was particularly
smart—it was kept by the State Senator and he fussed
over his dead bodies like a mother hen. He took
me first to the waiting-room and then up the stairs and
all round were frescoes from Bunyan's *Pilgrim's Progress*. The house, from the outside, was an ordinary
typical western house and in each room the furniture
and the decorations were different. There was a
Louis Quinze Room, a Renaissance Room, a Gothic
Room, and a Mother Goose Room for dead children
with toys in the corner. The family chose in which
room they would prefer their late lamented to lie,
and he could remain there often up to one week.

In each room I found a body, and they were in
coffins that had glass tops down to the waist, and
the dead were dressed in their Sunday day clothes,
the men often in black suits with large bow ties and
their heads lay on white taffeta. In one room, where
the family were sitting, they were asked to leave so
that I could come in, and I was shown how this embalmed man, 6 feet 4 inches, weighing 300 lbs. and
only 39, was not ready yet for his coffin, the body
and the skin being still too rigid. At this moment

the embalmer came in with a clean collar to put on the man, and I went out to go downstairs, past the basement where they kept infectious cases—through the room where you chose your coffin, and into the embalming chamber—which was like any operation room.

Here lay two shrouded bodies, and as the blood is drawn from beneath one arm, so is the embalming fluid injected into the other. To be an embalmer is a very definite art, and you have to undergo a course as well as take your degree at a University—a degree in embalming. And I understood it, for there was a dead boy there that had been kicked in the face and the embalmer was rebuilding the face, partly from a photograph, and partly from imagination, so that his parents could look once again on him as they knew him.

This last look takes place in the drawing-room upstairs, where the body is placed for a short funeral service and eulogy, pronounced by the mortician, in this case the Senator, and the relatives sit round like at a concert, in a semicircle, and there is an organ. Then the corpse is removed to one of the many mausoleums that are springing up through the West and the East.

With the negro parlours things are less elaborate, but otherwise not much different. In the smartest one, I found the All Seeing Eye in cardboard on the door, and inside, next the room for the body, was a well-furnished room with dining-room table and kitchenette adjoining, for here the negroes sit up all night before the funeral, eating, drinking, and having a mild form of wake. Here, too, they had a chapel, and the man who was showing it me did not come up at once so that I walked up the stairs alone. And as I went up I must have pressed a button or a spring

—for suddenly from the chapel the electrically worked pianola started to play Chopin's Funeral March and I was uncannily alone in the chapel with the music.

In front of the altar was the place for the coffin, so contrived that the moment the Service is completed —the coffin is lowered—the floor giving way and it is shot down to the hearse that is waiting in the open space underneath the chapel and the body is round at the front door before the negro women can have hysterics, or even get down to the door themselves. But perhaps there is even less privacy or respect for the dead body here than with the whites, for a friend of mine told me he once went to a negro parlour and walked into a room where lay a naked dead body, and the embalmer, resting from his labours, was quietly playing the guitar beside the corpse and singing a negro spiritual. I visited their embalming rooms, and over the door, as a mascot, was a still-born baby preserved and kept in a liquid bottle.

What happens to you after death in America has made me pray I never die there—yet morticians are popular, for in the West, they are often State Senators and amongst the negroes they are usually the richest citizens; whilst in New Orleans, the Negro King of Carnival—the Zulu King—seems always to be a mortician, and the Carnival procession invariably starts from a Funeral Home and stops at others *en route* for refreshments.

CHAPTER XXIV

AT SEA

My time was nearly up and my visa was running out. It was February and I must go home. I came down from Washington through the South. I saw much and I am afraid I was forced to miss much. I passed rather hurriedly through the old cities—and I was forced to miss Boston and most of New England—though I visited Connecticut. I stopped a little at Southern Pines in North Carolina where they hunted as in England and where the country reminded me of Hampshire and the New Forest. I left out Charleston, but I stopped a fortnight in New Orleans. I passed through the Cotton Country and the Black Belt—so called because of the soil, and I stopped in Montgomery.

Here I saw Anti-Bellum Houses—for down there they have never forgotten the Civil War, and I found one house given over by private charity to caring for the white, not black, unemployed—but there were no beds, 130 slept on planks and I spoke at a luncheon club after the Supreme Court Judge, who informed us in future he meant to take the jurors from the luncheon clubs—the city's groups of respectable men —and I visited a delightful lady in an old-world colonial style house, and not only her servants—all negroes—but the young men and women in the party called her "Miss Elsie," though she, the heiress of this plantation, had been thirty years married at the least.

And soon through to Mobile, that is on the Gulf of Mexico, where only a week before they had begun Community Chest relief for the unemployed; and then into New Orleans, where I was wonderfully entertained by French and English Americans, and shown and taken to all the balls of their Carnival that dates back nearly one hundred years in its ceremonies. One ball one night would be got up as from time immemorial by one group of families and one night another. Some old ladies, impoverished now that their plantations were no more, kept just one good dress for their family group ball and at the Boston Club I watched the processions and the entertainments of the Carnival Queen as she processed to lunch in a back room, from the gallery, with her maids, on the arms of old club members, and we all danced in the afternoon.

The Bishop and his wife told me how Charleston, New Orleans, Richmond and Boston have always linked themselves together as the social centres, and how they looked down on New York, finding it a foreign city and felt happier, some in London, others in Paris. And yet others told me Natchez, the home of the planters, had always looked down on New Orleans as a home of merchants.

The daughter of one house motored me out to their sugar plantation, and old Celestine, her negress nurse, and now cook, kissed her lovingly and gave such a meal as I had not eaten for a long time. She spoke to us too, this negress, in a French that was better almost than her English and we motored back below the Mississippi, below banks built to prevent her overflowing.

Our British Consul-General next arranged for me, with the Italian Consul, that I have the Director's cabin on an Italian freight boat, and in this I sailed down the Mississippi from New Orleans to the Gulf— eight hours down the river, and so across to Texas, to Galveston and up the Canal with oil stations all along to Houston, one of America's really coming cities.

Here, everything seems optimistic for a revival, and for a great future for this State. Their problem has been not so much Negroes as Mexicans, and since the depression, they have deported them wholesale. They recognise in Houston—that many now un-employed will never get back to work and they have arranged a ten year plan of small holdings for these people that shows a foresightedness I found nowhere else.

In Galveston the immigration official invited me to lunch with his family, and the whole district, especially the large German colonies, were particularly excited at the visit of the German destroyer *Karlsruhe*. I went on board, and at High Mass on the Sunday there was a sermon in German and we all sang "Die Wacht am Rhine."

From Galveston we cruised for a week around the coast of Florida and up to Wilmington, North Carolina, where I found the people mainly Anglo-Saxon, and some men had been to Oxford, and we talked of the strange group living in the forests near by, and from their language, they thought it might form the lost colony of Sir Walter Raleigh.

All this made me regret lack of time and that I had missed visiting the Kentucky Mountaineers where women do not ring chickens' necks, they just shoot off their heads with revolvers from the cabin door—where the men are crack shots and family vendettas are ancient history, where men frequently die in a café brawl, where drink is made, old English spoken of a type that is almost pure Elizabethan, and where Mrs. Breckenridge does such wonders with her mounted nursing service—all this I missed and no doubt much more.

And I was amused, as we sailed from one port, that the Customs official, the night before, asked the

Captain for a bottle of cognac. "That," replied the Captain, "is the second officer's job," and at five-thirty next morning the Customs officer was on board to see the second officer and to get his bottle, and I saw many more things of a like nature, as on the night before I left New Orleans—in a speak-easy on a Saturday, there came in two police officers. No, not to raid the place, but to get their "rake off"—ten dollars a week which kept the place from being raided, and the money went to the Police Widows Pension Fund.

And then on March 2 I sailed from America. I was three weeks at sea before landing in Europe—three weeks in which to think over all I had seen, and again to ask myself, what is America? Where is she going? I had seen her as a man in the street would see her—not an expert, and I have written about her for the man in the street, telling what I saw, enjoying every minute of the comforts and the discomforts, the hospitality, and the general friendliness of everyone.

I leave to those who have read this far to fill in for themselves this canvas. It is an uncompleted picture of an uncompleted country. Experts may say and prophesy as they like, America is always changing, she is not finished yet, she has scarcely begun—no one can generalise about her, no one can be dogmatic—but I will just describe what I think is at least the framework of this unfinished picture—what is common to all in America, and what seem to me Europe's biggest mistakes when judging her.

First of all if we are looking for an American Nation, as France, or Germany, or England—there is no such thing. The nearest approach is to say it is a slightly more homogeneous British Empire. Its economic solidarity has been made possible by slightly stronger political links. Otherwise, it seems to me the same. Forty-eight States that are extremely jealous of their own independence—up to the point when it does not hurt their pockets—and bigger groups—say half a dozen, whose interests are very similar and almost totally different from those of the other groups.

For instance, though the South and the North have little in common, only looking to Europe for many influences, yet they both have less in common with the Pacific States, that look anxiously at Asia. Then there is the Middle West whose politics will more and more be bounded by the Great Lakes and the Mississippi. And yet again there is Texas and the Oil States and there are the Mountain States, most of whose inhabitants have never seen the sea and hate the Panama Canal.

How, in reason, can Europe expect from all these different groups a constant National unchanging policy. They are all pulling against each other, and Europe petulantly says: "You must have a common policy, you are too big an influence in the world—you must have a definite policy and stick to it." "Not at all," answers America. "Yours is the argument of old, rather effete nations, everything with you is conservative, is settled—you do not like change; with us nothing is settled, we are not nearly finished, and we have no intention of doing anything else but going on experimenting and scrapping without hesitation what we don't find good—look at Prohibition." And that is just it.

If through this depression America can become more level-headed and less wasteful and less keen to rush into things too quickly and so over-produce—she can stand very much on her own, and not bother what Europe thinks of her—her real worries are in Asia, and she is to-day inwardly more ready to go to

war, it seemed to me, than any nation in Europe.
Over the Japanese trouble in Manchuria her more
ignorant majority talked freely of war and did not
seem anything but excited at the prospect. She has
never really experienced a war, as has Europe. She is
rich still and still has a wonderful future. She is
unlikely to be very influential in the world for the
next few years—at least positively—because she will
be too busy putting her own house in order to give
any lead elsewhere.

Given over to rapid change, she has oddly enough
never changed her Constitution which is, perhaps, one
hundred years out of date and devised for a few
colonies that were mainly agricultural. That Constitution will soon be changed and before America
can really be a united or a great influence, there must
be a thorough overhauling of her political system, and
also of the influence of Big Business.

It is coming, that change, and perhaps sooner than
we imagine, and when America decides to change,
she will do so with bewildering rapidity. We can
only hope she will not make too many mistakes and
that chaos will not ensue. She is such a virile country,
and as far as I could see, the farther West I went, at
bottom, so devoid of real Socialism—though she does
like working in groups—that there is no very serious
danger of revolution—but there is some danger with
her Eastern foreign unemployed. What the changes
will eventually be and what are the chief influences
to-day, again it is almost impossible to tell. I have
written of all I saw, for amongst the groups and the
peoples are influences perhaps to-day ignored, that
I saw and that to-morrow will be much more vital.

Of one thing am I certain, there is a spirit out in
the West that is the most original in the States and
perhaps when mellowed, it will be the spirit of the

eventual America. It is a spirit of independence, a frontier man's spirit—of determination that the simple things of life are the best and yet a spirit of great, perhaps too great, respect for education.

There will one day be an aristocracy of great influence in America—but it will never be an aristocracy of birth—it will be an aristocracy of educated University professors, of great scientists and of polished literary men.

Striving to join all this are the foreigners of very low birth and breeding in their own country, with an inferiority complex brought on by centuries of smallness. At home if they rose to any heights, these people were mellowed by the traditions of their surroundings, but in America there is no such mellowing influence—and as they rise they become more and more obnoxious and that is largely the type we notice in Europe. That obnoxious type—the others come quietly and go quietly and remain proudly American—will one day cease—for migration is closing down and three generations will make them different beings.

But will they last three generations? In the Eastern cities very few foreign families survive the strain of American living to the fourth generation, and almost no one takes seriously the sons of millionaires. It seems to be only the older stocks that survive, and the farmers of the West and South.

These people have an odd complex, especially in the North-West, of being extremely sentimental and liberal with other people, but hard, narrow and severe to themselves and their families—it is partly the influence of Puritanism and Nonconformity—an influence intensely marked in the new American.

To my mind, the influence of the religious sects is immense, and the seeking after religious knowledge and uncertainty about the next world after having worked hard to make a fortune in this one, is most noticeable, and should encourage the greater Churches to renewed activity amongst the very earnest youth. The youth is interested in religion, but not in politics which, unfortunately, they despise.

Undoubtedly the American thinks usually in terms of making money and dollars—but not just to possess money—rather to have the money to spend on other things. There is no hoarding of money in America— there is no more wasteful country; the need for money is because of an appreciation of its uses and it is as well to remember that speculation, depression, loans and so-called prosperity is largely window dressing— for we must not forget that over three-fifths of the American bank failures in the last ten years took place in the boom period before 1928. Lastly it has been said the American never takes anything as proved— not even that you cannot serve God and Mammon, and certainly the Bible Belt does its best to fit in both.

Where is America heading?—nobody knows. Is it keener on independence or on community life? It always talks of independence—but whenever there is any trouble or anyone really wants to do anything— they always get into groups or communities.

Chain Banks have never been a success—because they say there is no independence—but it is really because the people cannot borrow so easily or so cheaply. In every village the shop windows have the same dressing, changed each week and there are plenty of Chain Stores, and so the people get stuff cheaper, therefore they tolerate the Chain Store and other forms of mass production—because they get things cheaper.

America will not give a lead in the near future—she will be too busy, but at any moment she might quite quickly get worked into such a condition that she would join one side or another in a struggle and so she cannot be ignored. For England, at bottom, her best elements—the ones that will survive—have a real affection and respect. They like England's admiration, however much they may deny it, and they resent very bitterly the ignorant criticism and the insulting criticisms that often come out of England.

England has everything to gain and nothing to lose by being friends with America. But to be friends with America does not mean to be sycophants and to give way—or break from other nations as we did with Japan. America does not admire that sort of thing, she despises it. England and the British Empire must go their own way—acting fairly and honestly, and America will respect them. There is no need for either to cross the other's path, and one day if that western independent anglo-saxon or north european element becomes predominant, the British Empire and America will be the greatest powers on earth for good.

But England has got to hold her Empire together, and America has three big problems to solve. Her foreign unemployed, her politics and her constitution, and lastly her coloured problem, and all these things will take a lot of doing.

High tariffs with her will always have a following, usually a majority following; the West will never see, however small the difference, why Europe be let off her debts—if the West must pay hers to the bankers of the East; and the advice of Washington to keep away from Europe will long be a powerful one.

Sailing across the sea—I had landed at Wilmington, Los Angeles, and I departed from Wilmington, North Carolina—I felt sorry my journey had ended. America changes every day and its influence invigorates the European. But he needs to visit all America, not only

the Eastern States on which the West looks down—
as often as he can—soon he gets out of date.

Prohibition seemed then the predominant subject—
the attempt of this great group of peoples to alter
almost the laws of nature—but nature has been too
powerful for them and oddly enough as I landed at
Genoa I went first to the building of the "Bank of
St. George," the oldest bank in the world, and on its
walls I read the letter of Christopher Columbus before
his last voyage:

"I sail again for the Indies in the name of the Most Holy
Trinity, and I return at once; but as I know I am but a mortal,
I charge my son Don Diego to pay you yearly and for ever
the tenth part of all my revenue in order to lighten the toll on
wine and corn."

Had Don Diego inherited America, what wealth
would have poured into Genoa—what wine the
Genoese would have drunk. And to-day—if America
now starting on a new pattern to paint into her unfinished picture—can control her citizens' ambitions,
and make them think more often of their children's
future and their grandchildren's rather than the
immediate enjoyment of their own, what happiness
can be in store for 120,000,000 people—and through
them perhaps for the whole world.

Let America remember—it was through religious
zeal in North and South, that her pioneers first made
good—there is more need of some faith to-day. Her
first peoples went to America to suffer that their
descendants might be happy. To-day the people are
grasping too much for themselves—let them, too, think
of their descendants. And do not let a country gifted
as is no other country—the biggest Free Trade area on
earth—break up or degenerate because it cannot find
Utopia in a day.

Slowly but surely, if petty jealousies are buried and sectional interests withdrawn—then forty-eight States, united still in little else but an uncertain faith in their future—can come together, making a real League of Nations and can give the world an aristocracy of learning and a people whose ambitions are normal and quite simple. But for this—they must draw breath a little—and they must suffer a little.

Surely we have every reason to hope the depression of 1930–3 is the first step towards this new America—a new America that being a little chastened, may arouse less jealousy in her neighbours—less resentment—and may become a popular leader amongst the peoples of the world no matter what may be her eventual form of Government.

She may come in to redress the balance of the old world, not to disturb it.

THE END

INDEX

INDEX

Foreign Travelers in America
1810–1935

AN ARNO PRESS COLLECTION

Archer, William. **America To-Day**: Observations and Reflections. 1899.

Belloc, Hilaire. **The Contrast**. 1924.

[Boardman, James]. **America, and the Americans**. By a Citizen of the World. 1833.

Bose, Sudhindra. **Fifteen Years in America**. 1920.

Bretherton, C. H. **Midas, Or, The United States and the Future**. 1926.

Bridge, James Howard (Harold Brydges). **Uncle Sam at Home**. 1888.

Brown, Elijah (Alan Raleigh). **The Real America**. 1913.

Combe, George. **Notes on the United States Of North America During a Phrenological Visit in 1838-9-40**. 1841. 2 volumes in one.

D'Estournelles de Constant, Paul H. B. **America and Her Problems**. 1915.

Duhamel, Georges. **America the Menace**: Scenes from the Life of the Future. Translated by Charles Miner Thompson. 1931.

Feiler, Arthur. **America Seen Through German Eyes**. Translated by Margaret Leland Goldsmith. 1928.

Fidler, Isaac. **Observations on Professions, Literature, Manners, and Emigration, in the United States and Canada, Made During a Residence There in 1832**. 1833.

Fitzgerald, William G. (Ignatius Phayre). **Can America Last?** A Survey of the Emigrant Empire from the Wilderness to World-Power Together With Its Claim to "Sovereignty" in the Western Hemisphere from Pole to Pole. 1933.

Gibbs, Philip. **People of Destiny**: Americans As I Saw Them at Home and Abroad. 1920.

Graham, Stephen. **With Poor Immigrants to America**. 1914.

Griffin, Lepel Henry. **The Great Republic**. 1884.

Hall, Basil. **Travels in North America in the Years 1827 and 1828**. 1829. 3 volumes in one.

Hannay, James Owen (George A. Birmingham). **From Dublin to Chicago**: Some Notes on a Tour in America. 1914.

Hardy, Mary (McDowell) Duffus. **Through Cities and Prairie Lands:** Sketches of an American Tour. 1881.

Holmes, Isaac. **An Account of the United States of America,** Derived from Actual Observation, During a Residence of Four Years in That République, Including Original Communications. [1823].

Ilf, Ilya and Eugene Petrov. **Little Golden America:** Two Famous Soviet Humorists Survey These United States. Translated by Charles Malamuth. 1937.

Kerr, Lennox. **Back Door Guest.** 1930.

Kipling, Rudyard. **American Notes.** 1899.

Leng, John. **America in 1876:** Pencillings During a Tour in the Centennial Year, With a Chapter on the Aspects of American Life. 1877.

Longworth, Maria Theresa (Yelverton). **Teresina in America.** 1875. 2 volumes in one.

Low, A[lfred] Maurice. **America at Home.** [1908].

Marshall, W[alter] G[ore]. **Through America:** Or, Nine Months in the United States. 1881.

Mitchell, Ronald Elwy. **America:** A Practical Handbook. 1935.

Moehring, Eugene P. **Urban America and the Foreign Traveler, 1815-1855.** With Selected Documents on 19th-Century American Cities. 1974.

Muir, Ramsay. **America the Golden:** An Englishman's Notes and Comparisons. 1927.

Price, M[organ] Philips. **America After Sixty Years:** The Travel Diaries of Two Generations of Englishmen. 1936.

Sala, George Augustus. **America Revisited:** From the Bay of New York to the Gulf of Mexico and from Lake Michigan to the Pacific. 1883. 3rd edition. 2 volumes in one.

Saunders, William. **Through the Light Continent;** Or, the United States in 1877-8. 1879. 2nd edition.

Smith, Frederick [Edwin] (Lord Birkenhead). **My American Visit.** 1918.

Stuart, James. **Three Years in North America.** 1833. 2 volumes in one.

Teeling, William. **American Stew.** 1933.

Vivian, H. Hussey. **Notes of a Tour in America from August 7th to November 17th, 1877.** 1878.

Wagner, Charles. **My Impressions of America.** Translated by Mary Louise Hendee. 1906.

Wells, H. G. **The Future in America:** A Search After Realities. 1906.